COLLINS

HOW TO IDENTIFY

WILD FLOWERS

CHRISTOPHER GREY-WILSON • LISA ALDERSON

HarperCollins*Publishers*

CONTENTS

CONTENTS

Fig. 1: Plant profile

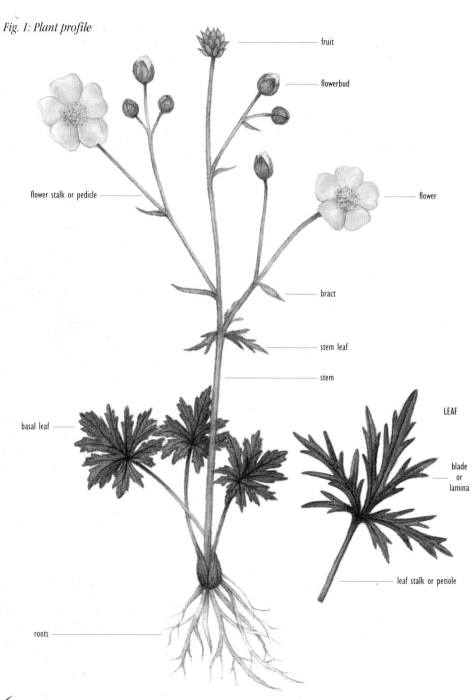

fruit

flowerbud

flower stalk or pedicle

flower

bract

stem leaf

stem

LEAF

basal leaf

blade
or
lamina

leaf stalk or petiole

roots

Types of Flowering Plant

THE MAJORITY OF FLOWERING PLANTS ARE EQUIPPED WITH ROOTS, STEMS, LEAVES AND FLOWERS and these sustain the plant through its life cycle with the ultimate goal being the production of seeds for future generations.

This book deals primarily with the identification of flowering herbs: trees and shrubs are omitted but they are to be found in another title in this series *How to Identify Trees.*

Flowering herbs can be divided into three main types:

Annual plants are those plants that germinate, flower, seed and complete their life cycle within a year. Good examples are Shepherd's Purse, Common Poppy and Groundsel. Annuals often grow on disturbed or open ground, sometimes in large numbers, and are usually capable of producing substantial numbers of seeds.

Biennial plants are those plants that germinate in the first year, flower and complete their life cycle in the second. Familiar examples are Alexanders, the Foxglove and Aaron's Rod. Biennials are the smallest group. They often form a leaf-rosette at ground level in their first season.

Perennial plants geminate in the first year and flower in the second and subsequent years. Perennials may live for many years, although some are relatively short-lived. Some may not flower for the first time until they are several years old. Perennials are by far the largest group of plants that make up the countryside.

PARTS OF THE PLANT
THE ROOTS
The roots serve two main functions: first they support the plant in the soil and second they take up nutrients and water and translocate it to all parts of the plant. Roots are often extensive and form an intricate network below ground, sometimes close to the surface but often they penetrate deep into the soil. Roots can be fine and thread-like, thick and fleshy or swollen and tuberous. Some plants can have several root types. A few parasitic plants such as Mistletoe grow on other plants and are rootless.

THE STEM
The stem can be simple or branched, stiff and erect to horizontal. Stems carry all the above ground plant parts, especially the leaves and flowers and give the plant height. Some plants like the common daisy are stemless with both leaves and flowers at ground level. Stems contain an intricate network of capillaries that carry water and nutrients to the leaves, flowers and fruits.

THE LEAVES
The leaves are one of the most visible parts of the plant. They are basically flat but they differ enormously in shape, size and texture from one species to another. Leaves are essentially chemical factories: they contain the green pigment chlorophyll which harnesses the sun's energy which, in combinations with the other nutrients taken up by the plant, produces the life-giving energy it requires for growth and reproduction.

THE FLOWERS
The flowers are often the most colourful and obvious part of the plant, although they can be small and inconspicuous. Flowers contain the sexual parts (male and female) organs and are concerned with reproduction and the continuation of the species for future generations. Flowers are complex structures and vary enormously in both shape and the number of different parts and positions of the various organs.

THE FRUITS
The fruits are the visible sign of plant reproduction. They come in many different types and forms and contain the seeds, few in some plants but numerous in others. The seeds are the individual units of reproduction; each is capable of establishing a new individual similar to the parent species, or occasionally a hybrid between two species.

Flowers and Inflorescences

SOME PLANTS LIKE THE PRIMROSE BEAR SOLITARY FLOWERS. HOWEVER, IN THE MAJORITY of plants the flowers are organised into more complex structures which can bear a few to very many individual flowers; these structures are called inflorescences. The inflorescence type is often diagnostic of a particular species or even an entire genus.

The inflorescence can be borne on various parts of the plant but they are either terminal to the shoot (main shoots or lateral shoots) or lateral, being borne from the leaf-axils.

Inflorescences generally carry hermaphrodite (bisexual) flowers but they may occasionally be entirely male or entirely female, or they may sometimes bear separate male and female flowers on the same inflorescence.

Inflorescences frequently carry bracts, leaf-like organs which arise at the points on the stem where the flower stalks (pedicels) join. Further, often smaller, bract-like organs located on the lateral branches of the inflorescence are called bracteoles.

INFLORESCENCE TYPES
SPIKE
The flowers are stalkless and arranged along a simple axis, usually with the lowermost flower opening first.

RACEME
Essentially similar to a spike but with the individual flowers stalked. Both spikes and racemes can occasionally be branched. Both the Foxglove and the Rosebay Willowherb bear racemes.

CYME
Cymes come in a number of different forms. In the basic type (a dichasium) the inflorescence is

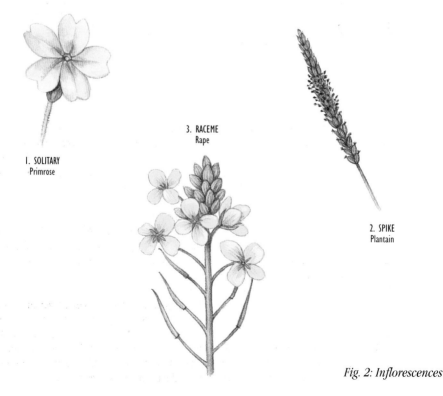

1. SOLITARY
Primrose

3. RACEME
Rape

2. SPIKE
Plantain

Fig. 2: Inflorescences

Fig. 2: (continued)

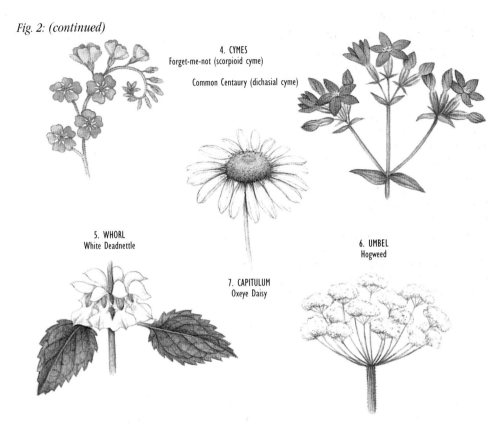

4. CYMES
Forget-me-not (scorpioid cyme)

Common Centaury (dichasial cyme)

5. WHORL
White Deadnettle

7. CAPITULUM
Oxeye Daisy

6. UMBEL
Hogweed

regularly branched with each branch terminating in a flower. The terminal flower of each branch opens before those on the secondary branches. Familiar examples include the campions and many of the buttercups. In the scorpioid cyme, typical of the Forget-me-not and related plants, the cyme is one-sided and coiled when young.

PANICLE
A much-branched compound inflorescence often forming a large pyramidal shape. St John's worts often have panicles.

UMBEL
Inflorescences in which all the branches arise from a single point like the spokes of an umbrella. Umbels are typical of the Carrot and Hogweed and other members of the cow parsley family, Umbelliferae.

CORYMB
Rather like an umbel but in effect a raceme in which the alternating flower stalks are progressively shorter, bringing the flowers up to the same level. Corymbs are generally flat-topped.

WHORL (*VERTICILLASTER*)
Common to members of the Labiatae in which the inflorescences are condensed, the flowers appearing as whorls around the stem at each node.

CAPITULUM
A compound inflorescences in which numerous small flowers (or florets) are crammed together symmetrically on a flattened or domed disk. Daisies have typical capitula in which the outer florets are rayed and petal-like, while the inner are short and form the central disk (*see* p. 13).

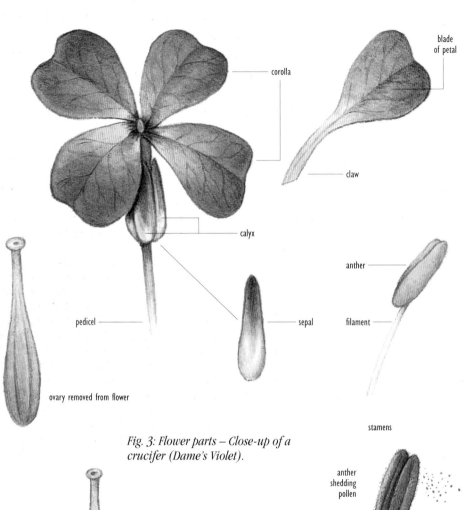

corolla

blade of petal

claw

calyx

anther

filament

pedicel

sepal

ovary removed from flower

Fig. 3: Flower parts – Close-up of a crucifer (Dame's Violet).

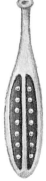

ovary (half-section) with ovules

stamens

anther shedding pollen

Flower Organs

FLOWERS ARE COMPOSED OF A NUMBER OF ORGANS THAT ARE ARRANGED IN WELL-DEFINED SERIES. The average flower has sepals, petals, stamens and an ovary or ovaries. The number, shape and exact position of the various organs is diagnostic of genera and sometimes whole families and are important in plant classification. In some species one or other organ, or several sets of organs may be reduced or missing. For instance, some flowers are without sepals and others without petals. In unisexual flowers the male or female organs are suppressed or missing altogether.

SEPALS

The outermost series of a flower are the sepals (collectively the calyx). The sepals are often small and greenish, sometimes brightly coloured, but generally not particularly conspicuous. The sepals, which are often 3,4 or 5 in number and the same number as the petals, can be separate from one another or variously joined to form a tube or funnel around the other flower parts.

PETALS

The showy part of most flowers, which are often brightly coloured, are the petals (collectively the corolla). Like the sepals, the petals can be separate from one another or variously united, often to form a tube or bell shape, as in the flowers of the Harebell. In more extreme forms the corolla becomes 2-lipped (e.g. the White Deadnettle) or with one prominent lip as in many orchids.

STAMENS (COLLECTIVELY CALLED THE ANDROECIUM)

The stamens are the male organs of the flower. They consist of a stalk or filament and a two-parted anther which contains the pollen. Flowers can contain as many stamens as the other flower parts or many more. In flowers like the Poppy and Buttercup there is a central boss of numerous stamens.

OVARIES (COLLECTIVELY CALLED THE GYNOECIUM)

The ovaries are the female part of the flower and consist of the ovary itself (containing the ovules which, after fertilisation, develop into the seeds) and a receptive apex or stigma. The stigma is often drawn out on a long slender stalk, the style. Ovaries vary enormously as do the resultant fruit types. They can consist of numerous separate little ovaries (as in the Buttercup) or they consist of one or a number of chambers in which the ovules are located. After fertilisation the ovary expands in various ways to produce a vast range of different shapes and styles of fruit. Identifying fruit types can be just as useful in diagnosing the correct species, as can be the flower.

Flower Shapes

ONE OF THE MOST FASCINATING THINGS ABOUT FLOWERS IS THE INFINITE VARIETY of shapes, sizes and colours that they present. As has been seen, the average flower is made up of several well-defined series of organs. It is the elaboration or suppression of these various organs that creates variety. For instance, in some species there may be even-sized petals, while in others the petals may be very uneven, or fused together in various ways to give a unique shape. Flowers may have few or many stamens and the structure of the ovaries and subsequent fruits is remarkably variable. Species within the same genus will share the same basic flower and fruit structure but may differ in details such as colour, size and patterning.

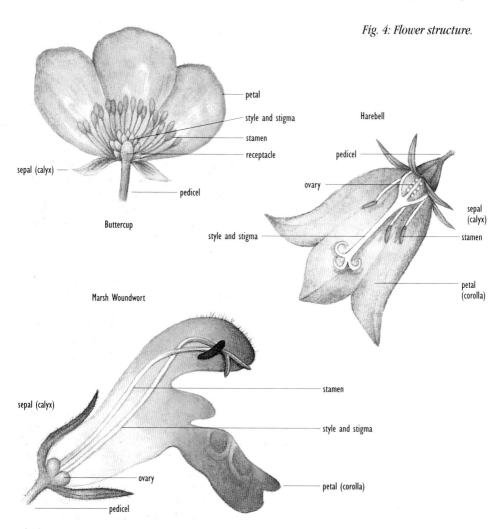

Fig. 4: Flower structure.

petal

style and stigma

stamen

receptacle

Harebell

sepal (calyx)

pedicel

pedicel

ovary

sepal (calyx)

Buttercup

style and stigma

stamen

Marsh Woundwort

petal (corolla)

stamen

sepal (calyx)

style and stigma

ovary

petal (corolla)

pedicel

Some typical shapes of European wild flowers are:

BOWL-SHAPED:
An open bowl shape typical of the buttercups and anemones.

CROSS-SHAPED (CRUCIFORM):
4-parted flowers in which the 4 petals form a distinctive cross-shape; typical of members of the cress family, Cruciferae.

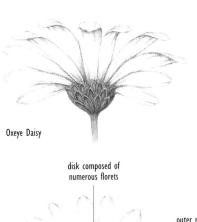

Oxeye Daisy

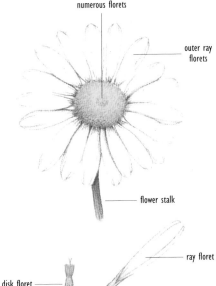

disk composed of numerous florets

outer ray florets

flower stalk

ray floret

disk floret

Fig. 4: (continued)

STAR-SHAPED:
5-parted flowers (sometimes 6-8-parted) flowers which form a typical star shape, e.g. stonecrops, many onions.

BELL-SHAPED:
Generally a pendent flower which is typically bell-shaped, as are many members of the Campanulaceae, e.g the common Harebell.

SALVER-SHAPED:
The corolla has a long tube with the lobes spreading out at right angles to form a distinctive limb, e.g. Primrose.

FUNNEL-SHAPED:
Forming a typical cone shape with the corolla narrowing to a neck, e.g. bindweeds.

PEA-SHAPED:
Restricted to members of the pea family, Leguminosae. In the pea-flower there are 5 petals: the upper one forms a standard and the two lateral ones wings, while the lower two petals are fused along the lower edge to form a keel that encloses the stamens and ovary.

TWO-LIPPED:
Typical of members of the deadnettle family, Labiatae, but not exclusive to that family are flowers in which the corolla is tubular but terminates in an upper and a lower lip; the upper lip generally forms a hood which houses the stamens and style, while the low lip forms a landing platform for visiting insects.

DAISY- OR THISTLE-SHAPED (COMPOSITE):
Members of the daisy family, Compositae, and the scabious family, Dipsacaceae, bear numerous small flowers (or florets) massed into dense heads of capitula which are surrounded by a series of flower-bracts. The individual florets have a corolla as well as stamens and an ovary, although the outer florets in the capitulum are often sterile and enlarged. The central florets often form a distinctive disk.

13

Fruits

FRUIT IDENTIFICATION CAN BE JUST AS IMPORTANT in the accurate naming of plants as the flowers and, like them, they are extremely complex and variable from one species to another.

Fruits develop from the maturing ovaries after fertilisation. The fruit structure may consist only of the ovary and the contained seeds, but other parts of the flower such as the receptacle, the corolla or the calyx may be elaborated into the fruit structure. For instance, in the fruit of the strawberry it is the swollen receptacle that forms the juicy part of the fruit with the seeds embedded on its surface. In the fruit of the clematis the style persists in the fruit and eventually becomes feathery and this aids the seeds in their dispersal by wind.

PRIME FRUIT TYPES:

ACHENES
Single-seeded dry fruit that does not split and falls from the plant in one piece. Achenes are sometime adorned with a feathery style as in the Pasque Flower, or with a pappus or parachute of hairs, as in the Dandelion.

POD
Typical of members of the pea family, Leguminosae, is the pod, a single-chambered fruit (containing a row of seeds) which normally splits along two opposing sides.

FOLLICLES
Rather like a pod but splitting along the inner edge only. Follicles are often arranged in groups, e.g. Columbine and Marsh Marigold.

CAPSULES
A very common type of fruit which is dry when mature, splitting for its entire length, or a part of, to release the seeds. Capsules can split by a few apical teeth (campions) or pores (poppies) and are extremely variable in size, shape and structure from one species to another. In the balsam fruit the capsule explodes elastically when ripe, flinging the seeds from the plant.

ACHENE

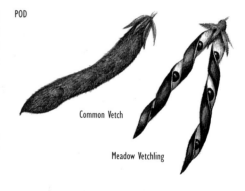

Pasque flower   Buttercup   Dandelion

POD

Common Vetch

Meadow Vetchling

CAPSULES

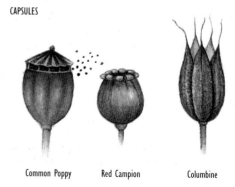

Common Poppy   Red Campion   Columbine

Fig. 5: Fruits

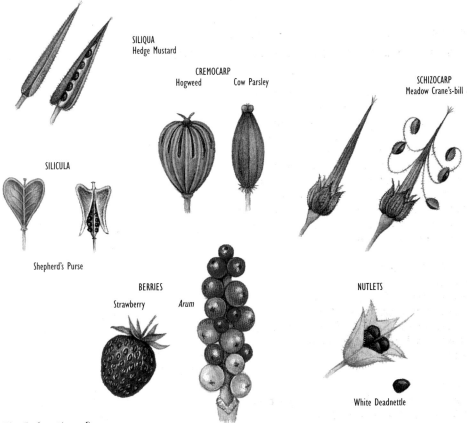

SILIQUA
Hedge Mustard

CREMOCARP
Hogweed   Cow Parsley

SCHIZOCARP
Meadow Crane's-bill

SILICULA

Shepherd's Purse

BERRIES
Strawberry   *Arum*

NUTLETS

White Deadnettle

Fig. 5: (continued)

SILIQUA

A long, often slender, two-valved fruit with the seeds attached to a central membrane (as in Honesty). When ripe the two valves split away form the centre of the fruit to release the seeds. Many members of the Cruciferae possess siliquas.

SILICULA

Essentially similar to the Siliqua but the fruits are short and often broad. The shape can vary immensely from species to species, with ovals, rounds and heart-shapes predominating. Many crucifers possess siliculas but the fruit type is not confined to that family.

SCHIZOCARP

Dry fruits that break up into one-seeded portions or mericarps. In the members of the Umbelliferae, the carrot family, the fruits split into two one-seeded pieces when ripe, leaving behind a central spindle. In the geranium fruit, five single-seed portions spring away from the central core but remain attached at the apex; this action flings the seeds away from the plant.

BERRY

A fleshy fruit that usually contains a single seed. Berries are often brightly coloured when ripe.

NUTLETS

Dry hard-walled little fruits containing a single seed and not splitting when ripe. Members of the mint family, Labiatae, and borage family, Boraginaceae, typically have nutlets (usually 4 or 5) which are located at the base of the persistent calyx.

15

Where to Look

LOOKING FOR WILD FLOWERS CAN BE A REWARDING AND ABSORBING PASTIME. There are many types of habitat that can be explored from fields and hedgerows, to woodland, hills and mountains. Rural areas are obviously the best to explore for seeing a wide range of wild flowers, but urban areas can also produce an extraordinary variety; even inner city areas and canal banks or industrial sites can harbour a surprising range of wild flowers, as well as alien species that have crept into the country from abroad.

It can be great fun going on walks to look for wild flowers and seeing how many different ones can be identified. Familiarity makes identification easier and, after a short while, it will be possible to put a name to many of the local wild flowers in your area. You can then start to move further afield to look for a great diversity of plants, looking especially for some of the more unusual or rarer ones.

Habitats play an important rôle: although some plants can grow happily in a variety of different habitats, others are more restricted and specialised. Exploring different types of habitat opens up a far greater range of plants. For instance, woodland will reveal a completely different range of plants to chalk grassland or mountain screes. Of the more accessible habitats, meadows, hedgerows and woodland offer the greatest variety for those starting to explore the world of wild flowers. For the naturalist, looking for flowers goes hand in hand with bird-watching, looking for insects and other wildlife and many happy hours can be spent on natural history jaunts, close to home or further afield.

Finds can be recorded in a nature diary, which can include brief descriptions of the plants and their habitats, as well as small diagnostic drawings. A camera can be a very useful tool and photographs can be a lasting reminder of plants and places.

CONSERVATION

Today, conservation of our wild flowers and habitats is vitally important if future generations are to see and appreciate the variety of wildlife that we enjoy. Habitats are under threat from development from new housing estates, factories and road improvements, as well as modern farm practices, particularly the widespread use of herbicides and land drainage. All this puts considerable pressure on our wildlife, with some habitats being increasingly squeezed into smaller and smaller areas.

Our wild flowers need to be treated with respect. In Britain and many European countries it is a punishable offence to dig up any wild flower, besides which, many of the rarer ones are given special protection from picking or the removal of seed. In addition, many areas are set aside as national parks and reserves; besides often being areas of outstanding natural beauty, these are often habitats of scientific interest where plants and animals can thrive unmolested.

When identifying wild flowers take the book to the plant; this avoids having to pick it for purposes of identification. Where identification requires more detailed investigation the removal of small plant portions (say a leaf, a flower or a fruit) for later analysis can do very little harm, provided the plant does not have special protection. It is always wise to leave a plant alone if its rarity value is not known.

Further Reading

HAVING IDENTIFIED THE COMMONER WILD FLOWERS you will doubtless want to move on to more detailed and comprehensive books. HarperCollins*Publishers* have a series of floras and field guides that provide full coverage. These include:

Mediterranean Wild Flowers, Marjorie Blamey and Christopher Grey-Wilson (HarperCollins*Publishers*)

Collins Pocket Guide Alpine Flowers of Britain and Europe, Marjorie Blamey and Christopher Grey-Wilson (HarperCollins*Publishers*)

Collins Pocket Guide Wild Flowers of Britain and Northern Europe, Richard Fitter, Alistair Fitter and Marjorie Blamey (HarperCollins*Publishers*)

ALSO:

New Flora of the British Isles, Clive Stace (Cambridge University Press)

The Illustrated Flora of Britain and Northern Europe, Marjorie Blamey and Christopher Grey-Wilson (Hodder & Stoughton)

Flora Europaea, 5 volumes, Ed. V. Heywood *et al*. (Cambridge University Press)

In addition there are numerous regional floras to the various European countries covered by this book and to individual regions (for instance, many British counties have their own flora).

Identification Keys

(BASED ON DETAILS OF THE FLOWERS AND FRUITS)

For flowers aggregated into dense heads or umbels *see* key on p.20

i. FLOWERS 3-PARTED (WITH PARTS IN THREES)

1. a) Flowers with 6 'petals', without a lip: **2**
   b) Flowers with 2 or 5 'petals' and a distinct lip: **5**

2. a) Flowers with 6 even 'petals': **3**
   b) Flowers with uneven 'petals', 3 large and 3 small and a different shape: **4**

3. a) Flowers star-shaped: ***Allium*** pp.228–9
   Scilla verna p.231
   b) Flowers bell- or urn-shaped:
   Convallaria majalis (white) p.233
   Hyacinthoides (blue, occasionally pink or white) pp.230–1
   Leucojum (white tipped green) p.235
   Polygonatum (white) pp.232–3
   c) Flowers flared, with a distinct trumpet:
   Narcissus (yellow) pp.246–7

4. a) Flowers nodding white with short inner 'petals': ***Galanthus nivalis*** p.234
   b) Flowers with large falls and smaller erect standards: ***Iris*** pp.248–9

5. a) Flowers spurred:
   Anacamptis pyramidalis (lip plain, 3-lobed) p.240
   Dactylorhiza (lip 3-lobed, spotted) pp.242–3
   Platanthera (lip unlobed, plain) p.241
   Orchis (lip 3-lobed, usually spotted) pp.238–9
   b) Flowers not spurred:
   Epipactis (lip not insect- or spider-like) pp.244–5
   Ophrys (lip insect- or spider-like) pp.236–7

ii. FLOWERS 4-PARTED (WITH 4 SEPARATE SEPALS AND/OR PETALS)

1. a) Petals absent; flowers green or greenish-yellow: **2**
   b) Petals present, 4: **3**

2. a) Leaves whorled, elliptic to oval, untoothed:
   Cruciata p.43
   Galium pp.42–3

b) Leaves mostly basal, rounded, lobed and toothed : ***Alchemilla*** p.91

3. a) Flowers with many stamens; petals not clawed:
   Glaucium flavum p.24
   Papaver pp.22–3
   Chelidonium majus p.25
   b) Flowers with 8 stamens:
   Chamerion angustifolium p.40
   Epilobium p.41
   c) Flowers with 6 stamens; petals clawed (crucifers): **4**
   d) Flowers with 2 stamens only:
   Veronica pp.44–7

4. a) Fruit slender, much longer than wide, a siliqua:
   Alliaria petiolata p.26
   Brassica pp.30–1
   Cardamine pp.34–5
   Cheiranthus cheri p.29
   Hesperis matronalis p.28
   Sinapis p.33
   Sisymbrium p.31
   b) Fruit short, generally as long as wide, or somewhat longer, a silicula:
   Capsella bursa-pastoris p.38
   Cochlearia p.37
   Thlaspi p.39

iii. FLOWERS 5-PARTED (WITH 5 (OCCASIONALLY 10) SEPALS AND/OR PETALS)

1. a) Flowers pea-shaped (with a standard petal two wings and a keel); legumes: **2**
   b) Flowers not pea-shaped: **3**

2. a) Leaves with tendrils: ***Lathyrus*** pp.134–5
   Ceratocapnos p.129
   Vicia pp.130–3
   b) Leaves without tendrils:
   Melilotus pp.136–7
   Lotus pp.138–9
   Trifolium pp.142–5
   Medicago pp.140–1
   Corydalis, Fumaria pp.128–9

3. a) Petals separate: **4**
   b) Petals joined or partly joined: **9**

4. a) Sepals 8–10 (in two whorls), fused towards the base:
   Fragaria (fruit a strawberry) pp.58–9
   Malva (fruit a ring of 'seeds') pp.70–1
   Potentilla (fruit a cluster of achenes) pp.54–7
   b) Sepals 3, separate, the lowermost elaborated into a spur:
   Impatiens (fruit an explosive capsule) pp.124–5
   c) Sepals 5, separate: **5**
   d) Sepals 5, fused into a tube: **8**

5. a) Flowers star-shaped, the petals not notched:
   Arenaria (fruit a capsule) p.74
   Saxifraga (fruit 2-parted) pp.76–8
   Sedum (fruit star-shaped) p.79
   Spergularia (fruit a capsule) p.75
   b) Flowers star-shaped, with notched petals:
   Cerastium p.73
   Stellaria p.72
   c) Flowers spurred:
   Aquilegia vulgaris p.177
   d) Flowers not as 5a–5c: **6**

6. a) Flowers not symmetrical: ***Viola*** pp.126–7
   b) Flowers symmetrical: **7**

7. a) Leaves unlobed: ***Anagallis*** p.109
   Helianthemum pp.68–9
   Hypericum pp.66–7
   Linum pp.64–5
   Lysimachia p.108
   Ranunculus (in part) pp.50–2
   Caltha p.53
   b) Leaves lobed: ***Filipendula*** pp.90–1
   Geranium pp.60–3
   Oxalis p.65
   Ranunculus (in part) pp.48–9

8. a) Calyx with pairs of bracts around the base:
   Dianthus pp.86–7

   b) Calyx bractless: ***Lychnis*** pp.80–1
   Saponaria officinalis p.81
   Silene pp.82–5

9. a) Corolla not 2-lipped: **10**
   b) Corolla 2-lipped: **14**

10. a) Flowers flat, cupped or salver-shaped: **11**
    b) Flowers not as above: **13**

11. a) Flowers borne on leafless stems (scapes):
    Armeria pp.110–11
    Limonium vulgare p.111
    Primula pp.106–7
    b) Flowers borne on leafy stems: **12**

12. a) Fruit a berry: ***Solanum*** p.117
    b) Fruit 4 nutlets at the base of the calyx:
    Borago officinalis p.116
    Lithospermum pp.112–13
    Myosotis pp.114–15
    c) Fruit a many-seeded capsule:
    Verbascum pp.118–19
    d) Fruit small, dry, not splitting:
    Valeriana pp.120–1

13. a) Corolla tubular; fruit 4 nutlets at the base of the calyx:
    Echium vulgare, Symphytum pp.100–1
    b) Corolla funnel-shaped; twining plants:
    Calystegia p.105
    Convolvulus arvensis p.104
    c) Corolla bell-shaped:
    Atropa belladonna (fruit a berry; corolla greenish, not netted) p.102
    Campanula (fruit a capsule; corolla bright blue or purple, not netted) pp.94–9
    Hyoscyamus niger (fruit a capsule; corolla sombre, netted) p.103

14. a) Fruit 4 nutlets at the base of the calyx; Labiatae: **15**
    b) Fruit a many-seeded 2-part capsule; Scrophulariaceae and Orobanchaceae: **18**

19

15. a) Upper lip of corolla much reduced:
      Ajuga pp.146–7
      Teucrium p.149
  b) Upper lip of corolla equal to the lower: **16**

16. a) Plants patch-forming, with stolons or runner:
      Glechoma hederacea p.150
      Lamiastrum galeobdolon p.155
      Lamium (in part) p.154
      Mentha pp.162–3
      Thymus p.165
  b) Plants tufted, without runners or stolons: **17**

17. a) Upper lip of corolla hooded (concave), as large or larger than the lower lip:
      Ballota nigra p.152
      Galeopsis pp.156–7
      Lamium (in part) pp.154–5
      Leonurus p.153
      Prunella p.147
      Salvia (the only genus in this group with 2 rather than 4 stamens) pp.158–9
      Scutellaria pp.148–9
      Stachys pp.160–1
  b) Upper lip of corolla flat or convex, generally shorter than the lower lip:
      Nepeta p.151
      Origanum vulgare p.164
      Teucrium p.149

18. a) Corolla spurred at the base:
      Kickxia p.169
      Linaria pp.168–9
  b) Corolla not spurred: **19**

19. a) Calyx with 4 even teeth or lobes:
      Melampyrum pp.174–5
      Odontites p.175
      Rhinanthus minor p.175
  b) Calyx 2-lipped or with teeth:
      Mimulus pp.170–1
      Pedicularis pp.172–3
      Scrophularia pp.166–7

iv. FLOWERS 6 OR MORE PARTED

1. a) Flowers solitary: ***Anemone*** pp.88–9
  b) Flowers whorled: ***Lythrum*** pp.92–3

v. FLOWERS AGGREGATED INTO DENSE HEADS OR UMBELS (COMPOSITES AND UMBELLIFERS)

1. a) Flowers borne in umbels: **2**
  b) Flowers borne in dense heads: **4**

2. a) Flowers greenish, small with distinctive glands and encircling bracts, borne in distinctive umbels: ***Euphorbia*** pp.188–9
  b) Flowers not as above, usually white or yellowish, rarely pinkish; fruit flat and 2-parted; umbellifers: **3**

3. a) Flowers yellow or greenish-yellow:
      Angelica pp.184–5
      Smyrnium pp.186–7
  b) Flowers white, occasionally pinkish:
      Aegopodium podograria p.183
      Anthriscus pp.178–9
      Chaerophyllum p.179
      Daucus carota p.180
      Heracleum sphondylium p.182
      Pimpinella p.181

4. a) Flowerheads thistle-like (florets all the same, usually 5-lobed, not strap-shaped): **5**
  b) Flowerheads cornflower- or scabious-like (florets similar but the outer often enlarged, not strap-shaped): **6**
  c) Flowerheads dandelion-like (florets all strap-shaped): **7**
  d) Flowerheads daisy-like (florets of two types, the outer strap-shaped): **8**

5. a) Flowerheads elongated, the florets with protruding stamens: ***Dipsacus*** pp.202–3
  b) Flowerheads flat to rounded, the florets with included and inconspicuous stamens:
      Arctium p.203
      Carduus pp.207, 210–11
      Carlina pp.204–5
      Cirsium pp.206–9

6. a) Florets with protruding stamens; Dipsacaceae:

> **Jasione** p.215
> **Knautia** pp.216–17
> **Scabiosa** p.217
> **Succisa pratensis** p.214

b) Florets with included and inconspicuous stamens; Compositae: **Centaurea** pp.212–13

7. a) Leaves primarily in a basal rosette:

> **Crepis** and **Hieracium** pp.226–7
> **Hypochaeris** p.225
> **Taraxacum officinale** p.224

b) Leaves primarily alternate on well-developed stems: **Cichorium intybus** p.219

> **Lactuca** pp.222–3
> **Lapsana communis** p.223
> **Sonchus** pp.220–1
> **Tragopogon** pp.218–19

8. a) Flowerheads white, with a yellow or brownish disk:

> **Achillea** (flowerheads occasionally with pink or reddish rays) pp.196–7
> **Anthemis** p.191
> **Bellis perennis** p.191
> **Leucanthemum vulgare** p.198
> **Tanacetum vulgare** p.199
> **Matricaria** and **Tripleurospermum** pp.190–1

b) Flowerheads yellow with a yellow or brownish disk: **Chrysanthemum segetum** p.199

> **Inula** p.193
> **Pulicaria dysenterica** p.192
> **Senecio** pp.200–1
> **Tussilago** p.195

c) Flowerheads pink, yellowish-white or reddish-violet overall: **Petasites** pp.194–5

vi. ODD ONES OUT

Several common wild flowers do not fit comfortably into any of the above groupings and are singled out here:

Arum has distinctive heart shaped leaves and a spike-like inflorescence with separated male and female flowers borne on a fleshy axis that is surrounded by a large spathe. pp.250–1

Digitalis purpurea, the foxglove, has basically 5-parted flowers, but the corolla is tubular and appears to be all one piece and scarcely lobed. p.176

Reseda has 4–8-parted flowers borne in slender spikes and petals that are deeply fringed. pp.122–3

Papaveraceae

Common Poppy
Papaver rhoeas

A very common and easily recognised plant typical of arable land and other disturbed sites. However, despite this, this attractive species has certainly declined in recent years due to agricultural practices, particularly the widespread use of herbicides. It will grow in association with other arable weeds such as Corncockle, Cornflower and Corn Marigold, all of which have suffered an even more severe decline.

The seeds of the Common Poppy can reside in the soil for many years waiting for the right conditions to germinate; disturbance of the land by some means or another normally triggers this.

NOTE:
Generally rather uniform in the wild but local variants can be seen from time to time. These include those with semi-double flowers or flowers in paler colours, especially lilac, pale pink or almost white, or petals with a paler edge. All poppies exude a whitish or yellowish latex when cut.

KEY FEATURES: Flowers large and bright scarlet, open throughout the day but individually short-lived. Sepals falling away as the buds open to reveal 4 large crumpled petals, which usually have a black blotch at the base.

HABITAT: Arable land, wasteland, disturbed sites such as recent road workings, motorway verges and where ditches have been cleared; most often on calcareous or sandy soils.

FREQUENCY: Locally common, sometimes abundant, especially on set-aside land. Throughout England but far more local in Wales, Scotland and Ireland.

SEASON: June to early September, but a few blooms sometimes persisting until October.

HABIT: Bristly annual to 60 cm tall, usually branched, but depauperate unbranched plants can be found on poor land.

LEAVES: Grey-green, pinnately lobed and with rather narrow, toothed segments.

FLOWERS: Solitary on long wiry stalks, 7–10 cm diameter. Calyx 2-parted and bristly, deciduous. Petals rounded, overlapping. Stamens numerous with bluish anthers, forming a prominent boss around the ovary.

FRUIT: A smooth rounded capsule with pores around the rim and through which the numerous seeds escape, like pepper from a pepperpot.

J
F
M
A
M
J
J
A
S
O
N
D

22

LOOKALIKES

Long-headed Poppy *Papaver dubium*
Very similar but flowers smaller, 3–7 cm diameter, and
pale scarlet, the petals often unblotched at the base. In
addition, the fruit capsule is oblong. Equally
widespread but rarely found in such large numbers.
June–August. Throughout except for the north of
Scotland.

Long-headed Poppy

Rough Poppy

Prickly Poppy

Prickly Poppy
Papaver argemone
A smaller plant to 40 cm tall
with pale scarlet flower 2–6
cm diameter with the petals
not overlapping but only
sometimes with a dark basal blotch. The fruit capsule is
oblong and bears a few erect bristles. Similar habitats but more
often on light sandy soils. May–August. Throughout except for the
far north.

Opium Poppy

Rough Poppy *Papaver hybridum*
Similar to the Prickly Poppy but flowers crimson, the petals always with
a dark basal blotch. The fruit capsules are rounded and densely covered
with pale yellowish bristles. Similar habitats; nearly always on well-drained
calcareous soils. June–August. Throughout except for much of the north
and Ireland.

Opium Poppy *Papaver somniferum*
Very distinct from the others, being a taller very upright annual to 1 m with fleshy,
smooth greyish leaves and large purple, pink or mauve flowers up to 15 cm diameter.
The large smooth, rounded fruit capsules are widely used for dried decoration and
contain the seeds widely used as a condiment. Cultivated and wasteland. June–August.
Throughout except for the far north.

23

Horned Poppy

Glaucium flavum

Papaveraceae

This distinctive member of the poppy family is a coastal inhabitant. Plants are both imposing and handsome with fleshy foliage and typical 4-petalled poppy flowers. The seed, like those of the common poppy, *Papaver rhoeas* (*see* p.22), can reside for a long time in the soil until condition are right for germination. When bruised the whole plant exudes a yellow sap. Poisonous.

NOTE:
The common name Horned Poppy refers to the long curved horn-like fruit pods.

J
F
M
A
M
J
J
A
S
O
N
D

KEY FEATURES: A large fleshy silvery-grey plant, with a waxy texture. Upper leaves clasping the stem. Flowers with 4 petals and numerous stamens. Sepals 2, completely enclosing the flower and falling away as the buds burst open. Fruit a long slender 2-parted capsule.

HABITAT: Primary coastal shingles and dunes, but occasionally on sea cliffs or inland.

FREQUENCY: Locally common along coastal Europe as far north as southern Norway; in Britain not north of Argyll.

SEASON: June–September.

HABIT: A stout silvery-grey, much-branched, biennial or short-lived perennial, to 90 cm tall.

LEAVES: Large and fleshy, with a waxy, rough-hairy surface; lower and basal leaves broadly lobed, stalked, while the upper leaves are smaller, less deeply lobed and clasp the stem with unstalked bases.

FLOWERS: Solitary, poppy-like, yellow, cup-shaped, 6–9 cm across, with a central boss of stamens and a single bilobed stigma.

FRUIT: A long linear capsule, sickle-shaped, to 30 cm long, smooth, splitting lengthways into two when ripe.

Lookalikes

Greater celandine *Chelidonium majus*
Superficially like a small version of the previous but a plant of moist shaded habitats, especially woodland and hedgebanks. A short-lived tufted perennial to 80 cm, with pinnately-lobed pale-green leaves. Flowers small but poppy-like, bright yellow, 15–25 mm across, borne in a small cluster at the top of a common stalk. Capsule linear-oblong, 30–50 cm long, splitting into two when ripe. Throughout, except Iceland. Poisonous.

Garlic Mustard
Alliaria petiolata

Cruciferae

Also commonly known as Jack-by-the-Hedge, this common and often gregarious plant has been long used as a flavouring in soups, stews and sauces because of its mild garlic flavour; the young shoots are used before they become too tough or the plants run up to flowering. *Alliaria* is one of a number of white-flowered crucifers in the area; fruit identification is important for accurate identification of many of them.

NOTE:
Members of the Cruciferae are frequently referred to as crucifers. This aptly describes the cross-like flowers with their typical 4 petals.

KEY FEATURES: A slender, stiffly erect biennial, occasionally annual, with a simple unbranched stem. Leaves nettle-shaped, smelling mildly of garlic when crushed. Flowers 4-parted, the spreading petals forming a cross. Fruit a linear, 2-parted, erect capsule.

HABITAT: Woodland margins, hedgerows, scrub, roadsides and waste places, often on calcareous soils.

FREQUENCY: Common and often forming large colonies; throughout except for the Faeroes and Iceland.

SEASON: April–June.

HABIT: Erect biennial to 1.2 m, though generally less, usually with a simple unbranched stem.

LEAVES: Alternate, kidney-shaped to heart-shaped, rather pale green, stalked and with a coarsely toothed margin.

FLOWERS: White, numerous borne in elongating racemes, each 3–5 mm across. Sepals green, half the length of the petals.

FRUIT: Linear, 2–7 cm long, eventually splitting into 2 valves and containing many seeds.

J
F
M
A
M
J
J
A
S
O
N
D

LOOKALIKES

Hoary Cress *Cardaria draba*
Has similar, but slightly larger white flower, but borne in broader, branched clusters. A greyish perennial generally with several stems from the base and oblong stem leaves that clasp the stem with unstalked bases. The fruit is entirely different, small and kidney-shaped, only 3–4.5 mm and somewhat inflated. Cultivated and waste ground, roadsides and hedgerows; May–June. Throughout, except for the Faeroes and Iceland.

Horse-radish *Armoracia rusticana*
A robust patch-forming perennial with very large deep green, oblong basal leaves, often in excess of 50 cm long. Flowers often sparsely produced, but borne in large panicle-like inflorescences; white, 8–9 mm across. Fruit rarely produced, but rounded and inflated, 4–6 mm across. Widely naturalised from S Russia in fields, verges, along streamsides, railways and on wasteland; May–June. Throughout except for most of the north and Iceland. Frequently cultivated.

Dame's Violet

Hesperis matronalis

Cruciferae

A lthough not native in the area, Dame's Violet has become so thoroughly naturalised that it can now almost be considered to be indigenous. The plant has been cultivated for many centuries; formerly in medieval and herb gardens, later as an important cottage garden flower; from these sources it must have escaped into the wild.

NOTE:
The flowers are visited by various insects, but particularly butterflies.

J
F
M
A
M
J
J
A
S
O
N
D

KEY FEATURES: A tall perennial branched only in the inflorescence. Leaves alternate, not divided. Flowers 4-parted, fragrant. Fruit a linear pod, curved upwards.

HABITAT: Grassy places, field boundaries, hedgerows and verges.

FREQUENCY: Locally common throughout apart from the far north.

SEASON: May–August.

HABIT: An erect tufted hairy perennial, occasionally biennial; stems stiff, branched only in the upper half, to 1.2 m tall.

LEAVES: Lanceolate, short stalked, with a coarsely toothed margin.

FLOWERS: White or purple, 15–20 mm across, borne in large panicle-like clusters, sweetly fragrant.

FRUIT: A linear pod, 2–10 cm long, smooth, upward curved.

LOOKALIKES

Perennial Honesty *Lunaria rediviva*
A lower plant to 70 cm with oval, pointed leaves and pale
purple to violet flowers, 20–25 mm across. Fruit very
distinctive, elliptical and pointed, pendent, 3.5–9 cm long,
splitting into 2 valves to leave a shiny silvery membrane. Damp
woods and shaded places; May–July. Continental Europe
from Denmark and Germany southwards. Widely cultivated.

Wallflower
Cheiranthus cheiri
A rather variable plant with oblong, untoothed
leaves and racemes of yellow or orange-brown,
sweetly scented flowers, each 20–25 mm
across. Fruit a linear, erect pod, 2.5–7.5
cm long. Widely naturalised in rocky
places and on old walls throughout
except for Scandinavia and Iceland,
but widely cultivated. March–June.

Treacle Mustard *Erysimum cheiranthoides*
A hairy annual with square stems and oblong to
lanceolate, toothed leaves. Flowers small and yellow,
5–6 mm across, borne in racemes. Fruit a linear pod,
1–5 cm long, curved upwards. Weed of arable and
cultivated land; June–August. Throughout, except the far
north and the Faeroes.

Black Mustard
Brassica nigra

Cruciferae

The brassicas are a widespread and rather confusing group in the area, all being rather lank, leafy herbs with yellow flowers. *B. nigra* is particularly common in some regions. It has been cultivated for many centuries as a source of mustard flour, ground from the seeds. This is often mixed with white mustard, *Sinapis alba* (*see* p.33).

J
F
M
A
M
J
J
A
S
O
N
D

KEY FEATURES: Tall and rather greyish plant, with stems bristly below. Lower leaves lobed, the upper unlobed and with a narrowed base, not clasping the stem, Flowers yellow, 4-parted. Fruit a short erect pod pressed close to the stem.

HABITAT: Cultivated and waste ground, river and ditch margins, sea cliffs.

FREQUENCY: Widespread and locally abundant in the area apart from the far north and Iceland.

SEASON: June–August.

HABIT: Tall greyish annual to 1.2 m, with erect stems that are branched in the inflorescence and bristly below.

LEAVES: The lower pinnately lobed while the upper are unlobed and narrow-oblong.

FLOWERS: Yellow, 12–15 mm across, borne in long, slender branched racemes.

FRUIT: An erect pod only 10–20 mm long, with a short peak, splitting into 2 valves to release the seeds.

LOOKALIKES

Rape *Brassica napus*
Similar to Black Mustard but with the upper leaves more heart-shaped and clasping the stem, the flowers a deeper greenish-yellow, 14–25 mm across, and the fruits spreading 5–10 cm long. Widely cultivated and naturalised throughout, except the far north. May–August.

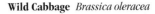

Wild Cabbage *Brassica oleracea*
A biennial or perennial with waxy, rather fleshy leaves, the lower of which are lobed, while the upper are unlobed and clasping the stem. Flowers yellow, 30–40 mm across, in branched racemes. Fruit pod linear. 5–7 cm long, with a cylindrical beak. Coastal habitats, particularly cliffs; May–September. Britain and France; naturalised in Holland and Germany.

Hedge Mustard *Sisymbrium officinale*
Superficially like a *Brassica* but a rough-hairy annual or biennial with spreading branches and lobed leaves with a large end lobe. Flowers yellow, small, only 3–4 mm across. Fruit pod erect, 1–2 cm long, linear, pressed close to the stem. Cultivated and waste ground; May–September. Throughout, except the far north.

Tall Rocket
Sisymbrium altissimum
Biennial with ascending branches, the upper leaves with linear segments. Flowers yellow, 10–11 mm across. Fruit pod linear 5–10 cm long. Waste and disturbed ground; naturalised throughout, except for the far north, Ireland and Iceland.

London Rocket
Sisymbrium irio
Like *S. altissimum*, but upper leaves with broad, toothed segments sand flowers pale yellow, small, 3–4 mm across, overtopped by the young linear fruits. Waste places, verges, old walls; June–August. Naturalised throughout, except for the far north.

31

Wild Radish

Raphanus raphanistrum

Cruciferae

A familiar plant of cultivated land, this is often a persistent agricultural weed and has been thoroughly naturalised in the region since prehistoric times. A coastal form, subsp. *maritimus*, the Sea Radish, which is taller and bushier with a carrot-like root with broader fruit pods, is native in Britain and Holland southwards.

NOTE:
The cultivated or garden radish is a different species R. sativus. *In* Raphanus *the fruits do not split into 2 valves as they do in most other crucifers.*

J
F
M
A
M
J
J
A
S
O
N
D

KEY FEATURES: A bristly annual or biennial, with most leaves pinnately lobed. Flowers 4-parted, the petals usually with violet veins. Fruit a beaded pod, prominently veined and with a long beak.

HABITAT: Cultivated, bare and waste ground, especially on clay soils.

FREQUENCY: Widespread and often common, sometimes gregarious; naturalised throughout, but possibly native in the south of the area.

SEASON: May–September.

HABIT: An erect bristly annual or biennial to 75 cm tall, simple or little branched.

LEAVES: All leaves blunt-toothed and stalked, the lower larger and pinnately lobed, but the upper unlobed.

FLOWERS: White or yellow, generally with violet veins, 15–30 mm across, borne in branched racemes.

FRUIT: An erect jointed and beaded pod, 3–9 cm long, with strong parallel veins and a prominent beak.

Garden Radish *Raphanus sativus*
Plants with a typical swollen fleshy rootstock
(radish) and white or lilac flowers. Fruit 2–9 cm
long, scarcely beaded. Cultivated and waste ground;
occasionally naturalised. Of unknown origin.

White Mustard *Sinapis alba*
Similar to *Raphanus*, but all the leaves are pinnately
lobed and the yellow flowers are 18–25 mm across.
Fruit pods 2–4 cm long, somewhat beaded, 2–4 cm
long, with a parallel-veined lower half and a flat-
beaked upper, splitting into 2 valves eventually; seeds
grey. Naturalised and cultivated almost throughout;
June–August.

Charlock *Sinapis arvensis*
Similar to *S. alba*, but upper leaves simple, lanceolate and
flowers smaller, 15–20 mm across. Fruit 1.5–4.5 cm long,
with a conical beak; seeds reddish-brown. Naturalised,
especially on cultivated and waste ground, throughout. An
injurious weed in some areas.

Cuckoo-flower
Cardamine pratensis

Cruciferae

A familiar plant of damp meadows, this attractive plant has acquired a host of local vernacular names including Lady's-smock, Milkmaids, May Flower and Fairy Flower. It comes into flower in the early spring when whole meadows can be stained from pink to mauve. The young leaves, like those of cress, have a peppery taste and can be used in salads.

NOTE:
Double-flowered forms 'Flore Pleno' occur occasionally in the wild and have been long cultivated in gardens.

J
F
M
A
M
J
J
A
S
O
N
D

KEY FEATURES: A hairless perennial with pinnate leaves. Flowers 4-parted with slightly notched petals. Fruit an erect linear pod.

HABITAT: Damp meadows and pastures, marshes, lake and stream margins, ditches and verges; occasionally in open woodland.

FREQUENCY: Widespread and locally abundant, often gregarious; throughout apart from the far north.

SEASON: April–June.

HABIT: An erect, tufted, hairless perennial to 50 cm tall, with a basal leaf-rosette.

LEAVES: All pinnate, the basal with rounded leaflets, but the upper with narrow-oblong leaflets.

FLOWERS: Pale pink, lilac or mauve, occasionally white, 12–18 mm across, borne in erect racemes; anthers yellow.

FRUIT: An erect linear pod 2.5–4 cm long, splitting into 2 valves when ripe.

34

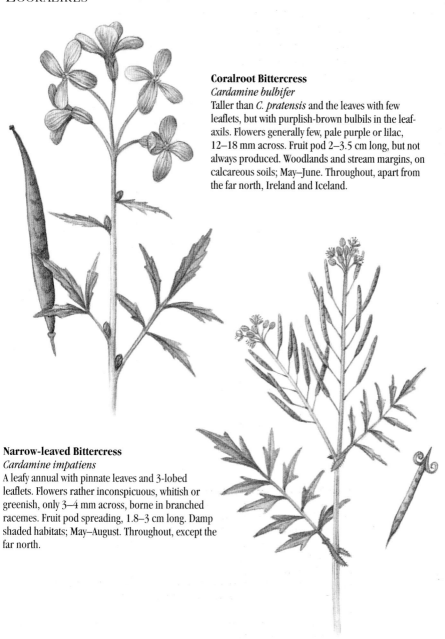

Coralroot Bittercress
Cardamine bulbifer
Taller than *C. pratensis* and the leaves with few leaflets, but with purplish-brown bulbils in the leaf-axils. Flowers generally few, pale purple or lilac, 12–18 mm across. Fruit pod 2–3.5 cm long, but not always produced. Woodlands and stream margins, on calcareous soils; May–June. Throughout, apart from the far north, Ireland and Iceland.

Narrow-leaved Bittercress
Cardamine impatiens
A leafy annual with pinnate leaves and 3-lobed leaflets. Flowers rather inconspicuous, whitish or greenish, only 3–4 mm across, borne in branched racemes. Fruit pod spreading, 1.8–3 cm long. Damp shaded habitats; May–August. Throughout, except the far north.

Tower Mustard

Arabis glabra

Cruciferae

A slender plant that is widespread yet often overlooked. It is one of a number of rather similar looking white- or cream-flowered cresses. In *Arabis* the fruits are long and slender but in the lookalike genera of *Iberis* and *Cochlearia* the fruits are very different. In the Cruciferae accurate identification of fruit types is critical to accurate determination.

KEY FEATURES: Stems simple. Leaves dimorphic, the basal stalked, deeply toothed and oblong, while the stem leaves are arrow-shaped and unstalked. Flowers 4-parted. Fruit a long slender erect pod.

HABITAT: Dry places, particularly woods and heaths.

FREQUENCY: Locally common throughout, except the far north, Ireland, the Faeroes and Iceland.

SEASON: May–July.

HABIT: An erect unbranched biennial to 1 m, though often less, with a basal leaf-rosette.

LEAVES: Grey-green, the basal oblong, stalked and with a toothed margin; stem leaves arrow-shaped, clasping the stem with an unstalked base and with an untoothed margin.

FLOWERS: Cream or greenish, 5–6 mm across, numerous borne in an elongating raceme.

FRUIT: A linear erect pod, 4–7 cm long, smooth.

J
F
M
A
M
J
J
A
S
O
N
D

36

LOOKALIKES

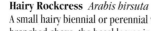

Hairy Rockcress *Arabis hirsuta*
A small hairy biennial or perennial with the stems branched above, the basal leaves in a rosette. Flowers white, 3–5 mm. Fruit pod 1.5–3.5 cm long, erect and held close to the stem. Dry grassy and rocky places, dunes; May–August. Throughout, except Iceland.

Wild Candytuft
Iberis amara
Distinctive annual of arable land with white or purplish flowers borne in flattish heads; each flower 6–8 mm across, with 2 long and 2 short petals. Fruit rounded, winged with triangular lobes, only 3–5 mm. S England (rare), Holland to Germany southwards.

Common Scurvy-grass
Cochlearia officinalis
A rather fleshy plant of primarily coastal habitats with kidney-shaped long-stalked basal leaves and clasping stem leaves. Flowers white, 8–10 mm across. Fruit a swollen rounded pod, 4–7 mm across. Throughout except the far north, Iceland and Finland.

English Scurvy-grass
Cochlearia anglica
Has oval, often slightly toothed, basal leaves and white flowers 9–14 mm across. Fruit pod elliptical, 8–15 mm. Muddy coastal habitats, particularly marshes; April–July. Throughout, except the far north and Iceland.

Danish Scurvy-grass *Cochlearia danica*
Basal leaves more triangular, while the upper are lobed. Flowers white to lilac-purple, only 4–5 mm across. Fruit pod oval, 3–6 mm. Coastal; January–September. Throughout, except the Faeroes and Iceland.

37

Shepherd's Purse

Capsella bursa-pastoris

Cruciferae

A very familiar and well-known weed of cultivated lands. The plant derives its common name from the heart-shaped seed capsules that remind one of the small purses or pouches attached to cords that were worn by medieval peasants around their waists.

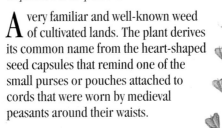

NOTE:
On poor and impoverished land plants may be very small, perhaps only 4–8 cm tall.

KEY FEATURES: Slight plant with a basal rosette of leaves. Flowers small, 4-parted. Fruit a heart-shaped capsule that splits into 2 when ripe.

HABITAT: Cultivated, bare and waste ground.

FREQUENCY: Common throughout.

SEASON: Flowering almost throughout the year, especially in lowland areas, except at more northerly latitudes.

HABIT: A very variable upright hairy to almost glabrous annual (sometimes overwintering) to 40 cm, often much smaller, with a simple or sparingly branched stem and a basal leaf rosette.

LEAVES: Basal leaves lanceolate to elliptical, pinnately lobed, with a winged stalk; stem leaves lanceolate, lobed or toothed, clasping the stem with an unstalked base.

FLOWERS: Small, white, 2–3 mm across, borne in lax elongating racemes with the lowermost flowering opening first. Sepals and petals 4, the latter twice the length of the former. Stamens 6.

FRUIT: A small flattish, triangular-heart-shaped capsule, 6–9 mm long, splitting into 2 valves when ripe to release the numerous coppery seeds.

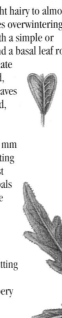

J
F
M
A
M
J
J
A
S
O
N
D

LOOKALIKES

Field Pennycress *Thlaspi arvense*
A more robust rather foetid plant of similar habit but with
larger, 4–6 mm flowers and quite large fruit capsules, 10–15
mm long, that are rounded with a broadly winged margin and
notched apex. Similar habitats, often on rather fertile soils;
May–August. Throughout, except for the far north and the
Faeroes.

Garlic Pennycress *Thlaspi alliaceum*
Similar to *T. arvense*, but the whole plant smelling of garlic when crushed
and the stem hairy below. In addition, the fruits are narrower and more
heart-shaped. Similar habitats in France and Germany; naturalised in SE
England; April–June.

Perfoliate Pennycress *Thlaspi perfoliatum*
Similar to *T. arvense*, but a slighter plant with rounded,
long-stalked, rosette leaves. Flowers smaller, 3–4 mm
across, and fruits only 4–6 mm. Throughout, except for
much of the north; in Britain rare and confined to bare
limestone areas in central-southern England.

Rosebay Willowherb

Chamerion angustifolium (syn. *Epilobium angustifolium*)

Onagraceae

NOTE:
A very variable plant that can be a serious and invasive weed in some places, especially in gardens.

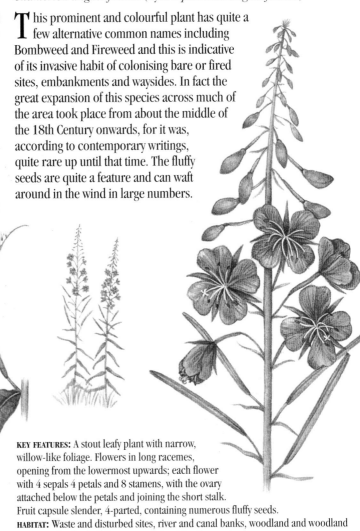

This prominent and colourful plant has quite a few alternative common names including Bombweed and Fireweed and this is indicative of its invasive habit of colonising bare or fired sites, embankments and waysides. In fact the great expansion of this species across much of the area took place from about the middle of the 18th Century onwards, for it was, according to contemporary writings, quite rare up until that time. The fluffy seeds are quite a feature and can waft around in the wind in large numbers.

KEY FEATURES: A stout leafy plant with narrow, willow-like foliage. Flowers in long racemes, opening from the lowermost upwards; each flower with 4 sepals 4 petals and 8 stamens, with the ovary attached below the petals and joining the short stalk. Fruit capsule slender, 4-parted, containing numerous fluffy seeds.
HABITAT: Waste and disturbed sites, river and canal banks, woodland and woodland margins, derelict buildings, on a variety of soils.
FREQUENCY: Common throughout, often gregarious and abundant.
SEASON: June–September.
HABIT: A stout patch-forming rhizomatous, almost hairless, perennial to 2 m tall, occasionally taller.
LEAVES: Alternate and crowded, lanceolate, slightly toothed, willow-like.
FLOWERS: Violet or rose-purple, 20–30 mm across, 4-parted; petals rounded and slightly notched, about the same length as the narrow, pointed sepals.
FRUIT: A linear capsule, often pinkish or purplish, splitting into 4 valves when ripe to release numerous fluffy seeds.

J
F
M
A
M
J
J
A
S
O
N
D

LOOKALIKES

Greater Willowherb *Epilobium hirsutum*
An equally robust plant but with hairy stems and leaves, the leaves
mostly paired or whorled. Flowers purple-pink, somewhat smaller.
Damp habitats and waste places; June–September. Throughout,
except the far north, Faeroes and Iceland.

▲ **Broad-leaved Willowherb** *Epilobium montanum*
A smaller plant to 60 cm, only slightly hairy and with mostly
opposite leaves. Flowers small, purplish-pink, 6–12 mm,
borne in a leafy raceme; petals deeply notched. Waste and
cultivated land, woodland, hedgebanks; May–August.
Throughout, except Iceland.

▶ **Spear-leaved Willowherb** *Epilobium lanceolatum*
Like *E. montanum*, but stems almost square (not round)
and leaves generally alternate. Flowers white changing to
pale pink. Similar habitats; June–September. Holland and
Germany southwards; widely naturalised in Britain.

41

Woodruff
Galium odoratum

Rubiaceae

This quiet yet attractive little mat-forming plant is typical of woodlands and shaded places. The plant has no appreciable odour when fresh but once dried it takes on a sweet new-mown hay scent that can last for many months. In medieval times the plant was much prized as an air freshener and was strewn around houses or placed in bunches in linen cupboards. It was also used in pot-pourris as well as pillows and for adding to wines and other drinks.

NOTE:
In most Galium *species the fruit barbs readily attach themselves to fur or clothing and aid in the dispersal of the seeds.*

KEY FEATURES: Stems square and rather brittle with a ring of hairs at each node. Leaves in distinct whorls of 6–9. Flowers small, 4-parted. Fruit a 2-lobed, with hooked, blackish bristles.
HABITAT: Deciduous woodland on calcareous soils; occasionally in shaded rocks or along hedgerows.
FREQUENCY: Common throughout, but absent from the Faeroes and Iceland.
SEASON: May–June.
HABIT: A low carpeting rhizomatous, practically hairless, perennial forming dense patches, with erect stems to 15 cm tall.
LEAVES: In whorls of 6–9, elliptical, untoothed but with a bristly margin.
FLOWERS: Small white, 4–7 mm, faintly scented, like a 4-pointed star, borne in broad, branched clusters.
FRUIT: Small, 2–3 mm, 2-lobed covered in hooked, black-tipped bristles.

LOOKALIKES

Common Marsh Bedstraw *Galium palustre*
A much larger and laxer plant with leaves in whorls of 4–6. Flowers white or greenish, with red anthers, 2–3 mm across. Fruit smooth, black when ripe. Moist and wet habitats; June–August. Throughout.

Lady's Bedstraw *Galium verum*
Has distinctive rounded stems with 4 raised lines and shiny leaves in whorls of 8–12. Flowers golden-yellow, 2–3.5 mm across, fragrant, in large narrow panicles. Fruit 2-lobed and smooth, black when ripe. Open habitats such as grassland, hedgebanks, verges and dunes; June–September. Throughout, except the Faeroes.

J
F
M
A
M
J
J
A
S
O
N
D

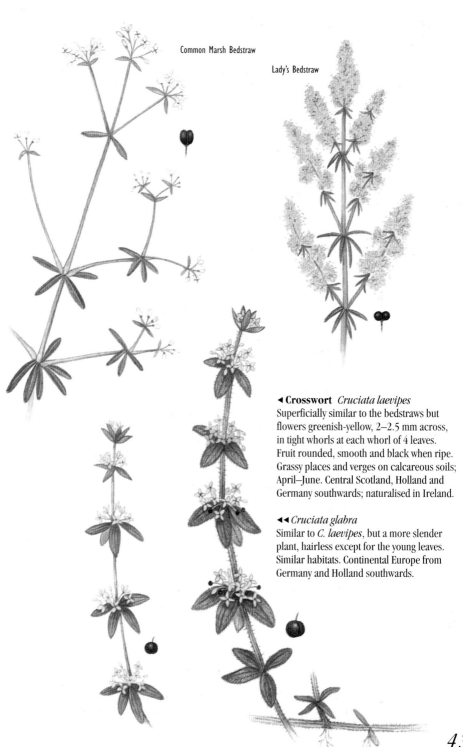

Common Marsh Bedstraw

Lady's Bedstraw

◀ **Crosswort** *Cruciata laevipes*
Superficially similar to the bedstraws but
flowers greenish-yellow, 2–2.5 mm across,
in tight whorls at each whorl of 4 leaves.
Fruit rounded, smooth and black when ripe.
Grassy places and verges on calcareous soils;
April–June. Central Scotland, Holland and
Germany southwards; naturalised in Ireland.

◀◀ *Cruciata glabra*
Similar to *C. laevipes*, but a more slender
plant, hairless except for the young leaves.
Similar habitats. Continental Europe from
Germany and Holland southwards.

43

Germander Speedwell

Veronica chamaedrys

Scrophulariaceae

A pretty little plant commonly seen along roadsides, pathways and lanes. In former times it was considered good luck to see the plant and it was said to speed you on your way on a journey, hence its common name; it was also called 'Farewell' and 'Goodbye' in parts of Britain.

NOTE:
There are quite a few similar speedwells which can be easily confused. Check flower and fruit details carefully.

KEY FEATURES: Leaves coarsely toothed, borne in pairs up the stem. Flowers borne in paired racemes, with 4 petals and only 2 stamens. Fruit 2-parted, heart-shaped capsule.

HABITAT: Grassy places, open woodland, verges, stony and waste places.

FREQUENCY: Common throughout the region except for the far north; sometimes abundant.

SEASON: March–July.

HABIT: A low spreading hairy perennial, sometimes sprawling, to 50 cm tall, though often less; stems with 2 opposite lines of hairs.

LEAVES: Paired, oval to oblong, short-stalked or unstalked, with a coarsely toothed margin.

FLOWERS: Small but bright blue, with a white centre, 9–10 mm across, 4-parted (but with only 2 stamens), borne in paired, long-stalked racemes.

FRUIT: A small compressed, heart-shaped capsule with a hairy margin.

J
F
M
A
M
J
J
A
S
O
N
D

LOOKALIKES

Wood Speedwell *Veronica montana*
Similar to *V. chamaedrys* but all leaves stalked and rather pale green. Flowers pale lilac-blue, 8–10 mm across, generally in alternating racemes. Damp woodland; April–July. Central Scotland, Denmark and S Sweden southwards.

◄ **Heath Speedwell** *Veronica officinalis*
A smaller more prostrate perennial than *V. chamaedrys*, with grey-green elliptical leaves and solitary racemes of small lilac-blue flowers, 6–8 mm across. Grassy places, woods and heaths; May–August. Throughout.

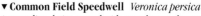

▼ **Common Field Speedwell** *Veronica persica*
A sprawling, hairy annual with most leaves alternate, heart-shaped and stalked. Flowers solitary, bright blue, 8–12 mm across, with the lowest petal white or pale. Cultivated ground, often abundant; throughout the year. Naturalised almost throughout from SW Asia.

Slender Speedwell *Veronica filiformis* ▶
Like *V. persica*, but a perennial rooting down at the nodes and mat-forming. Flowers pale lilac-blue, 10–15 mm across. Cultivated land and lawns; April–July. Naturalised in many areas from W Asia; absent from Iceland and much of Scandinavia.

45

Spiked Speedwell
Veronica spicata

Scrophulariaceae

An attractive species with distinctive spikes of flowers, that is widely grown in gardens. In cultivation it has been hybridised with *V. longifolia* to give a range of good garden plants. Unlike the previous speedwells, the inflorescence is terminal to the stem, rather than lateral.

NOTE:
In Britain the East Anglian plants (rarely exceeding 30 cm tall) are referable to subsp. spicata, *whereas all the other taller populations are referable to subsp.* hybrida.

J
F
M
A
M
J
J
A
S
O
N
D

KEY FEATURES: Erect stems with pairs of rather narrow leaves. Flowers borne in dense terminal spikes; each flower with 4 sepals, 4 pointed petals and 2 stamens. Fruit capsule heart-shaped.

HABITAT: Dry grassy places, woodland margins and rocky slopes.

FREQUENCY: Local in Britain (mainly confined to England), Scandinavia, Germany and France; occasionally naturalised elsewhere.

SEASON: July–October.

HABIT: A tufted, often mat-forming, hairy perennial, with erect stems to 60 cm tall, but often less.

LEAVES: Paired, grey-green, narrow-lanceolate to oval, blunt-toothed, usually short-stalked.

FLOWERS: Violet-blue, 4–8 mm across, borne in dense terminal, spike-like racemes.

FRUIT: A small rounded, notched, hairless capsule.

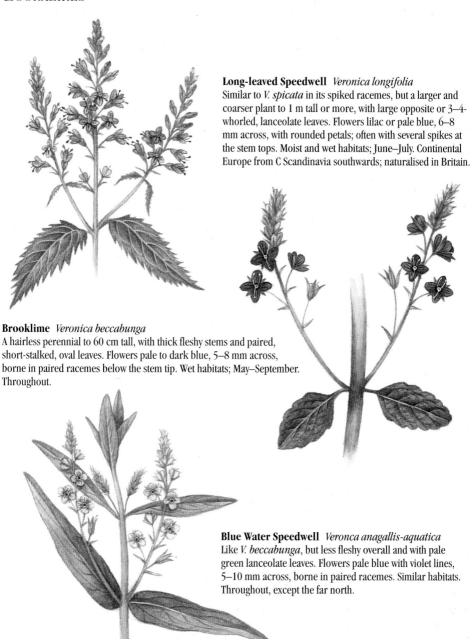

Long-leaved Speedwell *Veronica longifolia*
Similar to *V. spicata* in its spiked racemes, but a larger and coarser plant to 1 m tall or more, with large opposite or 3–4-whorled, lanceolate leaves. Flowers lilac or pale blue, 6–8 mm across, with rounded petals; often with several spikes at the stem tops. Moist and wet habitats; June–July. Continental Europe from C Scandinavia southwards; naturalised in Britain.

Brooklime *Veronica beccabunga*
A hairless perennial to 60 cm tall, with thick fleshy stems and paired, short-stalked, oval leaves. Flowers pale to dark blue, 5–8 mm across, borne in paired racemes below the stem tip. Wet habitats; May–September. Throughout.

Blue Water Speedwell *Veronca anagallis-aquatica*
Like *V. beccabunga*, but less fleshy overall and with pale green lanceolate leaves. Flowers pale blue with violet lines, 5–10 mm across, borne in paired racemes. Similar habitats. Throughout, except the far north.

Meadow Buttercup

Ranunculus acris

Ranunculaceae

A widespread and often abundant plant of grassy places, especially unimproved meadows. However, the Meadow Buttercup is just one of a number of buttercups that are widespread in the region in similar habitats which, with their showy yellow flowers, are easily confused. Like most species of *Ranunculus*, the leaves are poisonous and are avoided by livestock; the presence of the alkaloid Protoanemonin in the sap gives the leaves a bitter taste. They can also be confused with some species of *Potentilla* which, however, have an epicalyx as well as a calyx (*see* pp.54–7).

NOTE
In the north of Britain, Iceland and Arctic and Subarctic Europe the species is replaced by subspecies borealis which seldom grows more than 20 cm tall, has mainly 3-lobed basal leaves, and flowers often with brown-veined petals.

KEY FEATURES: Plant tufted, without runners. Basal leaves palmate, with 3–7 wedge-shaped, toothed segments. Flowers symmetrical, bowl-shaped, golden yellow, with 5 petals and with erect sepals below. Fruit a head of single-seeded achenes.

HABITAT: Damp meadows and pastures especially hay meadows and grazed land, verges and open woodland.

FREQUENCY: Common throughout, sometimes abundant and forming extensive colonies.

SEASON: April–September, occasionally with a few later blooms.

HABIT: A very variable tufted hairy perennial to 90 cm tall with erect, sparingly branched, stems, but dwarfer on poorer or drier soils.

LEAVES: Palmate, the basal with 3–7 wedged-shaped, acutely toothed segments, hairy like the leaves, long-stalked; stem leaves similar but smaller and less divided.

FLOWERS: Golden yellow, solitary on slender hairy stalks, cupped, 15–25 mm across, with rounded, slightly notched petals. Sepals 5, as petals, smaller and greenish, not reflexed.

FRUIT: Achenes in rounded heads, each 2–3.5 mm, with a hooked beak.

J
F
M
A
M
J
J
A
S
O
N
D

LOOKALIKES

Creeping Buttercup *Ranunculus repens*
Very similar in flower but plant not more than 60 cm tall, with long
creeping and rooting runners, and leaves with only 3 deeply toothed
segments. Damp or wet meadows, especially on slightly acid clay soils,
marshes, fens, verges, and as well as cultivated land. May–September.
Throughout the region, often common.

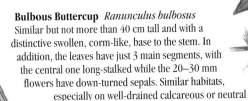

Bulbous Buttercup *Ranunculus bulbosus*
Similar but not more than 40 cm tall and with a
distinctive swollen, corm-like, base to the stem. In
addition, the leaves have just 3 main segments, with
the central one long-stalked while the 20–30 mm
flowers have down-turned sepals. Similar habitats,
especially on well-drained calcareous or neutral
meadows and pastures where
it can be abundant.
March–July. Throughout
the region, except parts of
Scotland and Ireland.

Corn Crowfoot *Ranunculus arvensis* ▶
A slighter, annual species to 60 cm with
smaller pale greenish-yellow flowers to
12 mm across. The achenes are very
distinctive, 6–8 mm, with spiny sides
and an almost straight beak. Local
on arable and disturbed land,
especially south of the Humber,
but always local. Decreasing.

◀ **Goldilocks Buttercup**
Ranunculus auricomus
Another annual but the stem leaves with 3–5
narrow lobes and 15–25 mm flowers in which
one or more of the petals is generally reduced in
size or missing altogether. Achenes 3–4 mm, hairy
but not spiny. Throughout in meadows, open
woodland and hedgerows, particularly on heavy
fertile soils; locally abundant. April–May.

49

Ranunculaceae

Lesser Spearwort
Ranunculus flammula

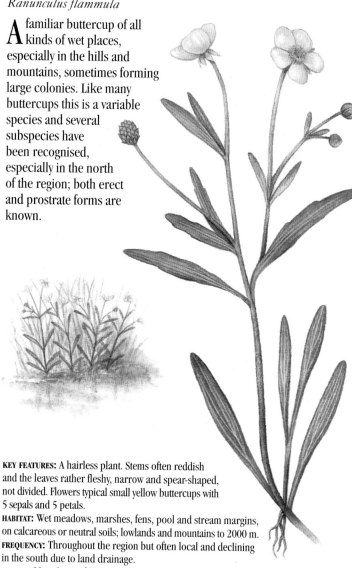

A familiar buttercup of all kinds of wet places, especially in the hills and mountains, sometimes forming large colonies. Like many buttercups this is a variable species and several subspecies have been recognised, especially in the north of the region; both erect and prostrate forms are known.

NOTE:
Plants with prostrate non-rooting stems and thicker leaves with a heart-shaped base, found in exposed coastal habitats in W Ireland and N and W Scotland are distinguished as subsp. minimus. *Plants found locally in N Scotland with smaller linear leaves and usually solitary flowers are referable to subsp.* scoticus.

J
F
M
A
M
J
J
A
S
O
N
D

KEY FEATURES: A hairless plant. Stems often reddish and the leaves rather fleshy, narrow and spear-shaped, not divided. Flowers typical small yellow buttercups with 5 sepals and 5 petals.
HABITAT: Wet meadows, marshes, fens, pool and stream margins, on calcareous or neutral soils; lowlands and mountains to 2000 m.
FREQUENCY: Throughout the region but often local and declining in the south due to land drainage.
SEASON: May–September.
HABIT: A tufted perennial, often erect and to 50 cm tall but sometimes with prostrate non-rooting stems.
LEAVES: Spear-shaped (lanceolate to narrow-oblong), rather thin, untoothed or slightly toothed.
FLOWERS: Few in branched clusters, each on a slender furrowed stalk, bright shiny yellow, cupped, 7–20 mm across. Petals rounded, twice as long as the small greenish sepals.
FRUIT: Achenes borne in rounded heads, small, 1–2 mm, with a short blunt beak.

50

LOOKALIKES

Great Spearwort *Ranunculus lingua*

Like a giant version of Lesser Spearwort, to 120 cm tall, with stout hollow stems with spear-shaped, toothed leaves; basal leaves more oval or heart-shaped, but withered by flowering time. The flowers are larger 30–50 mm across. Similar habitats, often growing in shallow water and spreading by long horizontal stems. June–September. Throughout, though rare in N Scotland. Cultivated.

Creeping Spearwort *Ranunculus reptans*

Like a smaller and more slender Lesser Spearwort but with creeping runners that root at the nodes. Leaves elliptical to paddle-shaped and flowers solitary, only 5–10 mm across. Confined to gravelly lake margins in the Faeroes, Iceland and Scandinavia. Replaced in Britain (Lake District northwards) by a hybrid, *R. × levenensis*, which looks very similar but has broader leaves, 1.5 cm wide or more.

Lesser Celandine

Ranunculus ficaria

Ranunculaceae

A harbinger of spring, the Lesser Celandine, comes into flower at the end of the winter and is often a feature at that time of year along country lanes and in woodland. Traditionally, the plant was used as a cure for haemorrhoids; the nobbly tubers were said to resemble piles, hence the obsolete common name Pilewort applied to the plant. This stemmed from the Doctrine of Signatures that stated that all plants had been 'signed' by the creator with some physical clue as to their medicinal use. The pile-like tubers readily break off and quickly aid in the distribution of the plant.

NOTE:
Widely cultivated; many forms exist in gardens including those with purple-bronze leaves and lemon, white or orange, single or double, flowers. These occasionally naturalise outside gardens.

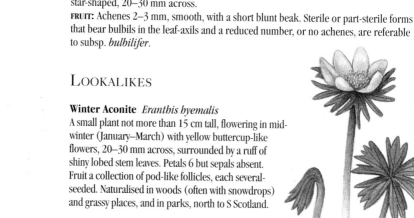

KEY FEATURES: A low tufted, hairless perennial with fleshy, heart-shaped leaves. Flowers bright yellow, with 7–12 narrow petals and only 3 smaller, pale green sepals. Fruit a head of small, single-seeded achenes.

HABITAT: Moist deciduous woodland, meadows, verges and other grassy places, river and stream banks.

FREQUENCY: Common throughout the region, particularly in the lowlands but up to 900 m in the mountains.

SEASON: Late February–May; soon dies down after flowering and fruiting.

HABIT: Low tufted tuberous-rooted perennial, rarely more than 20 cm tall.

LEAVES: Leaves heart-shaped, with a scalloped margin, long-stalked, dark green and often with dark brown markings.

FLOWERS: solitary, long-stalked, bright shiny yellow (often fading to white eventually), star-shaped, 20–30 mm across.

FRUIT: Achenes 2–3 mm, smooth, with a short blunt beak. Sterile or part-sterile forms that bear bulbils in the leaf-axils and a reduced number, or no achenes, are referable to subsp. *bulbilifer*.

J
F
M
A
M
J
J
A
S
O
N
D

LOOKALIKES

Winter Aconite *Eranthis hyemalis*
A small plant not more than 15 cm tall, flowering in mid-winter (January–March) with yellow buttercup-like flowers, 20–30 mm across, surrounded by a ruff of shiny lobed stem leaves. Petals 6 but sepals absent. Fruit a collection of pod-like follicles, each several-seeded. Naturalised in woods (often with snowdrops) and grassy places, and in parks, north to S Scotland.

Marsh Marigold
Caltha palustris

Ranunculaceae

A familiar plant of wet areas with large buttercup-like flowers that are borne early in the year. Before widespread land drainage this was a far more common plant than it is today. It is remarkably tough and is resistant to all the frost and winds which abound when it is in flower. It has been a popular plant amongst country folk for countless years and for this reason it has acquired numerous common names including Kingcup, Mayflower, May-blobs, Pollyblobs, Water-bubbles and Gollins.

KEY FEATURES: Stout fleshy plant with large heart-shaped leaves. Flowers in stalked clusters, large and buttercup-like but without obvious sepals. Fruit a cluster of pod-like follicles, each containing several seeds.

HABITAT: Wet places, particularly marshes, meadows, deciduous woodland, stream and pond margins, fens and ditches.

FREQUENCY: Locally common throughout. Smaller plants from northerly upland regions, with solitary, small flowers are referable to var. radicans.

SEASON: March–June, but often later in northerly upland areas.

HABIT: Tufted rhizomatous perennial, with stems rooting at the lower nodes, to 45 cm tall.

LEAVES: Large glossy deep green, heart-shaped, with a finely toothed margin and long stalk, but the uppermost rather smaller and clasping the stem with little or no stalk.

FLOWERS: Prominent and saucer-shaped, golden yellow, often greenish beneath, 15–50 mm across, with a boss of many stamens in the centre.

FRUIT: A cluster of up to 15 follicles which split down one side to release the seeds.

J
F
M
A
M
J
J
A
S
O
N
D

53

Rosaceae

Marsh Cinquefoil
Potentilla palustris

Perhaps the most distinctive of the species of *Potentilla* found in the British Isles, this is typically a plant of wet habitats. It is quite widespread, but despite this it is often overlooked because of its rather sombre flowers. The flowers are visited by various insects including bees, craneflies and mosquitoes.

NOTE:
Often grows in association with other typical marsh plants such as Myosotis scorpioides *and* Geum rivale.

KEY FEATURES: Hand-like leaves with 5 or 7 lobes, with papery stipules at the base. Flowers symmetrical, star-shaped, 5-parted, reddish or purplish, with large sepals and small petals; epicalyx present.

HABITAT: Wet meadows, marshes, fens, bogs and ditches; lowland and mountains.

FREQUENCY: Locally common but declining in some areas due to land drainage and pasture improvement.

SEASON: May–July.

HABIT: A rhizomatous, slightly hairy perennial, with erect flowering stems to 50 cm tall. Stem bases woody, rooting at the nodes.

LEAVES: All stalked, hand-like, with 5 or 7 separate, oblong, toothed lobes; uppermost leaves sometimes reduced to 3 or 1 leaflet.

FLOWERS: Upright, borne in lax-branched clusters, star-shaped, 20–30 mm across; sepals prominent, purplish or reddish, but green on the reverse, oval with a slender pointed apex; petals elliptical, half the size of the sepals, maroon or purple. Stamens numerous.

FRUIT: A rounded head of small single-seeded achenes.

J
F
M
A
M
J
J
A
S
O
N
D

Silverweed
Potentilla anserina

Rosaceae

A very widespread and common plant, especially of grassy places. Also known locally as Traveller's Ease and Traveller's Joy the leaves of this plant were placed in shoes to keep the feet cool and sweat-free. The roots were also used as a famine food in former times and could be dried and powdered to produce a poor 'flour'.

NOTE:
Often a weed of cultivated land. Various insects, especially bees, visit the flowers.

KEY FEATURES: Carpeting plant with long rooting leafy runners. Leaves silvery beneath. Flowers solitary, long-stalked, yellow, buttercup-like, but with an epicalyx.
HABITAT: Damp grassy and rocky places, pathways and tracks, verges, open woodland, waste ground and even sand dunes; lowland and mountains.
FREQUENCY: Common and widespread throughout the area, sometimes forming extensive colonies.
SEASON: May–August, sometimes into autumn.
HABIT: A prostrate perennial, often patch-forming, with long slender leafy runners which root at the nodes.
LEAVES: Stalked, pinnate, with 15–25 elliptical, sharply toothed leaflets, grey above but silky-silver beneath, the main leaflets alternating with smaller ones.
FLOWERS: Upright, 5-parted, symmetrical, bright yellow, 15–20 mm across, with 5 large rounded petals. Calyx green, with 5 elliptical sepals about half the length of the petals and more or less hidden below them; epicalyx lobes smaller and linear.
FRUIT: A rounded head of single-seeded achenes.

J
F
M
A
M
J
J
A
S
O
N
D

Tormentil

Potentilla erecta

Rosaceae

A widespread and often common species inhabiting a wide range of habitats and soils, and venturing onto cultivated lands, especially gardens, as a weed. It is one of a number of common creeping cinquefoils (*Potentilla*) found in the region. They are sometimes confused with the creeping buttercup. *Ranunculus repens*, which does not have an epicalyx, (*see* p.49).

NOTE:
A more robust form with slightly larger flowers and more coarsely toothed leaves found in upland regions of Britain northwards is distinguished as subsp. strictissima.

KEY FEATURES: Plant creeping and patch-forming, the slender stems not rooting at the nodes. Basal leaves long-stalked, generally withered by flowering time, but stem leaves present and unstalked or nearly so. Leaves with usually 3 segments (appearing to be 5 because of the pair of leaflet-like stipule at the base of each. Flowers symmetrical, bowl-shaped, characteristically with 4 petals. Calyx with an epicalyx.
HABITAT: Grassy places, including lawns, heaths, moors, open woodland and woodland rises on a wide range of soils except highly calcareous ones.
FREQUENCY: Common throughout, sometimes forming extensive colonies.
SEASON: May–September, sometimes with a few later blooms.
HABIT: Prostrate mat-forming downy perennial with slender leafy stems radiating out from a centre, but that do not root down to the ground.
LEAVES: Palmate with 3, occasionally 4–5 toothed leaflets, green or grey-green above but silky with hairs beneath.
FLOWERS: Yellow, few to many in lax terminal clusters, each borne on long slender stalks above the foliage, 7–11 mm across, with 4 rounded, slightly notched petals. Sepals 4, alternating with very narrow epicalyx segments. Stamens up to 20.
FRUIT: A small cluster of up to 8, occasionally more, tiny single-seeded achenes.

J
F
M
A
M
J
J
A
S
O
N
D

LOOKALIKES

Trailing Tormentil *Potentilla anglica*
A less sturdy plant with a persistent leaf-rosette, and stems rooting down at least at some of the nodes. The long-stalked stem leaves have 3–5 leaflets and the 4-petalled flowers are 14–18 mm across. June–September. Scattered throughout the region as far north as S Scandinavia.

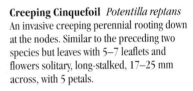

Creeping Cinquefoil *Potentilla reptans*
An invasive creeping perennial rooting down at the nodes. Similar to the preceding two species but leaves with 5–7 leaflets and flowers solitary, long-stalked, 17–25 mm across, with 5 petals.

Hoary Cinquefoil *Potentilla argentea*
Tufted perennial without rooting runners and erect to ascending stems bearing branched clusters of 5-petalled yellow flowers, 10–20 mm across. Leaves palmate, with 5 deeply toothed leaflets, deep green above but silvery-white with felt beneath, only the lowermost long-stalked. June–September. Throughout apart from the far north, Ireland and Iceland.

Herb Bennet *Potentilla urbanum*
A distinct and coarser erect perennial with the lower leaves pinnate and the upper ternate. Flowers pale yellow, 8–15 mm across, with 5 oval not-notched petals. Stipules large and leaf-like. May–September. Shaded habitats throughout, except far north.

57

Wild Strawberry
Fragaria vesca

A familiar and popular little plant much loved for its small succulent fruits. This species has nothing to do with the cultivated strawberry which is a hybrid between two American species. Although it is probably the commonest of the three *Fragaria* species found in the area, it is often confused with the others. The strawberry fruit is derived from the swollen receptacle with the seeds (achenes) embedded in the surface; as the receptacle ripens it changes from greenish-white to red.

NOTE:
The Alpine Strawberry, which is widely cultivated for its small sweet fruits, is a more robust form of F. vesca *that does not produce runners. It may sometimes become naturalised.*

KEY FEATURES: A tufted plant with long slender runners that root down at the nodes. Leaves 3-parted. Flowers potentilla-like, white with both a calyx and an epicalyx. Fruit a familiar strawberry but small.

HABITAT: Woodlands, banks and other dry grassy places, hedgerows, most often on calcareous soils.

FREQUENCY: Common, locally so in some parts of the south.

SEASON: April–July, occasionally later.

HABIT: Plant a patch-forming downy perennial, with a tuft of leaves from the base of which arise long slender runners that root down at the nodes.

LEAVES: Long-stalked, with 3 oval to rhombic, toothed, bright green leaflets, paler beneath.

FLOWERS: White, rather flat to slightly cupped, 12–18 mm across, borne in lax clusters about as long as the leaves. Petals 5, rounded, not-notched. Calyx with 5 sepals alternating with very narrow epicalyx segments.

FRUIT: Pendent, about 10 mm long, red and succulent when ripe, with the achenes raised over the surface. Good to eat.

J
F
M
A
M
J
J
A
S
O
N
D

58

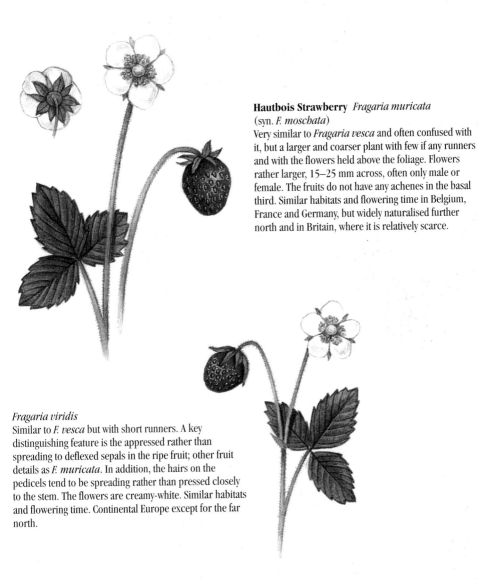

Hautbois Strawberry *Fragaria muricata*
(syn. *F. moschata*)
Very similar to *Fragaria vesca* and often confused with
it, but a larger and coarser plant with few if any runners
and with the flowers held above the foliage. Flowers
rather larger, 15–25 mm across, often only male or
female. The fruits do not have any achenes in the basal
third. Similar habitats and flowering time in Belgium,
France and Germany, but widely naturalised further
north and in Britain, where it is relatively scarce.

Fragaria viridis
Similar to *F. vesca* but with short runners. A key
distinguishing feature is the appressed rather than
spreading to deflexed sepals in the ripe fruit; other fruit
details as *F. muricata*. In addition, the hairs on the
pedicels tend to be spreading rather than pressed closely
to the stem. The flowers are creamy-white. Similar habitats
and flowering time. Continental Europe except for the far
north.

Meadow Crane's-bill
Geranium pratense

Geraniaceae

A familiar and widespread plant of grassy places which has long been grown as a cottage garden flower and has given rise to various colour forms in the garden, as well as those with double flowers. It is one of those plants associated with unspoilt meadows and flowery lanes during the summer months, favouring especially limestone areas, where it attracts bees as well as butterflies.

NOTE:
Variable in the wild where pale blue and occasionally white-flowered forms can be observed.

KEY FEATURES: Leaves deeply divided into 5–7 cut lobes. Flowers borne in pairs on a common stalk, with rounded not notched petals. Fruit a typical crane's-bill, with 5 seeds at the base of a long beak.

HABITAT: Grassy places, especially fields, meadows and road verges, more particularly on base-rich and calcareous soils.

FREQUENCY: Common, especially in the south of its range; absent for the far north.

SEASON: June–September.

HABIT: A tufted, hairy, perennial to 90 cm tall with erect stems that have rather swollen nodes.

LEAVES: Basal and lower long-stalked but the upper short-stalked; all rounded in outline, cut almost to the base into 5–7 deeply toothed lobes, deep green above, paler beneath.

FLOWERS: Bright violet-blue, bowl-shaped, 25–30 mm across, borne in pairs towards the stem tops, pendent in bud. Petals 5 rounded. Calyx with 5 elliptical pointed sepals that persist in fruit.

FRUIT: Long-beaked, with 5 seeds at the base within the calyx; eventually each seed springing apart with a section of the beak.

J
F
M
A
M
J
J
A
S
O
N
D

Wood Crane's-bill *Geranium sylvaticum*
Leaves less deeply cut and flowers reddish-purple
to pinkish-lilac or bluish, 22–26 mm across.
Similar although often moisture habitats and
damp woodland. Throughout but only on higher
ground in the south.

Bloody Crane's-bill *Geranium sanguineum*
A more spreading plant not more than 40 cm tall with solitary bright
reddish-purple flowers 25–30 mm across, the petals slightly notched.
Grassy and wooded as well as rocky places, generally over limestone.
Throughout except the far north and Iceland; in coastal N and W Britain
and C Ireland a variant with pale pink flowers is distinguished as var.
striatum.

Marsh Crane's-bill *Geranium palustre*
Like the Meadow Crane's-bill, but leaves
only divided for about two-thirds their
length and flowers purple or lilac, 22–30
mm across. Damp meadows. Continental
Europe north to S Sweden but not Holland.

Geraniaceae

Dove's-foot Crane's-bill

Geranium molle

A very common small-flowered species, particularly of cultivated and wasteland. It belongs to a group of closely allied and much confused European species all with a similar habit and size.

NOTE:
One of a number of similar-looking species found in the region. Flower size and leaf shape are important in identification.

KEY FEATURES: Semi-prostrate annual. Leaves rather small and rounded in outline, shallowly lobed, grey-green. Flowers borne in pairs, with 5 notched petals. Fruit a typical crane's-bill with 5 seeds at the base of a long beak.

HABITAT: Cultivated land (particularly arable), waste ground, dry grassy places and lawns, sand dunes.

FREQUENCY: Common, sometimes abundant, except for the far north.

SEASON: May–September.

HABIT: Prostrate or semi-prostrate densely hairy, rather grey-green, annual with stems radiating out from a central point, to 40 cm.

LEAVES: Grey-green, long-stalked, the blade circular in outline, with 5–7 shallow, wedge-shaped lobes, each itself 3-lobed at the top.

FLOWERS: Small, bore in branched pairs usually on a common hairy stalk, pinkish-purple, 6–10 mm across. Petals 5, slightly longer than the 5 pointed sepals, notched.

FRUIT: Borne on elbowed stalks, small grey-green, hairy cane's-bills.

J
F
M
A
M
J
J
A
S
O
N
D

LOOKALIKES

Round-leaved Crane's-bill
Geranium rotundifolium
A greener plant with pink, slightly larger flowers, 10–12 mm across; petals not or scarcely notched. Similar habitats. S Holland and Germany, C and S Britain southwards; also in S Ireland.

Small-flowered Crane's-bill *Geranium pusillum*
Like *G. molle*, but the leaves more finely cut and the flowers pale lilac, very small, 4–6 mm across. Similar habitats. Throughout except for the far north.

Herb Robert *Geranium robertianum.*
Distinctive plant with a disagreeable mouse-like smell. Leaves deeply cut and lobed, often flushed with red or purple. Flowers paired, bright pink, rarely white, 14–18 mm across, with petals scarcely notched and much longer than the sepals. Shaded rocky and woody places. Throughout.

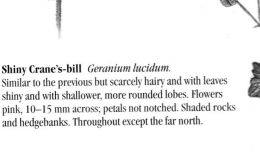

Shiny Crane's-bill *Geranium lucidum.*
Similar to the previous but scarcely hairy and with leaves shiny and with shallower, more rounded lobes. Flowers pink, 10–15 mm across; petals not notched. Shaded rocks and hedgebanks. Throughout except the far north.

Perennial Flax

Linum perenne

Linaceae

Few flowers have the grace and simplicity of the flaxes. The 5-petalled flowers, often in glorious shades of blue or lilac, have a certain fragility and the petals have generally fallen by the late afternoon. Yet, at the same time, plants produce a continuation of bloom over a number of weeks. Flaxes all have simple, often narrow, untoothed leaves and may be annual or perennial, or even shrubby.

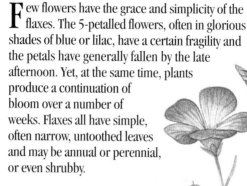

NOTE:
The British plant, which is referred to as subsp. anglicum *(syn.* L. anglicum*), is rare, but is found in scattered localities north as far as Durham and Kirkcudbright.*

KEY FEATURES: Slender fibrous stems bearing linear, pointed leaves. Flowers 5-parted with 5 small greenish sepals and 5 large showy petals, borne in lax racemes. Fruit a small capsule.
HABITAT: Dry permanent grassland on calcareous soils.
FREQUENCY: Locally common, but generally decreasing in Western Europe.
SEASON: May–July.
HABIT: A tufted, hairless perennial with a number, sometimes many, slender ascending unbranched stems arising from a common base.
LEAVES: Alternate, linear to linear-lanceolate, with a single vein and an untoothed margin.
FLOWERS: Dark blue, funnel-shaped to bowl-shaped, 20–26 mm across. Sepals greenish, the outer 3 pointed but the inner 2 broader and blunt. Petals thin and satiny, oval, lightly veined, with 5 stems within the corolla.
FRUIT: A small, many-seeded greenish capsule that splits into 10 valves when ripe.

J
F
M
A
M ❁
J ❁
J ❁ ✦
A ✦
S ✦
O
N
D

LOOKALIKES

Pale Flax
Linum bienne
A slighter plant biennial or perennial with pale blue or lilac-blue flowers 16–24 mm across; sepals uneven but all pointed. Similar habitats, but generally close to the coast. Confined to France, S Britain (Lancashire and N Wales southwards) and SE Ireland.

Flax *Linum usitatissimum*
Widely cultivated, rather robust, annual, occasionally naturalised,
grown for its fibre (linen) and for its oily seeds (linseed). Plants
usually with a single stem. Flowers similar to *L. bienne* but the
sepals larger, 6–9 mm long (not 4–6 mm).

Wood Sorrel *Oxalis acetosella*
Flowers rather similar to a flax, but the plant a low tufted,
creeping perennial with characteristic trifoliate leaves and
heart-shaped leaflets. Flowers white to pale lilac, bell-shaped,
8–15 mm long, half-nodding, solitary on slender stalks from
the base of the plant like the leaves. Shaded places, particularly
woodland, on moist humus soils. Throughout. April–June.

Procumbent Yellow Sorrel
Oxalis corniculata
A low, patch-forming perennial with the stems rooting down at the nodes.
Leaves trifoliate, long-stalked, from the base of the plant or on short stems. Flowers
upright, bright yellow, 10–15 mm across, with 5 rounded petals. Fruit capsule oblong.
Naturalised throughout much of the area; of uncertain origin.

Perforate St John's-wort

Hypericum perforatum

Hypericaceae

A widespread and familiar bright wild flower, golden throughout the summer months in woodlands and along hedgerows. The 'perforate' refers to the translucent dots which speckle the leaves when they are viewed against the light. The plant has another curious property in that it exudes a blood-red juice when the stems are cut. It is readily confused with other similar species (*see* the lookalikes).

NOTE:
The translucent leaf dots contain an essential oil, Hypericin.

J
F
M
A
M
J
J
A
S
O
N
D

KEY FEATURES: A hairless plant. Stems round with 2 raised lines. Leaves untoothed, speckled all over with translucent dots. Flowers 5-parted, but with numerous stamens in 5 bundles.

HABITAT: Woods, woodland verges, hedgerows, rough grassy places and open scrub, riverbanks, on neutral to calcareous soils.

FREQUENCY: Common throughout apart from the far north.

SEASON: May–September.

HABIT: A tufted perennial with erect stems to 70 cm tall; stem bases somewhat spreading and rooting at the nodes.

LEAVES: Opposite, narrow- to broad-oval, covered in relatively large translucent dots, unstalked; margin untoothed.

FLOWERS: Borne in large terminal panicles, bright yellow, large upright and saucer-shaped, 18–22 mm across, with elliptical petals which have a few black dots along the margin usually. Sepals linear and pointed, much shorter than the petals.

FRUIT: Fruit a 5-valved capsule, containing numerous seeds.

Imperforate St. John's-wort *Hypericum maculatum*
Similar but stems square in cross-section with a line down
each corner, and leaves net-veined, without translucent
dots, or occasionally with a few on the uppermost leaves.
Damp places, particularly woodland margins and
hedgerows. Throughout, except the far north (in Britain
mainly represented by subsp. *obtusiusculum*).

Hairy St. John's-wort *Hypericum hirsutum*
Taller, to 110 cm with downy stems and leaves. Stems with
2 raised lines and leaves with tiny translucent dots. Flowers
pale yellow, 15–22 mm across, sometimes with reddish veins.
Similar habitats to *H. perforatum*. Throughout, except for the far
north; absent from SW Britain.

Square-stalked St. John's-wort *Hypericum tetrapterum*
Like *H. maculatum*, but stems narrowly winged on the
corners and leaves often half-clasping the stem, with
translucent dots. Flowers small and pale yellow, 8–12 mm
across. Damp habitats, particularly marshes and riverbanks.
Throughout, except for N Scotland, Iceland and much of
Scandinavia.

Cistaceae

Common Rockrose
Helianthemum nummularium

The rockroses are familiar and cheerful wild flowers of dry sunny habitats throughout much of Europe, especially favouring calcareous soils. The Common Rockrose can often be found growing in large drifts, its flowers particularly attractive to bees and butterflies. It has been much used in cultivation, and is a feature of old cottage gardens where both single and double-flowered forms can be seen.

NOTE:
In some forms the petals have a distinctive orange spot at the base.

J
F
M
A
M
J
J
A
S
O
N
D

KEY FEATURES: Small evergreen shrublet, often prostrate. Leaves paired, small and untoothed. Flowers 5-parted but with numerous stamens, with rounded petals. Sepals 5, the outer two smaller and narrower.

HABITAT: Dry grassy, often short-grazed, meadows and banks, rocky places, over calcareous soils usually. Most often in hilly and mountainous districts or on cliffs.

FREQUENCY: Locally common throughout except the far north, Iceland and Norway (absent from much of SW and NW Britain).

SEASON: June–September.

HABIT: Low shrublet to 30 cm but often prostrate, with branched stems radiating outwards from a centre, becoming quite woody with age.

LEAVES: Paired, small, oblong to lanceolate, green or greyish above, but greyish- or white-hairy beneath, the margin untoothed and slightly rolled under.

FLOWERS: Bright yellow, occasionally cream or orange, saucer-shaped, 12–20 mm across, borne in racemes of up to 12.

FRUIT: A small 3-valved capsule.

LOOKALIKES

White Rockrose *Helianthemum apenninum*
Flowers white with a distinctive yellow centre. The leaves are generally grey-green. Similar habitats in Belgium and Germany southwards; in Britain confined to the south-west.

Hoary Rockrose *Helianthemum canum*
A dwarf tufted perennial to 20 cm with elliptical to linear grey leaves and small yellow flowers only 8–15 mm across. Confined to S Sweden southwards on the continent, W Britain and W Ireland.

Musk Mallow
Malva moschata

Malvaceae

T he musk-like fragrance of this widespread European plant is especially attractive, more noticeable when the plant is brought indoors; both the flowers, and to a lesser extent, the foliage is scented. This is typically a plant of dry places and the large flowers have a soft and pastel look in contrast to some of the harsher coloured native mallows.

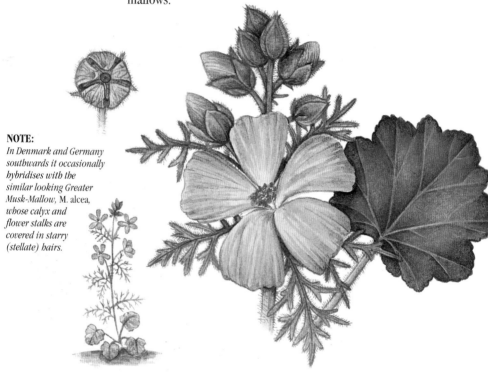

NOTE:
In Denmark and Germany southwards it occasionally hybridises with the similar looking Greater Musk-Mallow, M. alcea, *whose calyx and flower stalks are covered in starry (stellate) hairs.*

J
F
M
A
M
J
J
A
S
O
N
D

KEY FEATURES: A robust hairy erect perennial. Stem leaves deeply lobed. Flowers softly coloured, with a calyx as well as an epicalyx. Stamens characteristically bunched together below the styles on a single column.

HABITAT: Dry places, pastures and field boundaries, roadsides and hedgerows.

FREQUENCY: Frequent in the south but rare in parts of Ireland and Scotland; naturalised in Scandinavia.

SEASON: July–August.

HABIT: Tufted perennial to 80 cm, with erect, rather stiff leafy stems.

LEAVES: Basal and lower leaves heart-shaped, shallowly lobed and toothed, long-stalked. Middle and upper stem leaves deeply lobed and toothed with rather narrow segments, short-stalked or unstalked.

FLOWERS: Large and bowl-shaped, 35–60 mm across, soft bright pink to almost white, borne among the upper leaves. Petals 5, broad wedge-shaped with a notched apex. Calyx with 5 broad sepals and 3 narrow epicalyx segments.

FRUIT: A ring of closely packed seeds (actually mericarps) within the persistent calyx.

Dwarf Mallow *Malva neglecta*
A dwarf, rather sprawling annual, very different in habit to
the Musk Mallow, with all the leaves kidney-shaped in
outline, with 5–7 shallow, toothed lobes. Flowers also pale,
pale lilac to white, only 15–25 mm across, borne in
clusters of 3–6. In similar dry habitats, including coastal.
May–September. Throughout except for
the far north; commoner in the
south of its range.

Common Mallow *Malva sylvestris*
A robust plant like the Musk Mallow but all the leaves with
3–7 shallow, rather rounded, toothed lobes, and flowers
satiny, bright pink-purple with darker veins. Similar habitats.
June–September. Throughout except for the far north, the
Faeroes and Iceland.

Caryophyllaceae

Greater Stitchwort

Stellaria holostea

A common spring and early summer plant of woodland and hedgerows with its white starry flowers. Despite this, it is rather a fragile plant and the stems are easily snapped, although the surrounding vegetation normally supports them. The plant has a host of local common names including Brassy Buttons, Poor-man's-buttonhole and Poppers. The last refers to the fruit capsule, which explode when ripe with an audible pop, like a distant gun.

NOTE:
The flowers are visited by a variety of insects including bees, butterflies, various beetles and moths.

KEY FEATURES: A rather rough-feeling plant with square stems and paired long-tapered leaves. Flowers starry, 5-parted, with deeply cleft petals. Stamens 10, styles 3 and the capsule splitting at the end with 6 teeth. *Cerastium* (*see* lookalikes below) are similar but with 5 styles and capsules with 10 teeth.

HABITAT: Woods and hedgerows, banks and verges, on a variety of soils except very acid ones.

FREQUENCY: Widespread and locally abundant, throughout except for the far north.

SEASON: April–June, occasionally later.

HABIT: A patch-forming stoloniferous perennial of rather straggly habit, to 60 cm, with rough square stems and paired leaves.

LEAVES: Narrow-lanceolate, tapered gradually to a fine tip, rough on margins, untoothed and unstalked.

FLOWERS: In lax-branched clusters, white, starry, 18–30 mm across, on long slender stalks. Petals narrow-oval, deeply cleft. Sepals elliptical, pointed, half the length of the petals.

FRUIT: A capsule, splitting at the top by 6 teeth and containing numerous seeds.

J
F
M
A
M
J
J
A
S
O
N
D

LOOKALIKES

Wood Stitchwort *Stellaria nemorum*
Stems round and hairy bearing oval, mostly stalked, leaves. Flowers similar to *S. holostea*, 20–24 mm across. Damp woods and streamsides; May–July. Throughout, except the far north.

Common Chickweed *Stellaria media*
An annual with a sprawling to prostrate habit. Stems with a line of hairs down each internode. Leaves oval, the lower stalked. Flowers like *S. holostea* but very small, 8–10 mm across. Widespread weed of cultivation and waste or bare places.

▶▶ **Field Mouse-ear** *Cerastium arvense*
A low, slightly hairy, laxly matted annual with narrow-lanceolate paired leaves. Flowers white, 12–20 mm across, the petals cleft into two rounded lobes. Sepals shorter than the petals. Dry open habitats, grassy places and hedgebanks; April–August. Throughout; rare in Wales and Ireland.

▶ **Common Mouse-ear** *Cerastium fontanum*
Rather like a lax *Stellaria media* but the bracts are white-edged, the flowers have 5 styles and the fruit capsule is noticeably curved. Grassy places, shingle and sand dunes; April–November. Throughout.

◀ **Sticky Mouse-ear** *Cerastium glomeratum*
Also rather like *Stellaria media*, but a rather yellowish-green very sticky plant with flowers in compact clusters; flowers not opening properly, with the sepals as long as the petals. Cultivated land, sand dunes and pathways. Throughout.

Thyme-leaved Sandwort
Arenaria serpyllifolia

Caryophyllaceae

A small white-flowered plant that is widely distributed yet easily overlooked. It is one of a number of similar looking species in the region with 4–5-parted flowers and unnotched petals. The genus *Arenaria*, commonly called sandworts are annuals or perennials; all have flowers with 10 stamens and 3 styles. In *Spergularia* (see lookalikes below) the leaves are rather fleshy and appear to be in whorls, while the flowers are often pink or purple rather than white, and the fruit capsule bears only 3 teeth.

NOTE:
In coastal Britain, especially the south-west, a sand-dune form which is more robust and with denser flower clusters is sometimes distinguished as subsp. lloydi.

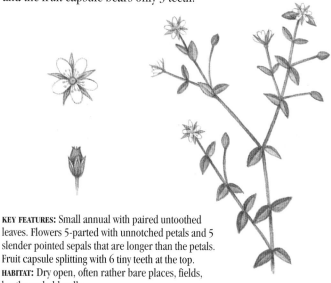

J
F
M
A
M
J
J
A
S
O
N
D

KEY FEATURES: Small annual with paired untoothed leaves. Flowers 5-parted with unnotched petals and 5 slender pointed sepals that are longer than the petals. Fruit capsule splitting with 6 tiny teeth at the top.

HABITAT: Dry open, often rather bare places, fields, heaths and old walls.

FREQUENCY: Common throughout except for the far north.

SEASON: April–September.

HABIT: A low bushy to prostrate, rough-hairy, annual to 30 cm, with stems generally much-branched.

LEAVES: Paired, oval to elliptical, pointed.

FLOWERS: Numerous, white, starry, 5–8 mm across, borne in small leafy spreading clusters. Sepals narrow-elliptic, pointed, twice the length of the petals.

FRUIT: A small capsule containing numerous seeds, splitting at the top into 6 tiny teeth.

LOOKALIKES

Lesser Thyme-leaved Sandwort
Arenaria leptoclados
A more delicate plant with sepals less than 3 mm long (not 3–4.5 mm) and capsule equalling sepals, not longer. Scattered throughout the area, sometimes in association with *A. serpyllifolia*.

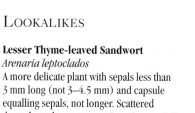

Great Sea-spurrey *Spergularia media*
Almost hairless perennial with linear leaves and white or pale bluish-pink flowers 7–12 mm across; petals slightly longer than the sepals; stamens 10. Saline habitats, especially on the coast. Throughout except the far north.

Lesser Sea-spurrey *Spergularia marina*
Less robust than *S. media* and often annual, the flowers smaller, 5–8 mm across, pink with a white centre; stamens not more than 5. Less common and confined to coastal Europe apart from the Faeroes.

Sea-spurrey *Spergularia rubra*
A stickily hairy annual or perennial with bristle-tipped linear leaves, silvery stipules and uniformly pale pink flowers only 3–6 mm across; stamens 10. Coastal habitats and inland on heaths and commons. Throughout, except the far north.

Greek Sea-spurrey *Spergularia bocconii*
Like *S. marina*, but an annual or a biennial with white flowers or pink with a white centre, 5–6 mm across, with the petals generally shorter than the sepals; stipules not silvery. S Britain, Holland and Germany southwards.

Meadow Saxifrage
Saxifaga granulata

Saxifragaceae

A widespread meadow plant, once a familiar sight in many areas but today declining in many due to the widespread use of herbicides and the ploughing up of ancient meadows. It is a good indicator plant of healthy and vibrant meadows and has long been cultivated in gardens, particularly in its double-flowered forms. The plant is sometimes mistaken for a member of the Caryophyllaceae (*see* pp.80–87), but the presence of 2 styles in the centre of the flower and the 2-parted fruit capsule is very characteristic.

NOTE:
The bulbils found on the plant naturally become detached from the parent plant and can, under the right conditions, grow to form new plants.

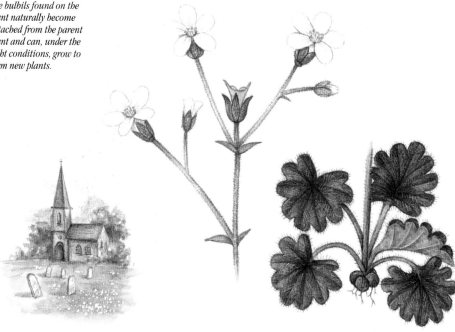

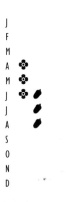

J
F
M
A
M
J
J
A
S
O
N
D

KEY FEATURES: Leaves deeply scalloped, the basal in a lax rosette, each leaf with a few bulbils at the base. Flowers 5-parted, with 10 stamens and 2 styles. Fruit a 2-parted capsule.
HABITAT: Old meadows and pastures, banks and road verges, sometimes in rocky places.
FREQUENCY: Locally common throughout, but absent from the Faeroes and Iceland. Generally declining in the south of its range.
SEASON: April–June.
HABIT: An erect hairy perennial 50 cm, often less, with a solitary stem or several in a tuft, leafy only in the basal part.
LEAVES: Basal in a lax rosette with lateral bulbils, rounded to kidney-shaped, deeply blunt-toothed, stalked.
FLOWERS: White or cream, 18–30 mm across, borne in lax, branched clusters; bulbils sometimes replace some or most of the flowers in the inflorescence.
FRUIT: A small greenish, 2-parted capsule containing many tiny seeds.

Starry Saxifrage *Saxifaga stellaris*
Densely tufted perennial to 20 cm tall, with all the leaves in a basal
rosette, the leaves oblong, toothed and scarcely stalked. Flowers
starry, 10–15 mm, borne in lax clusters, the pointed petals with a
pair of yellow spots towards the base and the sepals down-turned.
Moist mountain habitats. Arctic and sub-Arctic Europe, N Britain
(including N Wales) and Ireland.

Rue-leaved Saxifrage *Saxifraga tridactylites*
Rather like a small version of *S. granulata*, but
rarely more than 10 cm tall, very sticky with hairs
and leaves with 3 or 5 deep lobes. Flowers white,
small, only 3–5 mm across, and borne in leafy
clusters. Widespread but often overlooked; field
boundaries, sand dunes, bare and grassy places,
generally on calcareous soils. Not in Iceland or
the Faeroes.

Yellow Mountain Saxifrage
Saxifraga aizoides

Saxifragaceae

An interesting upland species, common on the mountains in the region, but descending to lower altitudes at more northerly latitudes. The species has a very wide distribution throughout the Northern Hemisphere, growing particularly in wet mountain habitats. It is sometimes mistaken for a stonecrop (*Sedum, see* p.79), but the slightly toothed leaves, spotted flowers and 2-parted ovary are good distinguishing characters.

J
F
M
A
M
J
J
A
S
O
N
D

KEY FEATURES: Leaves fleshy and slightly toothed. Flowers with spotted petals and 10 stamens. Sepals almost as large as the petals.
HABITAT: Wet places, rocks, streamsides, seepage zones and wet flushes in particular.
FREQUENCY: Locally common except in lowland areas and absent from the Faeroes; in Britain confined primarily to N England and Scotland.
SEASON: June–September.
HABIT: A low tufted and leafy plant to 20 cm tall, with stems branched near the base.
LEAVES: Fleshy and alternate, narrow-oblong or elliptic, with a few small teeth along the margin.
FLOWERS: Flowers bright yellow or orange, the petals often red-spotted, starry, 7–12 mm across, borne in lax terminal clusters. Petals elliptical, slightly longer than the greenish sepals.
FRUIT: A small 2-parted capsule containing numerous small seeds.

LOOKALIKES

Marsh Saxifrage
Saxifraga hirculus
A loosely tufted perennial with spoon-shaped to lanceolate non-fleshy, untoothed leaves that are hairy towards the base. Flowers bright yellow, 20–30 mm across, the petals sometimes red-spotted, borne on slender sparsely leafy stems to 20 cm tall; petals elliptical with a rounded, not pointed, apex. Wet grassy meadows and moors, mainly in the mountains. Throughout except for S Britain, the Faeroes, Holland and Belgium; in N Britain, generally rare and decreasing.

Wall-pepper
Sedum acre

Crassulaceae

Sometimes also commonly called Biting Stonecrop, this is a characteristic plant of rocky rather dry places, and for that reason it is equally at home on old walls and rooftops, where it can make a bright display in early summer. The sedums or stonecrops are a group of mostly succulent perennials that are closely related to the saxifrages, differing primarily in their succulent habit and in possessing a cluster of carpels equal to the number of petals.

NOTE:
The pale green young shoots have a peppery taste.

KEY FEATURES: Small succulent plant with alternate, swollen, little leaves. Flowers starry with 5 pointed petals and 10 stamens. Fruit a 5-parted starry capsule.
HABITAT: Dry rocky and sandy places, especially beaches and cliffs, old walls and rooftops.
FREQUENCY: Common throughout the areas, but scarcer in the far north.
SEASON: May–July.
HABIT: A low tufted, hairless perennial to 10 cm tall, but spreading much wider, with fleshy stems which become thin, brown and woody with age.
LEAVES: Green or brownish-green or bronze, fleshy and egg-shaped, only 3–5 mm long.
FLOWERS: Bright yellow and starry, 10–12 mm across, borne in small terminal clusters; styles 5 in the centre of the flower.
FRUIT: A 5-parted, starry capsule.

J
F
M
A
M
J
J
A
S
O
N
D

LOOKALIKES

Reflexed Stonecrop
Sedum rupestre (syn. *S. reflexum*)
A more robust plant to 20 cm tall with greyish, linear-cylindrical leaves to 20 mm long and dense heads of pale to bright yellow flowers that nod in bud. Flowers 14–15 mm across, often with 7 petals. Similar habitats; June–August. Continental Europe north as far as southern Scandinavia; naturalised in Britain and Ireland.

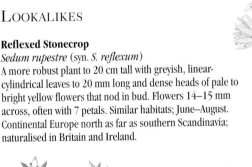

English Stonecrop *Sedum anglicum*
Rather like *S. acre* in habit, but generally smaller, the leaves blue-green, often flushed with pink. Flowers white, pink beneath, 9–12 mm across, borne in small clusters. Similar habitats but usually on acid soils; June–September. Throughout, except the far north, the Faeroes and Iceland.

79

Caryophyllaceae

Ragged Robin
Lychnis flos-cuculi

A catchfly (*Silene*) -like (*see* pp.82–84) species that inhabits damp and wet habitats. The common name derives from the cut and rather 'ragged' appearance of the flowers which are greatly sought after by both butterflies and long-tongued bees.

NOTE:
Dwarf variants are found in some exposed mountain and coastal habitats.

KEY FEATURES: A rough-hairy plant. Leaves narrow and paired. Flowers 5-parted; calyx tubular with 5 teeth; petals deeply cut into 4 narrow, pointed lobes. Fruit a capsule with 5 teeth when ripe.

HABITAT: Damp and wet places, particularly, marshes, fens and wet woodland, generally on peaty or mineral-rich soils.

FREQUENCY: Throughout; locally common, sometimes abundant.

SEASON: May–August, occasionally later.

HABIT: A thin-stemmed erect perennial to 75 cm tall with simple or branched stems, smooth to hairy.

LEAVES: Lower spoon-shaped and stalked, while the middle and upper are linear-lanceolate, unstalked and with a pointed apex; all leaves untoothed.

FLOWERS: Pale to bright purplish-pink, occasionally white, 30–40 mm across, borne in lax, branched clusters. Petals clawed, the limb deeply dissected into 4 lobes. Stamens 10.

FRUIT: A small 5-toothed capsule containing many seeds.

J
F
M
A
M
J
J
A
S
O
N
D

LOOKALIKES

Sticky Catchfly *Lychnis viscaria*
A more densely tufted shorter plant with the stems sticky just below
each pair of leaves. Flowers bright rose-purple, 18–22 mm across,
borne in a moderately dense oblong panicle; petals notched, not
deeply cut. Dry rocky and stony places on acid soils; May–August.
Throughout, except Ireland and the far north.

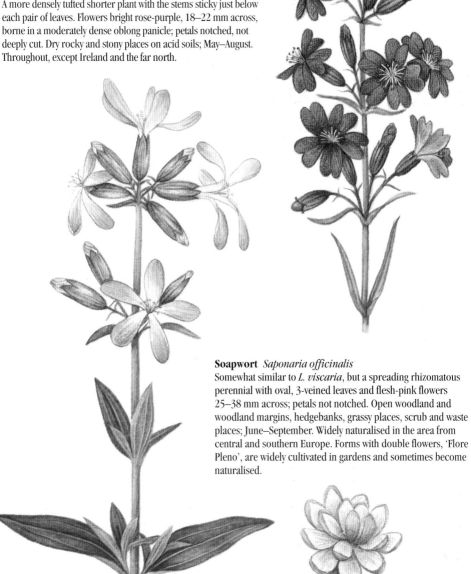

Soapwort *Saponaria officinalis*
Somewhat similar to *L. viscaria*, but a spreading rhizomatous
perennial with oval, 3-veined leaves and flesh-pink flowers
25–38 mm across; petals not notched. Open woodland and
woodland margins, hedgebanks, grassy places, scrub and waste
places; June–September. Widely naturalised in the area from
central and southern Europe. Forms with double flowers, 'Flore
Pleno', are widely cultivated in gardens and sometimes become
naturalised.

'Flore Pleno'

81

Red Campion

Silene dioica (syn. *Melandrium dioicum*)

Caryophyllaceae

A common and readily recognised plant whose relatively large deep pink flowers cannot be confused with any other plant in the region, often growing in association with other common woodland and hedgerow species such as Yarrow (*see* p.196), Cow Parsley (*see* p.178), Agrimony and Wood Avens. A good insect plant, the flowers are especially attractive to various long-tongued bees and hoverflies.

NOTE:
Hybridises widely with White Campion wherever the two grow in close proximity, especially bordering cultivated land. Hybrids, S. × hampeana, have varying pale or mid-pink flowers, are fully fertile and sometimes completely replace the parent species.

KEY FEATURES: Flowers bright rose-pink, open throughout the day, not scented. Sepals united into an urn-shaped calyx. Petals 5 with a long claw and a deeply notched limb with scales at the base.

HABITAT: Hedgerows and deciduous woodland, sometimes in rocky places, usually in shaded places; on calcareous soils usually.

FREQUENCY: Widespread and common, sometimes forming extensive colonies, particularly along hedge banks; scarcer in E Anglia, N Scotland and Ireland.

SEASON: May–August, then intermittently through to November.

HABIT: Hairy biennial or perennial with erect flowering stems, not sticky. Height 60–100 cm.

LEAVES: paired, deep green, paler beneath, oblong to elliptical, with an untoothed margin; lower stalked, the upper short-stalked or unstalked.

FLOWERS: numerous in symmetrically forked clusters, opening in succession, 18–25 mm across; calyx hairy. Male and female flowers borne on separate plants the male with 10 stamens and a 10-veined calyx, the female with 5 styles and a 20-veined calyx.

FRUIT: A papery capsule partly concealed by the expanded persistent calyx, opening at the apex by 10 recurved teeth and containing numerous seeds.

J
F
M
A
M ✿
J ✿
J ✿ ✦
A ✿ ✦
S ✿ ✦
O ✿ ✦
N ✿ ✦
D ✦

82

LOOKALIKES

Related campions all have hairy stems and leaves and deeply notched petals with scales at the base of the limb.

White Campion *Silene latifolia* (syn. *S. alba*)
Very similar, but a sticky plant with pure white flowers, 25–30 mm across, scented and only fully expanded in the evening or in dull weather. Mainly arable and wasteland on dry calcareous soils. Common throughout except for the far north; scarcer in the west and Ireland.

Night-flowering Catchfly *Silene noctiflora*
Plant sticky in the upper half, with strongly fragrant hermaphrodite flowers that unfurl in the evening, pale pink but yellowish beneath, 17–19 mm across; styles 3 and fruit capsule with 6 teeth only. June–August in dry sandy places and on arable land. Central and southern Britain from the Tees southwards; scarce elsewhere.

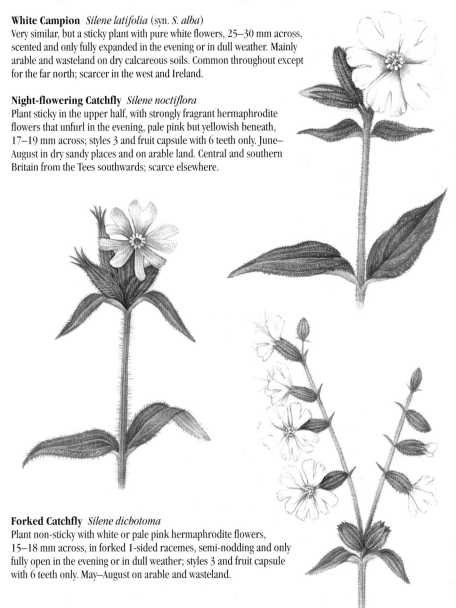

Forked Catchfly *Silene dichotoma*
Plant non-sticky with white or pale pink hermaphrodite flowers, 15–18 mm across, in forked 1-sided racemes, semi-nodding and only fully open in the evening or in dull weather; styles 3 and fruit capsule with 6 teeth only. May–August on arable and wasteland.

Bladder Campion

Silene vulgaris

Caryophyllaceae

A familiar wayside weed that looks like a larger more upright version of the Sea Campion, *S. uniflora*. For a long time botanists included both these within the same species, but today they are generally recognised as two, albeit closely allied, species. The Bladder Campion, is the favourite food plant of the small frog-hopper insects whose enveloping froth, generally referred to as cuckoo spit, is well known.

KEY FEATURES: A hairless or only slightly hairy plant with paired leaves. Calyx tubular and inflated and bladder-like, becoming papery as the fruits develops. Petals deeply notched. Fruit a small capsule with 6 erect teeth.

HABITAT: Grassy and waste places, particularly woodland margins, banks, verges and hedgerows.

FREQUENCY: Common throughout, sometimes abundant; absent from some of the more northerly islands.

SEASON: May–September.

HABIT: An erect greyish perennial, somewhat woody at the base and with stout stems to 80 cm.

LEAVES: Leaves oval to elliptical, with an untoothed margin, the lowermost stalked but the middle and upper unstalked.

FLOWERS: Inflorescence a lax leafy cluster often with many stalked, 5-parted, white flowers, each 16–18 mm across and fragrant. Calyx balloon-like, smooth and net-veined, with 5 teeth at the top. Petals with a long claw and a deeply notched, more or less heart-shaped limb. Stamens 10 and styles 3.

FRUIT: A small 6-toothed capsule hidden with the persistent calyx, many-seeded.

J
F
M
A
M
J
J
A
S
O
N
D

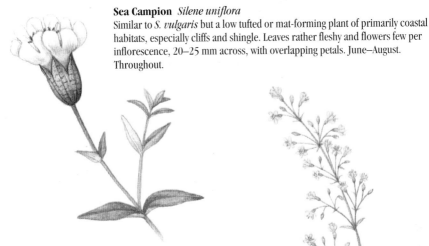

Sea Campion *Silene uniflora*
Similar to *S. vulgaris* but a low tufted or mat-forming plant of primarily coastal habitats, especially cliffs and shingle. Leaves rather fleshy and flowers few per inflorescence, 20–25 mm across, with overlapping petals. June–August. Throughout.

Spanish Catchfly *Silene otites*
An erect tufted biennial or perennial, rather sticky with hairs in the lower part. Flowers small and greenish-yellow, only 3–4 mm across, in large panicle-like inflorescences. June–September. E Britain, Holland and Germany southwards.

Sand Catchfly *Silene conica*
A stickily hairy erect annual with whitish to rose-pink, 4–5 mm flowers with the petals only shallowly notched. Calyx 30-veined, narrow at first but becoming broad and inflated as the fruits develop. Sandy and waste places, particularly coastal. May–August. S Britain, Holland and Germany southwards.

Small-flowered Catchfly *Silene gallica*
Like *S. conica* but flowers 6–10 mm across, with sticky 10-veined calyces. Arable land, waste and sandy places. June–October. W France and the Channel Islands, but casual in S England and near Edinburgh.

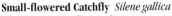

85

Deptford Pink

Dianthus armeria

Caryophyllaceae

T his interesting pink is closely related to the Sweet William (*Dianthus barbatus*), and looks rather like a scaled down version of that plant. The common name is misleading for it is fairly certain that the plant never grew in or near Deptford in the east end of London, although the Maiden Pink (*see opposite*) probably did.

NOTE:
Once far more common and widespread but declining in most of its localities due to modern farming techniques and the disappearance of former habitats due to development.

J
F
M
A
M
J
J
A
S
O
N
D

KEY FEATURES: Stiffly branched rough-hairy plant. Leaves in narrow and paired. Flowers clustered in tight heads, 5-parted, the petals with a distinct beard at the base of the limb; calyx with equally long pointed bracts around its base.

HABITAT: Dry grassy places, banks and verges, hedgerows, on rocky or calcareous soils.

FREQUENCY: Local and often rather rare; scattered localities in England, Wales and southern Scotland; generally decreasing.

SEASON: June–August.

HABIT: An erect, hairy, annual or biennial to 60 cm, with rather stiff branches.

LEAVES: Paired, deep green, linear, tapered to a pointed tip, hairy.

FLOWERS: Bright reddish-pink, 8–15 mm across, borne in dense terminal heads; calyx tubular with 5 teeth, surrounded at the base by 2–3 pairs of finely pointed bracts. Petals with a long claw, and an oval, slightly toothed, limb, with a beard towards the base. Styles 2.

FRUIT: Fruit a 5-toothed capsule containing numerous seeds.

Cheddar Pink *Dianthus gratianopolitanus*
A lower and laxer, tufted, hairless perennial
with narrow grass-like grey-green leaves.
Flowers solitary, plain pink, 20–30 mm across;
petals bearded towards the base of the limb,
with a deeply fringed margin. Exposed sunny
rocks and cliffs, usually on limestone; May–July.
S Britain (primarily around Cheddar Gorge),
Belgium to C Germany southwards.

Maiden Pink *Dianthus deltoides*
Similar in habit to the Cheddar Pink, but often more
spreading and with shorter, blunter, blue-green leaves.
Flowers deep pink, spotted in the centre, 15–20 mm
across. Grassy and rocky places, on light sandy or
calcareous soils; June–September. Throughout, except
the far north, Ireland and Iceland and most of the
smaller islands.

87

Wood Anemone

Anemone nemorosa

Ranunculaceae

A familiar woodland plant of early spring flowering at the same time as the Primrose, *Primula vulgaris* (*see* p.106). The Wood Anemone has been long associated with cottage gardens and today many cultivated forms are grown including those with violet, pink and blue, as well as white, flowers. The plants are very poisonous, especially to cattle, due to the presence of the narcotic Anemonin; this gives the plants a sharp, bittter taste.

NOTE:
In Anemone *there are no true petals and the petal-like organs are in reality sepals. The flowers tend to follow the sun.*

KEY FEATURES: A patch-forming woodland plant with a whorl of 3 stem leaves beneath the flower and separate basal leaves arising as the flowers fade. Flowers nodding, but become erect in bright sunshine, with 6–12 'petals'. Fruit a pendent cluster of small achenes.

HABITAT: Woodland (especially deciduous) and woodland clearings, copses, hedgerows, occasionally in more open grassy places, especially where trees have been cleared; generally on neutral to calcareous soils.

FREQUENCY: Locally abundant.

SEASON: March–May.

HABIT: A patch-forming, generally hairless, perennial with branching underground rhizomes, forming a leafy ground cover long after the flowers have finished; stems to 25 cm, often less.

LEAVES: Basal leaves appearing as the flowers fade, long-stalked, generally 2, with 3 deeply lobed and toothed segments. Stem leaves 3 in a whorl beneath the solitary flower, similar to the basal leaves but short-stalked.

FLOWERS: Pendent at first and closed but becoming erect and wide-open in sunshine, 20–40 mm across, white, but often flushed with pink or blue on the outside. 'Petals' 6–12, oval. Stamens numerous, pale yellow.

FRUIT: A pendent cluster of small greenish achenes, held on an arched stem just below the foliage.

J
F
M
A
M
J
J
A
S
O
N
D

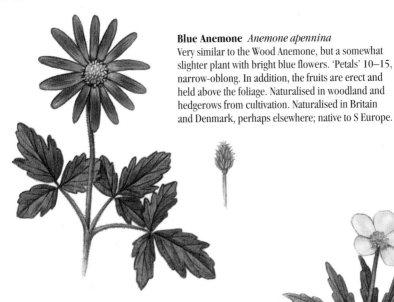

Blue Anemone *Anemone apennina*
Very similar to the Wood Anemone, but a somewhat slighter plant with bright blue flowers. 'Petals' 10–15, narrow-oblong. In addition, the fruits are erect and held above the foliage. Naturalised in woodland and hedgerows from cultivation. Naturalised in Britain and Denmark, perhaps elsewhere; native to S Europe.

Yellow Wood Anemone *Anemone ranunculoides*
Similar in habit to the Wood Anemone but tending to make denser less wide-spreading patches. The plant is generally hairy with very short stem leaves, but the bright yellow, 5-'petalled' flowers are very distinctive, often 2–3 together. Similar habitats and flowering time. Widespread in Continental Europe apart from the far north but naturalised in England.

Common Pasque Flower
Pulsatilla vulgaris (syn. *Anemone vulgaris*)
A distinctive plant with finely divided rather feathery foliage. The solitary pale to dark purple flowers are erect at first then half-nodding, bell-shaped, 5–7 cm across. Fruit a distinctive head of achenes with long feathery tails. Local short-grass meadows, generally over calcareous rocks; S England and S Sweden southwards.

89

Rosaceae

Meadowsweet
Filipendula ulmaria

The frothy white heads of the Meadowsweet are a characteristic of the countryside in the height of summer. The flowers have a pleasing fragrance which is difficult to place but 'musk', 'marzipan' and 'honey' have all been suggested, or perhaps it is a mixture of all three.

NOTE:
The flowers are especially attractive to different types of flies.

KEY FEATURES: Leaves pinnate, with large leaflets interspersed with smaller ones. Flowers small, usually 5-parted, and numerous, in branched clusters. Fruit a small cluster of achenes.

HABITAT: Damp meadows, marshes, fens and swamps, ditches, roadsides and woodland margins; often on neutral to calcareous soils.

FREQUENCY: Throughout, often gregarious and sometimes abundant.

SEASON: June–September.

HABIT: A robust tufted perennial, with stiff erect stems to 1.5 m.

LEAVES: Pinnate with up to 5 pairs of large leaflets interspersed with much smaller ones; leaflets oval to elliptical, coarsely toothed.

FLOWERS: Small, white or cream, sweetly, often rather sickly, scented, 4–8 mm across, usually with 5 petals; borne in dense, branched, rather upright clusters.

FRUIT: A small collection of achenes, each with 1–2 seeds.

J
F
M
A
M
J
J
A
S
O
N
D

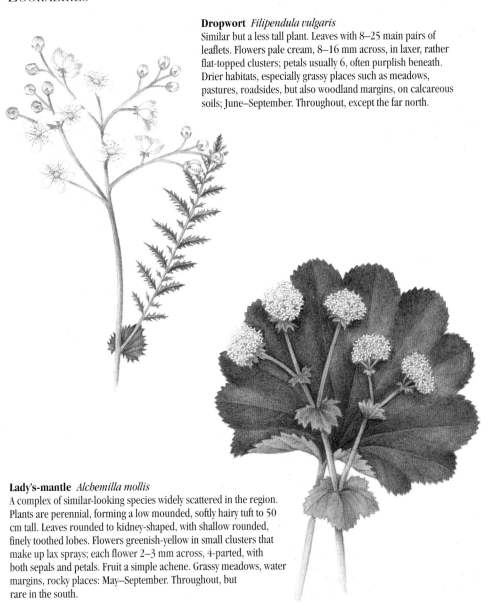

Dropwort *Filipendula vulgaris*
Similar but a less tall plant. Leaves with 8–25 main pairs of
leaflets. Flowers pale cream, 8–16 mm across, in laxer, rather
flat-topped clusters; petals usually 6, often purplish beneath.
Drier habitats, especially grassy places such as meadows,
pastures, roadsides, but also woodland margins, on calcareous
soils; June–September. Throughout, except the far north.

Lady's-mantle *Alchemilla mollis*
A complex of similar-looking species widely scattered in the region.
Plants are perennial, forming a low mounded, softly hairy tuft to 50
cm tall. Leaves rounded to kidney-shaped, with shallow rounded,
finely toothed lobes. Flowers greenish-yellow in small clusters that
make up lax sprays; each flower 2–3 mm across, 4-parted, with
both sepals and petals. Fruit a simple achene. Grassy meadows, water
margins, rocky places: May–September. Throughout, but
rare in the south.

Lythraceae

Purple Loosestrife

Lythrum salicaria

A prominent plant of damp habitats, which adds colour to the summer landscape, often growing in association with other moisture-loving perennials such as Meadowsweet (*see* p.90). The name 'loose-strife' comes from a direct translation from the Greek name for the plant, for it was thought to bring peace and harmony; a bunch placed on a yoke was thought to pacify oxen.

NOTE:

The flowers are trimorphic; there are three types of flower, looking similar but with the stamens and styles set at different levels. They are borne on separate plants.

KEY FEATURES: An upright plant with both leaves and flowers in distinct whorls. Flowers usually with 6 petals and 12 stamens. Fruit a many-seeded capsule.

HABITAT: Wet freshwater habitats, especially river and lake margins, but rarely on acid soils.

FREQUENCY: Throughout, except the far north, the Faeroes and Iceland; locally common.

SEASON: June–August.

HABIT: An erect, clump-forming, hairy, perennial, with stems to 1.5 m with 4 or more raised lines.

LEAVES: Grey-hairy, oval to lanceolate, paired or in whorls of 3, unstalked and untoothed.

FLOWERS: Bright reddish-purple in whorls forming long spikes with the uppermost whorls opening first. Flowers 10–15 mm across, usually with 6 petals.

FRUIT: Capsule oval, 10–15 mm long, containing numerous seeds.

J
F
M
A
M
J
J
A
S
O
N
D

LOOKALIKES

Grass-poly *Lythrum hyssopifolia*
A closely related but a far slighter, practically hairless, branched annual, not more than 25 cm tall. The alternate, rather pale green, linear to narrow-oblong leaves are semi-erect. Flowers pink, only 5 mm across. Solitary or paired at the base of the upper leaves and forming slender spikes. Disturbed and seasonally flooded land, at low altitudes; June–September. Throughout except for the far north, the Faeroes and Iceland; naturalised in Scandinavia. Rather scarce and erratic in appearance.

Harebell

Campanula rotundifolia

Campanulaceae

Known in Scotland appropriately as Bluebell, this charming and rather delicate wild flower is tolerant of a wide range of conditions, sometimes growing in the most harsh and exposed places. It is altogether charming and is undeniably a firm favourite amongst flower-lovers.

NOTE:
A very variable plant. The flowers are visited by various species of bee, but may also be self-pollinating.

KEY FEATURES: Stems thread-like. Leaves dimorphic, the basal broad, the others narrow. Flowers nodding, bell-shaped, with the petals joined together. Style 3-lobed.

HABITAT: Dry grassy places, hills, commons, heaths, rocky places and fixed sand dunes, on a wide variety of soils except wet ones.

FREQUENCY: Widespread and often common, sometimes abundant throughout the region.

SEASON: July–September.

HABIT: A stoloniferous, patch-forming, usually hairless, perennial, to 50 cm tall; stems thread-like, round.

LEAVES: Variable, the basal rounded to oval or kidney-shaped, toothed, long-stalked, while the stem leaves are narrow-lanceolate to linear and often untoothed.

FLOWERS: Pendent bells, blue, occasionally white, 12–20 mm long, borne in lax, branched panicles or racemes; calyx teeth linear, usually recurved.

FRUIT: A small capsule, splitting by 5 basal pores and containing numerous tiny seeds.

J
F
M
A
M
J
J
A
S
O
N
D

94

LOOKALIKES

Campanula scheuzeri
Similar to the Harebell, but all the leaves are narrow-lanceolate to linear and unstalked. Similar habitats, mainly in the mountains; June–September. Scandinavia, Germany and France.

Campanula rhomboidalis
Rather like a large Harebell but with rather angular stems and oval to lanceolate, toothed, stem leaves. Flowers pale to deep blue, 16–22 mm long, borne in few-flowered racemes; flowers erect in bud. Mountain meadows and other grassy places; June–September. In the Alps, but widely naturalised in Belgium, Holland and Germany.

Nettle-leaved Bellflower
Campanula trachelium

Campanulaceae

Also amusingly called Bats-in-the-Belfry, this imposing bellflower has rough heart-shaped leaves rather like the Stinging Nettle, but without the sting. Unusually, the uppermost flowers in the inflorescence are the first to open.

NOTE:
The flowers are hairy inside and these hairs provide a secure foothold for visiting insects, especially bees.

J
F
M
A
M
J
J
A
S
O
N
D

KEY FEATURES: A stout plant with nettle-shaped leaves. Flowers large and bell-shaped, ascending to erect; style 3-lobed. Sepals narrow-triangular.

HABITAT: Woodland margins, hedgerows and scrub, generally on calcareous soils.

FREQUENCY: Throughout except for Scandinavia, the Faeroes and Iceland; absent from N Scotland and rare in Ireland.

SEASON: July–September.

HABIT: A stout hairy perennial to 80 cm tall, sometimes taller; stems branched or unbranched, bristly, sharply angled.

LEAVES: Alternate, rough to the touch, broad-lanceolate to heart-shaped, with an irregularly toothed margin, only the lower stalked.

FLOWERS: Large bells, 25–40 mm long, violet-blue to pale blue, usually ascending, borne in a leafy raceme; calyx-teeth narrow-triangular, half the length of the corolla.

FRUIT: A pendent capsule, dehiscing by 5 basal pores and containing numerous tiny seeds.

LOOKALIKES

Giant Bellflower *Campanula latifolia*
Similar to *C. trachelium*, but to 1.2 m tall and with oval to oblong leaves that are often narrowed towards the base. Flowers blue, occasionally white, 40–55 mm long, erect to ascending. Woods, river and stream banks, mountain meadows; July–August. Continental Europe, except the far north, and Britain; naturalised in Belgium and Holland.

Creeping bellflower *Campanula rapunculoides*
A more slender and elegant plant with long spike-like racemes of pendent bluish-violet flowers, 20–30 mm long. A patch-forming perennial to 80 cm tall; styles 5-lobed. Woodland margins, meadows, hedgerows, embankments and cultivated land; July–September. Continental Europe, except the far north; naturalised in Britain.

◄ **Clustered Bellflower** *Campanula glomerata*
A distinctive patch-forming perennial with stiff stems to 70 cm tall, though often less. Leaves rounded to heart-shaped, stalked, but the upper stem leaves generally smaller and narrower. Flowers erect to ascending, deep blue, 15–30 mm long, clustered tightly at the stem tops. Grassy habitats, woodland, scrub and waste places, usually on calcareous soils; June–August. Throughout, except the far north, Ireland, the Faeroes and Iceland.

Campanula cervicaria ►
Like *C. glomerata*, but a more bristly plant with lanceolate leaves which have winged stalks. Flowers pale blue, 14–16 mm long, with a protruding style. Similar habitats and flowering time. Continental Europe, except the far north.

Campanulaceae

Peach-leaved Bellflower

Campanula persicifolia

This attractive flower has long been cultivated and is often associated with cottage gardens, where various forms can be found, including those with double flowers.

NOTE:
The flowers are visited by various species of bee.

J
F
M
A
M
J
J
A
S
O
N
D

KEY FEATURES: Plant with slender erect stems and narrow leaves. Flowers relatively large, broad bells, not nodding. Style 3-lobed.

HABITAT: Meadows and open woodland, waste places and cultivation.

FREQUENCY: Continental Europe, except the far north; naturalised widely in Britain.

SEASON: June–August.

HABIT: A patch-forming stoloniferous, hairless perennial; stems rather slender, erect, usually unbranched.

LEAVES: Lanceolate to narrow-oval, with blunt teeth and a tapered stalk, the upper leaves generally small, often linear and unstalked.

FLOWERS: Large broad bells, 30–40 mm long, blue or white, horizontal to ascending, borne in lax racemes; calyx-teeth narrow-triangular, one third the length of the corolla; buds erect.

FRUIT: An erect capsule, splitting at the top by 5 pores and containing numerous tiny seeds.

LOOKALIKES

Spreading Bellflower *Campanula patula*
A rough-hairy biennial or perennial, not spreading. Leaves oval, broadest above the middle; upper leaves few and linear-lanceolate, unstalked. Flowers erect wide violet to pale blue bells, 20–25 mm long, with the pointed corolla-lobed spreading widely apart, borne in a wide-spreading, branched inflorescence; calyx-teeth linear; buds pendent. Similar habitats; July–September. Britain, Holland to Germany and S Finland southwards, but widely naturalised elsewhere, especially in Scandinavia.

Rampion Bellflower *Campanula rapunculus*
Rather similar to *C. patula*, but a taller biennial with smaller flowers, 10–20 mm long. Flowers pale blue to white, broad erect bells, borne in a lax, occasionally branched, narrow-pyramidal inflorescence. Similar habitats and flowering time. Belgium, France, Holland and Germany; naturalised in Britain and Scandinavia.

Common Comfrey
Symphytum officinale

Boraginaceae

A bold bushy perennial of damp habitats, familiar in many regions. It has a long history as a healing herb being used in poultices in breaks, sprains and abrasions and is still much advocated today by herbalists. In addition, the plant is widely used today as a green manure and as a herbal tea. Its numerous common names, including Knit-bone and Bone-set bear witness to its useful medicinal properties.

NOTE:
The flowers are visited by a variety of insects although most prominently by various species of bee.

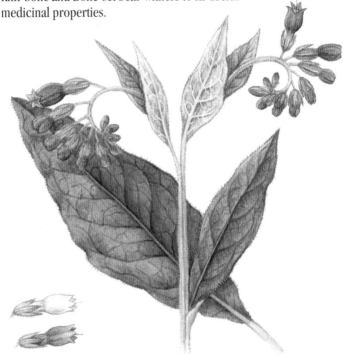

KEY FEATURES: A bold rough-bristly perennial with very large basal leaves. Leaves untoothed and net-veined. Flowers borne in spiralled cymes, 5-parted. Corolla tubular, broadening into 5 short lobes. Fruit 5 small nutlets.

HABITAT: Damp places, particularly river and stream margins, ditches, woodland, fens and verges.

FREQUENCY: Common, often locally abundant, but only naturalised in much of the north and in Ireland.

SEASON: May–July.

HABIT: A robust perennial to 1.5 m tall, with erect, widely winged stems.

LEAVES: Alternate, large and coarse, oval to lanceolate, with an untoothed margin, the lower stalked but the upper smaller and unstalked.

FLOWERS: Violet-purple, pinkish or white, tubular-bell-shaped, 12–18 mm long, borne in branched, spiralled clusters, nodding to half-nodding. Corolla tubular, with 5 short lobes at the expanded top, and a protruding style; stamens enclosed within the corolla-tube.

FRUIT: 5 small nutlets located at the base of the half-tubular, persistent calyx.

J
F
M
A
M
J
J
A
S
O
N
D

Rough Comfrey *Symphytum asperum*
A taller and rougher plant than *S. officinale*, without winged stems. Flowers pink in bud, but opening blue 10–17 mm long. Margins of cultivated land and waste places; June–July. Naturalised in Britain and C Scandinavia southwards (native to Iran and the Caucasus).

Russian Comfrey *Symphytum × uplandicum*
A hybrid between *S. asperum* and *S. officinale* to 2 m tall, with narrowly winged stems; flowers pink at first but becoming blue or violet. Common, often abundant along roadsides, hedges, woodland and waste places; June–August. Naturalised throughout except for the north.

Viper's Bugloss *Echium vulgare*
A bristly biennial, often with a solitary stem and lanceolate to elliptical, grey-green leaves. Flowers pale to bright blue or violet-blue, pink in bud, bell-shaped, 15–20 mm long with a wide-open mouth and protruding stamens. Dry open places; June–September. Throughout except for the far north.

Deadly Nightshade

Atropa bella-donna

Solanaceae

A large and imposing leafy plant with subdued flowers with cherry-like fruits that are extremely poisonous due to the presence of high quantities of hyoscyamine. The plant has been used traditionally in herbal remedies, especially as a stomach sedative, but the juice has long been used to dilate the pupils.

NOTE:
All parts of the plant are extremely poisonous.

KEY FEATURES: A large, much-branched perennial. Leaves large and untoothed. Flowers bell-shaped, nodding below the foliage. Fruit a succulent globose berry, black and shiny when ripe.

HABITAT: Damp and shaded places, particularly woodland, scrub and rocky areas, often on calcareous soils.

FREQUENCY: C and S Britain, Holland to Germany southwards, where it is quite common; elsewhere naturalised, scattered and local.

SEASON: June–September.

HABIT: A robust much-branched, leafy, hairless perennial.

LEAVES: Leaves plain green, alternate or opposite, oval, pointed and short-stalked.

FLOWERS: Bell-shaped, brownish-violet or greenish, nodding, 25–30 mm long, solitary from the upper leaf-axils and generally partly concealed by the foliage. Flowers 5-parted, with the sepals fused together only at the base, but the corolla tubular with 5 short, spreading lobes.

FRUIT: A globose berry, 15–20 mm across, black and shiny when ripe and surrounded by the star-like persistent calyx.

J
F
M
A
M
J
J
A
S
O
N
D

LOOKALIKES

Henbane *Hyoscyamus niger*
An equally poisonous plant but a stickily-hairy annual or perennial, to 80 cm tall.
Leaves oval to oblong, coarsely toothed or lobed, the stem leaves unstalked and
clasping. Flowers borne in 1-sided, branched spikes, irregularly trumpet-shaped,
pale yellow netted with purple veins. Fruit a capsule located at the base of the persisted,
stiff-papery calyx. Bare and waste ground, especially close to the sea or close to farm
buildings, often on nutrient-rich soils. Throughout, except for the far north, but often
local; May–September.

Bindweed

Convolvulus arvensis

Convolvulaceae

A very familiar wayside flower and often a troublesome weed of cultivation with typical funnel-shaped flowers that are short-lived and only open during the day. Bindweed gets its common name from its closely entwining stems that envelop any suitable support close at hand.

NOTE:
A very variable plant which can be very large and invasive in fertile soils but smaller and more discreet, sometimes forming small mats, in more exposed rocky or coastal habitats.

J
F
M
A
M
J
J
A
S
O
N
D

KEY FEATURES: A robust perennial with twinning stems. Leaves arrow-shaped. Flowers solitary, funnel-shaped, 5-parted but the corolla scarcely lobed. Fruit a small rounded, multi-seeded capsule.

HABITAT: Grassy, waste and cultivated places, hedgerows, coastal habitats.

FREQUENCY: Common almost throughout, but absent from the far north; sometimes abundant and making extensive colonies.

SEASON: June–September.

HABIT: A vigorous hairy or hairless, climbing or sprawling perennial, to 2 m, with twinning stems and far-reaching underground rhizomes.

LEAVES: Alternate, arrow-shaped, deep green, with a short stalk, the margin untoothed, although often somewhat undulate.

FLOWERS: Funnel-shaped, white or pink with white stripes, 15–25 mm across, the calyx with 5 equal sepals but the corolla with 5 more or less indistinguishable, fused petals.

FRUIT: A small rounded capsule, surrounded at the base by the persistent calyx.

Hedge Bindweed *Calystegia sepium*
A very vigorous entwining perennial to 3 m with arrow-shaped bright green leaves. Flowers white, funnel-shaped, 30–50 mm across; calyx surrounded by large bract-like scales. Coastal salt-marshes, sandy and waste places; June–September. Throughout except the far north.

▶ **Great Bindweed** *Calystegia silvatica*
Has larger flowers, 50–90 mm across, white, sometimes striped with pink; calyx scales widely overlapping and pouched at the base. Hedgerows, around buildings and waste places; July–September. Naturalised in Britain from S and SE Europe.

Hairy Bindweed *Calystegia pulchra*
Similar to *C. silvatica*, but both stems and leaf-stalks hairy and flowers always pink, 50–75 mm across. Hedges, scrub and waste places; July–September. Naturalised from gardens from Britain to Denmark and Germany southwards.

Primrose
Primula vulgaris

Primulaceae

O ne of the prettiest and most popular wild flowers of the area which has been widely selected and hybridised in gardens for many years. It has become, over many centuries, a symbol of spring and renewal. Indeed the very name Primrose or *prima rosa* indicates the first flower of the year.

NOTE:
In most species of Primula *plants exhibit heterostyly: plants either have a long (pin-eyed flowers) or short style (thrum-eyed flowers), with the anthers placed accordingly low or high in the corolla-tube. Hybrids between the Primrose and Cowslip,* P. × tommasinii, *or False Oxlip, can often be found where the two species grow in close proximity.*

KEY FEATURES: A rosette-forming, stemless, plant with the flowers set posy-like in the middle of the leaves. Flowers solitary 5-parted, the corolla tubular with a broad limb, the lobes of which are clearly notched.
HABITAT: Woodland and grassy banks, scrub, embankments, cliffs and ditches, on heavy but not wet soils.
FREQUENCY: Widely distributed and often gregarious, sometimes locally abundant.
SEASON: February–May, occasionally later.
HABIT: A tufted, rosette-forming, softly hairy plant with all the leaves and flowers basal.
LEAVES: Oval, tapered to a winged stalk, with a finely toothed margin, bright green above but paler and downy beneath.
FLOWERS: Scented, pale yellow, 20–40 mm across, solitary from the centre of the leaf-rosette, borne on downy stalks. Calyx bell-shaped with 5 short, pointed teeth. Corolla with a long slender tube and broad almost flat limb; lobed heart-shaped.
FRUIT: A 5-parted capsule hidden at the base of the persistent calyx, many-seeded.

J
F
M
A
M
J
J
A
S
O
N
D

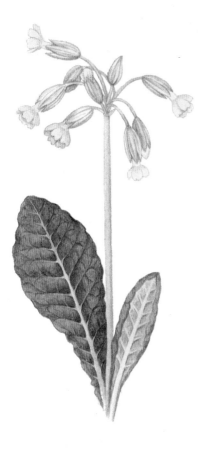

Cowslip *Primula veris*
A tufted plant with the leaves very similar to those of the Primrose, but abruptly narrowed into the stalk. Flowers sweetly scented, deep yellow with orange marks in the centre, 9–15 mm across, a number clustered on a common stalk in a 1-sided umbel. Grassy habitats, scrub and open woodland, banks, on drier (usually calcareous) soils than the Primrose; April–early June. Throughout, except the far north and Iceland.

Oxlip *Primula elatior*
Similar to the Primrose but leaves broader and more rounded and more abruptly narrowed into the stalk. Flowers pale yellow, 15–25 mm across, a number borne on a common stalk in a 1-sided umbel. Moist habitats, woodland, coppices and ditches, streamsides; April–May. E England, S Sweden and Denmark southwards.

Yellow Loosestrife

Lysimachia vulgaris

Primulaceae

A typical summer perennial of moist habitats, often growing with its purple, yet unrelated, namesake *Lythrum salicaria*. The simple 5-parted flowers somewhat resemble those of the St. John's-wort (*see* p.66), but the petals are joined into a short tube at the base, and there are only 5 stamens.

KEY FEATURES: Leaves untoothed, borne in whorls or 3–4 up the stem, or opposite; leaf surface dotted with orange or black glands. Flowers 5-parted, borne in large terminal panicles.

HABITAT: Moist habitats such as marshes, fens, lake and river margins, ditches, on neutral to calcareous soils.

FREQUENCY: Throughout except for the Faeroes and Iceland.

SEASON: June–August.

HABIT: A tufted stoloniferous, softly hairy, perennial with erect stems to 1.5 m.

LEAVES: Opposite or in whorls of 3–4, oval to lanceolate, with an untoothed margin, mostly unstalked.

FLOWERS: Numerous, yellow, salver-shaped, 15–20 mm across, with wide-spreading petals; sepals linear, much shorter than the petals, orange-edged.

FRUIT: A small 5-parted capsule containing numerous seeds.

J
F
M
A
M
J
J
A
S
O
N
D

LOOKALIKES

Yellow Pimpernel *Lysimachia nemorum*
Similar in flower but very different in habit; a creeping hairless perennial with pale green pairs of leaves. Flowers bright yellow, solitary on slender stalks, 10–15 mm across. Fruits borne on curved stalks. Damp and shaded habitats; may July. Throughout, except the far north and Iceland.

Dotted Loosestrife *Lysimachia punctata*
Robust perennial of similar height. Most leaves in distinct whorls of 3–4. Bright yellow flowers 18–26 mm across are borne in dense clusters at the upper leaf whorls; petals fringed with glands and rather more pointed. Naturalised from gardens in many parts except the far north. Native to SE Europe.

Scarlet Pimpernel *Anagallis arvensis*
A sprawling to prostrate annual with square stems and pairs of small oval leaves.
Flowers solitary, long-stalked, loosestrife-like but scarlet (occasionally pink or blue)
4–7 mm across; petals with a hairy margin. Cultivated, disturbed and wasteland;
May–October. Throughout, except for the Faeroes and Iceland.

Blue Pimpernel *Anagallis foemina* (syn. *A. arvensis* subsp. *caerulea*)
Similar to the previous but upper leaves narrow-lanceolate and flowers blue, the petals
without a hairy margin. Similar habitats, especially arable fields and gardens.
Throughout, except for Ireland, Iceland and the Faeroes.

Thrift
Armeria maritima

Plumbaginaceae

A familiar plant of coastal locations, the thrift has long been cultivated in gardens, its neat rather prim habit being long-favoured for edging flower borders. Its other common names include Cliff Clover, Ladies' Cushions and Sea-pink.

NOTE:
A taller version, to 50 cm in flower, with hairless scapes (flower stems) is distinguished as subsp. elongata *and is found primarily on rough pastures and rocky places in E England, Denmark, Holland, NW Germany and neighbouring parts of S Scandinavia, including Finland.*

J
F
M
A
M
J
J
A
S
O
N
D

KEY FEATURES: A low cushion-forming plant. Leaves tough and linear. Flowers clustered on top of a common leafless stalk or scape. Corolla 5-parted with the lobes fused together towards the base.

HABITAT: Maritime cliffs and meadows, salt marshes and mountain rocks.

FREQUENCY: Common throughout, sometimes abundant.

SEASON: April–August.

HABIT: Dense deep green cushion-forming perennial, to 30 cm tall in flower.

LEAVES: Linear, tough and leathery, borne in dense tufts, generally with a single vein.

FLOWERS: Borne in dense rounded, long-stalked heads, 15–25 mm across, pink, red or white. Corolla 5-lobed with spreading, rounded lobes. Flowers much visited by bees and butterflies.

FRUIT: Dry and 1-seeded, not splitting when ripe and surrounded by the persistent papery calyx.

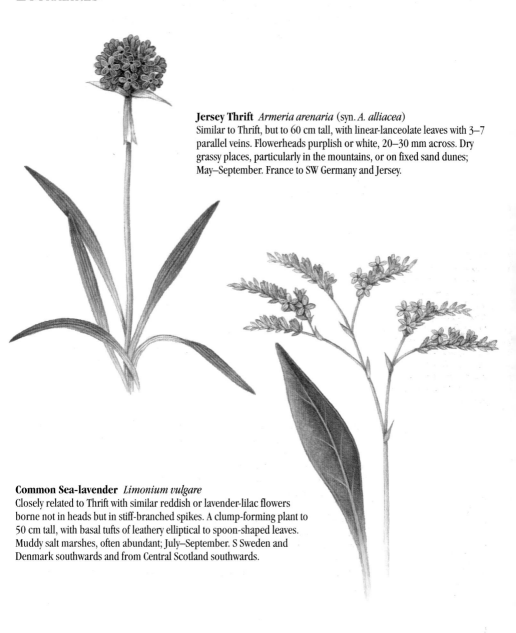

Jersey Thrift *Armeria arenaria* (syn. *A. alliacea*)
Similar to Thrift, but to 60 cm tall, with linear-lanceolate leaves with 3–7 parallel veins. Flowerheads purplish or white, 20–30 mm across. Dry grassy places, particularly in the mountains, or on fixed sand dunes; May–September. France to SW Germany and Jersey.

Common Sea-lavender *Limonium vulgare*
Closely related to Thrift with similar reddish or lavender-lilac flowers borne not in heads but in stiff-branched spikes. A clump-forming plant to 50 cm tall, with basal tufts of leathery elliptical to spoon-shaped leaves. Muddy salt marshes, often abundant; July–September. S Sweden and Denmark southwards and from Central Scotland southwards.

Field Gromwell

Lithospermum arvense (syn. *Buglossoides arvensis*)

Boraginaceae

A common plant of arable land and other dry habitats whose seeds, like those of the Common Poppy (*see* p.22), can reside in the soil for many years until conditions are suitable for germination. Unlike the poppy, however, this is not a spectacular plant and it is easily overlooked.

NOTE:
In most borages (members of the borage family) the calyx is persistent and protects the fruits as they develop.

J
F
M
A
M
J
J
A
S
O
N
D

KEY FEATURES: A stiff-stemmed, rather bristly, plant. Leaves untoothed. Flowers 5-parted, forget-me-not like, white or cream, often with a purplish tube. Fruit 4 small nutlets.
HABITAT: A weed of arable and other cultivated land, waste and open grassy places.
FREQUENCY: Locally frequent in England and on Continental Europe except for the far north; local and rarer in Ireland, Wales and Scotland.
SEASON: April–September.
HABIT: An erect stiff-stemmed annual, little-branched, to 50 cm tall, though often less.
LEAVES: Oblong to linear, bristly, with an untoothed margin, short-stalked or unstalked.
FLOWERS: White or cream, 6–9 mm across, borne in small spiralled clusters at the uppermost leaves; corolla 5 lobed, the lobes fused below into a short purplish tube.
FRUIT: 4 small greyish-brown nutlets located at the base of the persistent calyx.

LOOKALIKES

Common Gromwell *Lithospermum officinale*
A taller perennial plant to 100 cm tall with oval to lanceolate, prominently veined and pointed leaves. Flowers cream or greenish-white, 3–6 mm across. Fruit with shiny white nutlets. Woodland margins, scrub and hedgerows; May–August. Throughout, except the far north, but local and generally scarce in the west, particularly in Wales and Ireland.

Boraginaceae

Wood Forget-me-not
Myosotis sylvatica

The forget-me-nots are well known and much-loved plants. In Europe there are quite a few species which tend to look rather alike and are easily confused. Many occupy discreet habitats and these alone can aid in accurate identification.

NOTE:
This is the common forget-me-not of gardens, where it can be found in a range of colours from blue to pink and white.

KEY FEATURES: A softly hairy biennial or perennial. Basal leaves in a rosette; all leaves untoothed and alternate. Flowers 5-parted, with a flat limb with a small hole into the short tube beneath. Fruit consisting a 4 tiny nutlets.

HABITAT: Damp woodland and mountain grasslands.

FREQUENCY: Local, but sometimes abundant, from S Scandinavia southwards; in Britain rarer in the south.

SEASON: April–July.

HABIT: A hairy, tufted perennial, occasionally biennial, to 50 cm, with erect to ascending stems.

LEAVES: Oval to lanceolate, untoothed, the lowermost in a distinct rosette, the upper narrower, pointed and unstalked.

FLOWERS: Bright sky-blue, 6–10 mm across, borne in tight spiralled cymes; corolla with a flat limb.

FRUIT: 4 brownish nutlets at the base of the open persistent calyx, which is adorned with hooked hairs in the lower part.

J
F
M
A
M
J
J
A
S
O
N
D

LOOKALIKES

Field Forget-me-not *Myosotis arvensis*
An annual or biennial to 40 cm with small, 3–5 mm, grey-blue
flowers. Nutlets concealed at the base of the closed calyx. Dry
habitats, particularly arable and cultivated land and sand dunes;
April–October. Throughout.

◄ **Changing Forget-me-not**
Myosotis discolor
A slender annual not more than
25 cm tall, often branched from the
base and with the lowermost leaves
paired. Flowers very small, only 2 mm
across, at first pale yellow or cream but
ageing to pink, violet or blue. Bare and
open grassy places, open woodland, on
light well-drained soils; May–September.
Britain and S Scandinavia southwards.

Water Forget-me-not *Myosotis scopioides*
A rhizomatous perennial to 70 cm with slightly hairy to
hairless stems. Flowers sky-blue, occasionally pinkish or
white, 5–9 mm across; corolla with a flat limb and slightly
notched lobes. Wet habitats, especially pond and river
margins and ditches; May–September. Throughout.

115

Borage
Borago officinalis

Boraginaceae

Αn attractive and widely cultivated and naturalised plant with its familiar shooting star flowers. Despite its bristly habit the young leaves are sometimes added to salads and have a fresh cucumber taste. Both leaves and the colourful flowers are added to summer fruit cups to give interest. Today it is also grown as a field crop; oil is extracted from the seeds.

NOTE:
The flowers are visited by many insects, but bees in particular.

J
F
M
A
M
J
J
A
S
O
N
D

KEY FEATURES: A robust, very bristly, rather leafy annual. Leaves alternate, with wavy margins. Flowers 5-parted, borne in broad branched cymes; corolla star-shaped. Fruit a cluster of 4 nutlets.

HABITAT: Cultivated and waste land, waysides.

FREQUENCY: Native to C and S France but widely naturalised elsewhere; in Britain scattered in many areas.

SEASON: May–September.

HABIT: An upright bristly annual, with thick stems which are generally branched above, to 60 cm tall.

LEAVES: Oval to lanceolate, the lower stalked but the upper unstalked and clasping the stem; all with wavy untoothed margins.

FLOWERS: Star-shaped, 20–25 mm across, nodding to half-nodding, bright blue with a white centre and with a prominent cone of purple-black anthers projecting forwards.

FRUIT: 4 nutlets exposed at the base of the bristly calyx that enlarges as the fruits develop.

116

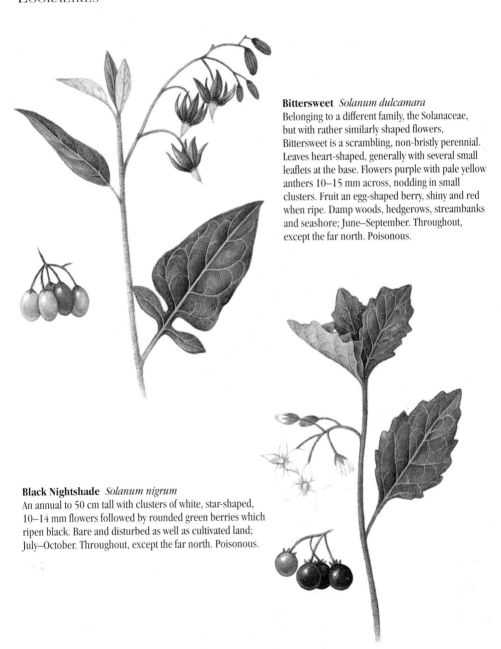

Bittersweet *Solanum dulcamara*
Belonging to a different family, the Solanaceae,
but with rather similarly shaped flowers,
Bittersweet is a scrambling, non-bristly perennial.
Leaves heart-shaped, generally with several small
leaflets at the base. Flowers purple with pale yellow
anthers 10–15 mm across, nodding in small
clusters. Fruit an egg-shaped berry, shiny and red
when ripe. Damp woods, hedgerows, streambanks
and seashore; June–September. Throughout,
except the far north. Poisonous.

Black Nightshade *Solanum nigrum*
An annual to 50 cm tall with clusters of white, star-shaped,
10–14 mm flowers followed by rounded green berries which
ripen black. Bare and disturbed as well as cultivated land;
July–October. Throughout, except the far north. Poisonous.

Great Mullein
Verbascum thapsus

Scrophulariaceae

A stately plant also locally known as Aaron's Rod. However, the furry nature of the foliage has also earned it a host of other common names including Adam's Flannel, Donkey's Ear or Hare's-beard. It is one of a number of interesting biennial species that passes the first year as a handsome evergreen leaf-rosette, before running up to flower in the second.

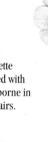

KEY FEATURES: Plant with a large leaf-rosette in the first year. Leaves and stems covered with woolly, fur-like, hair. Flowers 5-parted, borne in long dense spikes; stamens with white hairs. Fruit a 2-parted capsule.

HABITAT: Rough grassy and waste places, hedgebanks, scrub and verges, on light stony or calcareous soils.

FREQUENCY: Throughout, except the far north, sometimes locally abundant.

SEASON: June–August.

HABIT: A large grey- or white-woolly biennial to 2 m tall in flower, but spending the first year as a neat large leaf-rosette.

LEAVES: Basal elliptical to oblong, with a winged stalk, and usually with a finely toothed margin. Stem leaves alternate, smaller and unstalked, with the leaf base running characteristically down the stem to the leaf below.

FLOWERS: Yellow, 12–35 mm across, with 5 spreading rounded lobes, borne in dense woolly spikes that are sometimes branched towards the base.

FRUIT: A small 2-parted capsule splitting lengthways to expel numerous tiny seeds.

J
F
M
A
M
J
J
A
S
O
N
D

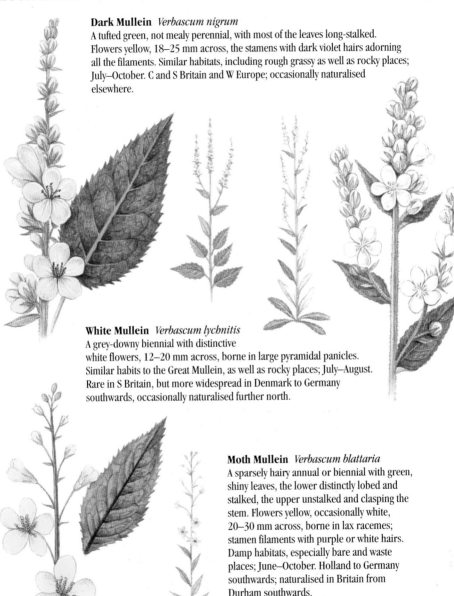

Dark Mullein *Verbascum nigrum*
A tufted green, not mealy perennial, with most of the leaves long-stalked.
Flowers yellow, 18–25 mm across, the stamens with dark violet hairs adorning
all the filaments. Similar habitats, including rough grassy as well as rocky places;
July–October. C and S Britain and W Europe; occasionally naturalised
elsewhere.

White Mullein *Verbascum lychnitis*
A grey-downy biennial with distinctive
white flowers, 12–20 mm across, borne in large pyramidal panicles.
Similar habits to the Great Mullein, as well as rocky places; July–August.
Rare in S Britain, but more widespread in Denmark to Germany
southwards, occasionally naturalised further north.

Moth Mullein *Verbascum blattaria*
A sparsely hairy annual or biennial with green,
shiny leaves, the lower distinctly lobed and
stalked, the upper unstalked and clasping the
stem. Flowers yellow, occasionally white,
20–30 mm across, borne in lax racemes;
stamen filaments with purple or white hairs.
Damp habitats, especially bare and waste
places; June–October. Holland to Germany
southwards; naturalised in Britain from
Durham southwards.

Common Valerian
Valeriana officinalis

Valerianaceae

An attractive vanilla-scented plant formerly much used in herbal medicines; the extracts have a tranquillising or sedative effect. Cats are attracted to the plant in the same way as they are to Catmint.

NOTE:
The flowers are much visited by both bees and butterflies.

KEY FEATURES: Plant with pinnately-lobed leaves. Flowers small, tubular, with 5 spreading lobes and 3 protruding stamens.
HABITAT: Dry grassy habitats, especially meadows and waysides, sometimes in ditches.
FREQUENCY: Throughout, except for the far north.
SEASON: June–August.
HABIT: An erect perennial to 2 m, though often less, with hairless, unbranched stems.
LEAVES: Pinnately lobed, the lower long-stalked, while the upper are smaller and unstalked; leaflets green, toothed or not.
FLOWERS: Small, pink or white, 2.5–5 mm long, borne in dense rounded and branched clusters.
FRUIT: Small and not splitting, adorned with a small and rather inconspicuous persistent calyx.

J
F
M
A
M
J
J
A
S
O
N
D

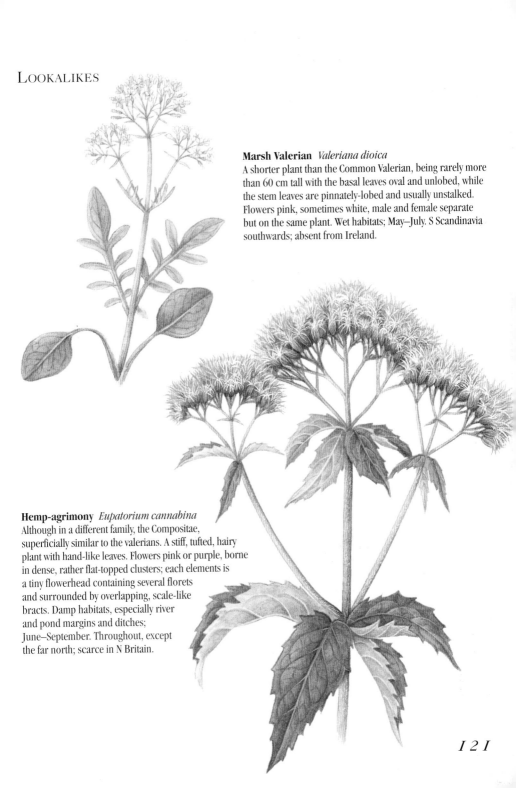

Marsh Valerian *Valeriana dioica*
A shorter plant than the Common Valerian, being rarely more than 60 cm tall with the basal leaves oval and unlobed, while the stem leaves are pinnately-lobed and usually unstalked. Flowers pink, sometimes white, male and female separate but on the same plant. Wet habitats; May–July. S Scandinavia southwards; absent from Ireland.

Hemp-agrimony *Eupatorium cannabina*
Although in a different family, the Compositae, superficially similar to the valerians. A stiff, tufted, hairy plant with hand-like leaves. Flowers pink or purple, borne in dense, rather flat-topped clusters; each elements is a tiny flowerhead containing several florets and surrounded by overlapping, scale-like bracts. Damp habitats, especially river and pond margins and ditches; June–September. Throughout, except the far north; scarce in N Britain.

Weld
Reseda luteola

Resedaceae

An alternative common name, Dyer's Rocket, indicates that in former times this was an important dye plant. The plant was grown on a field scale and all parts were used to dye cloth yellow. Today it is occasionally still used for dyeing, but it is more often seen as a wild plant in the countryside with its characteristic long feathery spires of flower. The seed can reside in the soil for many years until conditions, especially disturbance of the soil, are right for germination.

NOTE:
The flowers are visited primarily by bees. Plants form a leafy rosette at ground level in their first year.

J
F
M
A
M
J
J
A
S
O
N
D

KEY FEATURES: Tall plant with narrow spikes of flower. Leaves unlobed, wavy-edged. Flowers with 4 deeply cut petals. Fruit an erect 3-parted capsule.

HABITAT: Stony and sandy places, field boundaries, waste ground and old quarries, on calcareous soils.

FREQUENCY: Throughout, except the far north; probably naturalised in much of the north of the region.

SEASON: June–September.

HABIT: Tall, hairless biennial to 1.3 m, leafy in the lower half and branched in the upper.

LEAVES: Lanceolate, deep green, rather crowded, unlobed but usually with a wavy margin.

FLOWERS: Yellowish-green, 4–5 mm across, borne in very long tapered spikes; sepals and petals 4, the petals deeply lobed.

FRUIT: A 3-parted globular capsule, 3–4 mm long, erect and containing numerous seeds.

Wild Mignonette *Reseda lutea*
Similar to Weld, but a generally bushier plant with pinnately-lobed leaves (leaves usually with 1–2 pairs of lobes on each side). Flowers yellow, with 6 sepals and petals. Fruit capsule larger, 7–12 mm long, oblong and erect, less obviously lobed. Similar habitats, as well as cultivated ground, on calcareous soils; June–September. Britain, Ireland and Holland southwards; naturalised in Germany and further north.

White Mignonette *Reseda alba*
Leaves with 10 or more lobes, often rather grey-green. Flowers white, 8–9 mm across, with 5–6 sepals and petals. Fruit capsule 8–15 mm long, 4-parted, with persistent filaments around the base. Dry rocky ground, waste places, old walls, often near seaports; June–August. France, but naturalised in Britain, Holland and Germany; casual elsewhere.

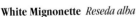

123

Himalayan Balsam

Impatiens glandulifera

Balsaminaceae

This Himalayan plant has become so much at home in some regions that it makes an impressive sight when in bloom, especially along waterways. It is probably the largest annual to be found in the countryside. An alternative common name 'Policeman's Helmet' aptly describes the shape of the flower. The flowers emit a rather sickly balsam scent that is highly attractive to bumblebees. Children love to flick the fruits that explode suddenly when ripe.

NOTE:
The balsam flower consists usually of a small lateral pair of sepals, an enlarged, often pouched lower sepal with an attached spur, and 5 petals. The upper petal forms a hood or helmet, while the lateral ones are fused in pairs. The stamens (5 in all) are closely united around the obscured ovary, but eventually fall off in one piece.

KEY FEATURES: Stems succulent and hollow. Leaves mostly whorled. Flowers with a pouch terminating in a short spur, and with a helmeted upper petal. Fruit a capsule, exploding when ripe.

HABITAT: Moist and semi-shaded places, particularly along lake margins and waterways, waste and cultivated land.

FREQUENCY: Naturalised throughout north as far as C Scandinavia, gregarious and locally abundant; from the W and C Himalaya.

SEASON: July–October.

HABIT: A stout succulent, hairless, annual to 2.5 m tall, with thick a pale green hollow stem, branched only in the inflorescence.

LEAVES: Whorled, generally 3–5 per whorl, lanceolate to elliptic, with a toothed margin, deep green above but paler beneath.

FLOWERS: Purple, pink, or occasionally reddish or white, 25–40 mm, borne in racemes of 5 or more from the upper nodes; flower pouched, with a short incurved spur, the upper petal forming a helmet over the stamens and ovary; throat spotted and marked within.

FRUIT: A club-shaped capsule, exploding elastically to eject the relatively large seeds, often some distance from the plant.

J
F
M
A
M
J
J
A
S
O
N
D

Touch-me-not *Impatiens noli-tangere*
A less tall annual, occasionally reaching 1.8 m, generally
less, with alternate, oval to elliptical leaves. Flowers 3–6,
on slender stalks, yellow with small brown spots, 20–35
mm, with a gradually incurved spur. Capsule linear. Moist
places, particularly by streams and rivers,
but also in wet woods and other damp places;
July–September. Throughout, except the far north;
in Britain mainly from Cumbria northwards.

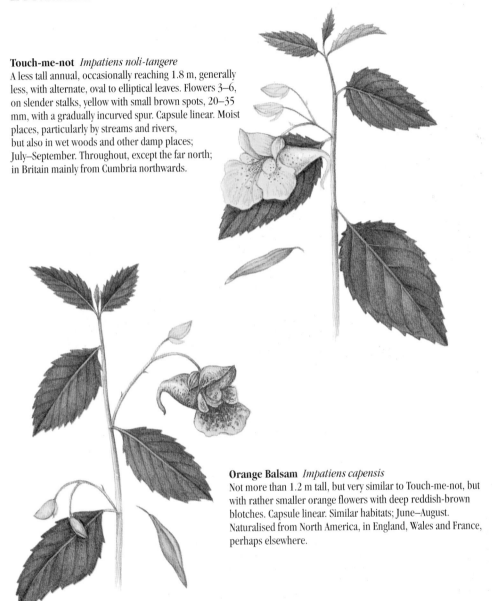

Orange Balsam *Impatiens capensis*
Not more than 1.2 m tall, but very similar to Touch-me-not, but
with rather smaller orange flowers with deep reddish-brown
blotches. Capsule linear. Similar habitats; June–August.
Naturalised from North America, in England, Wales and France,
perhaps elsewhere.

Sweet Violet

Viola odorata

Violaceae

V iolets are amongst the most treasured of our wild flowers, none more so than the Sweet Violet, long prized for its delightful perfume. It is not surprising that the plant was cherished by the ancient Greeks for perfumery, and in medieval times in Britain and elsewhere it was one of a number of strewing herbs used in homes to make the air generally more pleasing to breathe.

NOTE:
The species is widely cultivated in gardens and commonly escapes. In the summer insignificant cleistogamous flowers are borne, as they are in many other Viola *species; these fail to open but are able to set seed.*

J
F
M
A
M
J
J
A
S
O
N
D

KEY FEATURES: A low plant with long rooting runners. Leaves heart-shaped. Flowers solitary on the downturned end of slender stalks, 5-parted, the lowest petal forming a small lip; corolla spurred behind the calyx. Fruit a 5-parted capsule.

HABITAT: Woods, coppices, hedgerows, plantations and churchyards, on neutral to calcareous soils.

FREQUENCY: Throughout, except the far north, sometimes locally abundant.

SEASON: February–May.

HABIT: A low tufted, somewhat hairy, perennial to 10 cm tall, forming patches by long rooting runner.

LEAVES: Heart-shaped, pale green, long-stalked, the margin bluntly toothed.

FLOWERS: Dark violet or white; typical violet-shaped, 13–15 mm, with 2 upward-facing petals and 3 downward facing, the lowermost forming a small lip. Spur usually violet, 5–6 mm long. Flower stalk with a pair of small bracts in the middle.

FRUIT: A 5-parted capsule, splitting into a star-shape when ripe and containing numerous seeds.

Common Dog-violet *Viola riviniana*
Plants form leafy tufts without runners, with the flowers borne on short leafy shoots. Leaves hairless or almost so. Flowers deep bluish-violet, 14–25 mm, unscented, with a furrowed, whitish or pale purple spur. Deciduous woodland and grassy places, often over chalk or limestone; April–June. Throughout.

Heath Dog-violet *Viola canina*
This species lacks a basal leaf-rosette and bears bright blue or violet flowers, 10–18 mm, with a whitish to greenish-yellow spur. Dry places, woods, heaths, fens, sandy areas, generally on acid soils; April–July. Throughout.

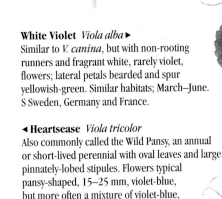

White Violet *Viola alba* ▶
Similar to *V. canina*, but with non-rooting runners and fragrant white, rarely violet, flowers; lateral petals bearded and spur yellowish-green. Similar habitats; March–June. S Sweden, Germany and France.

◀ **Heartsease** *Viola tricolor*
Also commonly called the Wild Pansy, an annual or short-lived perennial with oval leaves and large pinnately-lobed stipules. Flowers typical pansy-shaped, 15–25 mm, violet-blue, but more often a mixture of violet-blue, yellow and white. Cultivated land and waste places, rough grassland; April–October. Throughout.

Field Pansy *Viola arvensis*
Smaller than *V. tricolor*, with 10–15 mm flowers that are basically white or cream, but sometimes with the upper petals flushed with violet-blue. Common weed of arable land and other cultivated or waste places, on neutral to calcareous soils; April–October. Throughout, except the Faeroes and Iceland.

Yellow Corydalis

Corydalis lutea (syn. *Pseudofumaria lutea*)

Fumariaceae

Although not a native species the Yellow Corydalis is so thoroughly naturalised in the region that it has almost become to be regarded as indigenous. It favours rocky places, especially old walls and appears to flower almost throughout the year and, being a prodigious seeder, it is a rapid coloniser.

KEY FEATURES: Soft rather sappy plant. Leaves divided into numerous small leaflets. Flowers 2-lipped with a backwards-facing spur. Fruit a narrow 2-parted capsule.

HABITAT: Old walls, pavements and rocky places, sometimes in woodland.

FREQUENCY: Widely naturalised but often locally common; throughout, apart form much of the north and Scandinavia. Native to the central and eastern Alps.

SEASON: April–October, sometimes later.

HABIT: A densely tufted greyish-green plant to 40 cm, often less, with pale sappy, much-branched stems.

LEAVES: Dissected into numerous small oblong, lobed leaflets.

FLOWERS: Golden yellow, 12–20 mm long, including the spur, borne in long-stalked racemes opposite the uppermost leaves; upper lip recurved but the lower lip almost straight.

FRUIT: A narrow-elliptical, pendent capsule exploding suddenly to release the numerous black seeds.

J
F
M
A
M
J
J
A
S
O
N
D

LOOKALIKES

Climbing Corydalis
Ceratocapnos claviculata
Similar in leaf and flower, but a slender climbing pale green annual with tendrils. Flowers smaller, only 4–6 mm long, cream. Rocky and wooded places, heaths, generally on acid soils; June–September. S Scandinavia southwards, but rare in Ireland.

Common Fumitory *Fumaria officinalis*
A corydalis-like plant but with a rounded 1-seeded fruits that do not split. A erect to rather sprawling annual to 25 cm, with racemes of purplish-pink flowers with a reddish-black apex, each flower 7–9 mm long. Fruit wider than long, slightly notched at the apex. Cultivated land and waste places; May–October. Throughout, but only casual in the Faeroes and Iceland.

Common Ramping Fumitory *Fumaria muralis*
Similar to the Common Fumitory, but flowers larger, 9–10 mm long, and the fruit not wider than young, with a rounded apex. Similar habitats; April–October. S Norway southwards.

Fine-leaved Fumitory *Fumaria parviflora*
Readily distinguished by its small, white to pale pink 5–6 mm long flowers; racemes very short-stalked. Arable land, usually on calcareous soils; June–September. Britain (mostly in the south and east), Holland to Germany southwards.

Tufted Vetch
Vicia cracca

Leguminosae/Fabaceae

A common and often rampant herb seen in a variety of habitats during the summer months, especially clambering over other herbage. There are quite a few different vetches to be found in the region. They are characterised by their finely pinnate leaves that generally bear tendrils at the tip, and by their clusters or racemes of small pea-flowers. These are followed by pea-pod fruits that vary a lot from one species to another; they can be very useful in accurate identification.

NOTE:
One of the commonest vetches in the region. The flowers are visited primarily by different species of bee.

KEY FEATURES: Clambering plant with pinnate leaves bearing leaf-tendrils. Stipules present at leaf-bases. Flowers pea-shaped with a standard petal uppermost, 2 wings at the sides and a keel beneath. Fruit a pod, splitting lengthways when ripe.
HABITAT: Rough grassy places, meadows, scrub, woodland margins and hedgerows, as well as roadsides.
FREQUENCY: A common plant throughout, sometimes forming extensive colonies.
SEASON: June–August.
HABIT: A clambering perennial to 2 m, though often less, with thin, ridged, hairy or hairless stems.
LEAVES: Pinnate, with 6–15 pairs of small linear to oblong, untoothed leaflets; leaves terminating in a branched tendril.
FLOWERS: Bluish-violet, 10–12 mm long, borne in long-stalked 1-sided racemes at the upper leaves; calyx small and green, much shorter than the corolla, with 5 unequal teeth.
FRUIT: A small smooth pod, 10–25 mm long, brown when ripe.

J
F
M
A
M
J
J
A
S
O
N
D

LOOKALIKES

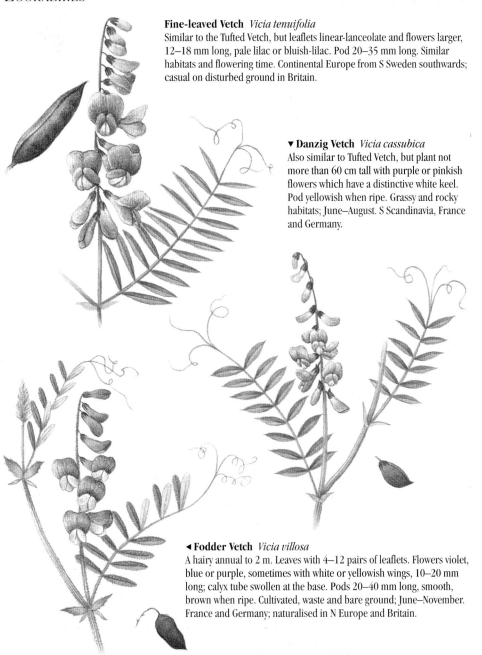

Fine-leaved Vetch *Vicia tenuifolia*
Similar to the Tufted Vetch, but leaflets linear-lanceolate and flowers larger, 12–18 mm long, pale lilac or bluish-lilac. Pod 20–35 mm long. Similar habitats and flowering time. Continental Europe from S Sweden southwards; casual on disturbed ground in Britain.

▼ **Danzig Vetch** *Vicia cassubica*
Also similar to Tufted Vetch, but plant not more than 60 cm tall with purple or pinkish flowers which have a distinctive white keel. Pod yellowish when ripe. Grassy and rocky habitats; June–August. S Scandinavia, France and Germany.

◄ **Fodder Vetch** *Vicia villosa*
A hairy annual to 2 m. Leaves with 4–12 pairs of leaflets. Flowers violet, blue or purple, sometimes with white or yellowish wings, 10–20 mm long; calyx tube swollen at the base. Pods 20–40 mm long, smooth, brown when ripe. Cultivated, waste and bare ground; June–November. France and Germany; naturalised in N Europe and Britain.

Wood Vetch

Vicia sylvatica

Leguminosae/Fabaceae

An attractive and widely distributed vetch, but rarely abundant. The flowers are pale but delightfully etched. It is a typical clambering species with clinging tendrils, preferring wooded places to any other habitat, although only thriving in the more open, partly sunny, areas.

NOTE:
Plants found on shingle and other coastal habitats may be dwarf and with few-flowered racemes.

J
F
M
A
M
J
J
A
S
O
N
D

KEY FEATURES: A clambering plant with pinnate leaves and leaf-tendrils. Flowers pea-shaped, with delicately purple-etched veins. Fruit a pod, splitting lengthways when ripe.

HABITAT: Woodland, often in rocky places, scrub, sometimes in coastal habitats or on cliffs.

FREQUENCY: Widely distributed throughout except for the far north, Iceland, Belgium and Holland; local in Britain, and only occasionally abundant.

SEASON: June–August.

HABIT: A clambering perennial to 2 m, though often less, with slender ridged, usually hairless stems.

LEAVES: Pinnate, with 5–12 pairs of small oblong leaflets and with terminal, branched tendrils.

FLOWERS: White or pale lilac with purple veins, especially on the upper (standard) petal, 12–20 mm long, borne in a rather 1-sided, long-stalked raceme.

FRUIT: Pod 25–30 mm long, smooth, and black when ripe.

LOOKALIKES

Wood Bitter-vetch *Vicia orobus*
An erect perennial to 60 cm with unridged stems and pinnate leaves ending in a point, not a tendril. Flowers white with purple or lilac veins, 12–15 mm long. Pods 20–30 mm long, yellowish-brown when ripe. Rough grassy places, scrub and hedgerows, roadsides or embankments; May–June. Throughout, except the far north, Iceland, Holland, Finland and Sweden.

▲ **Bush Vetch** *Vicia sepium*
A clambering, hairy perennial. Leaves with 3–9 pairs of leaflets; stipules with a black spot near the base. Flowers purplish-blue, 12–15 mm long, borne in very short-stalked clusters at the leaf-bases. Pod 20–35 mm long, black when ripe. Similar habitats to the Wood Bitter-vetch; May–November. Throughout, except the Faeroes.

▼ **Common Vetch** *Vicia sativa*
Similar to the Bush Vetch but flowers solitary or paired, pink to dark reddish-purple, larger, 18–30 mm long. Pod yellowish-brown to brown, 25–70 mm long, usually hairy. Cultivated and bare ground, meadows, pastures and hedgebanks; April–September. Throughout; naturalised in Iceland.

Spring Vetch *Vicia lathyroides* ▶
A hairy annual, often prostrate. Leaves with only 2–4 pairs of leaflets, tendrilled. Flowers purple, solitary, small, only 5–8 mm long. Arable land, grassy places, heaths, verges and waste places; May–June. Throughout, except the Faeroes and Iceland.

Broad-leaved Everlasting Pea
Lathyrus latifolius

Leguminosae/Fabaceae

A rampant, yet extremely attractive, coloniser of banks and verges, this climbing pea is also widely cultivated in gardens and has been for many centuries, and probably escaped into the wild from cottage gardens. The lasting quality of the blooms, in comparison to the rather fleeting blooms of the well-loved Sweet Pea, gives the plant its common name.

J
F
M
A
M
J
J
A
S
O
N
D

KEY FEATURES: Vigorous climber with broadly winged stems. Leaves with a single pair of large leaflets and a branched tendril. Flowers pea-shaped, and relatively large. Fruit a long slender pod.

HABITAT: Rough grassy places, scrub, hedgerows, verges and embankments.

FREQUENCY: Naturalised widely in S Britain, Belgium and Germany; native to France and S Europe.

SEASON: June–September.

HABIT: A rampant climber to 3 m, but sometimes sprawling over banks. Stems green with a wide wing on either side.

LEAVES: Alternate, with a pair of elliptical, untoothed leaflets, with strong parallel veins, and a branched tendril.

FLOWERS: Large pea-shaped, magenta-purple, pink or occasionally white, 20–30 mm across, borne in 1-sided, long-stalked racemes, unscented; petals thick.

FRUIT: A pendent hairless pod, 5–11 cm long, dark brown when ripe.

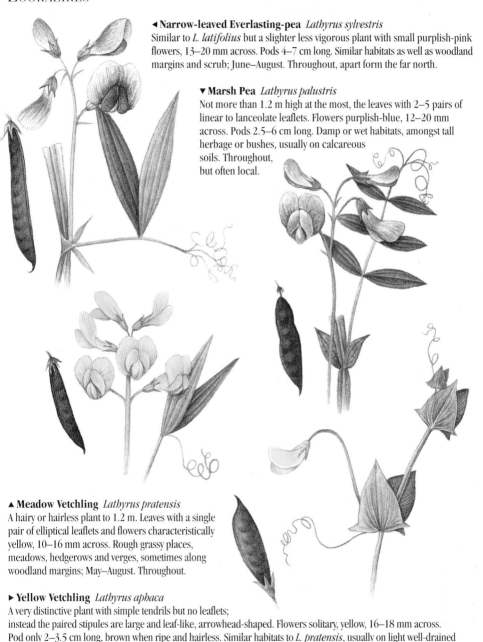

◄ **Narrow-leaved Everlasting-pea** *Lathyrus sylvestris*
Similar to *L. latifolius* but a slighter less vigorous plant with small purplish-pink flowers, 13–20 mm across. Pods 4–7 cm long. Similar habitats as well as woodland margins and scrub; June–August. Throughout, apart form the far north.

▼ **Marsh Pea** *Lathyrus palustris*
Not more than 1.2 m high at the most, the leaves with 2–5 pairs of linear to lanceolate leaflets. Flowers purplish-blue, 12–20 mm across. Pods 2.5–6 cm long. Damp or wet habitats, amongst tall herbage or bushes, usually on calcareous soils. Throughout, but often local.

▲ **Meadow Vetchling** *Lathyrus pratensis*
A hairy or hairless plant to 1.2 m. Leaves with a single pair of elliptical leaflets and flowers characteristically yellow, 10–16 mm across. Rough grassy places, meadows, hedgerows and verges, sometimes along woodland margins; May–August. Throughout.

► **Yellow Vetchling** *Lathyrus aphaca*
A very distinctive plant with simple tendrils but no leaflets; instead the paired stipules are large and leaf-like, arrowhead-shaped. Flowers solitary, yellow, 16–18 mm across. Pod only 2–3.5 cm long, brown when ripe and hairless. Similar habitats to *L. pratensis*, usually on light well-drained calcareous soils; May–August. France, but naturalised widely in Britain and much of NW Europe except for Scandinavia.

135

Ribbed Melilot
Melilotus officinalis

Leguminosae/Fabaceae

T he melilots are a handsome group of peas inhabiting a variety of different places in the wild. They all have trefoil leaves and lateral racemes of small pea-flowers. Although they are native in parts of Continental Europe, in Britain they were introduced many years ago as fodder crops and have subsequently become thoroughly naturalised.

J
F
M
A
M
J ❖
J ❖
A ❖ 🌰
S ❖ 🌰
O 🌰
N
D

KEY FEATURES: Slender-stemmed plant with alternate trefoil leaves. Flowers in slender racemes at the upper leaves. Fruit a small 1–2-seeded pod which does not split open when ripe.
HABITAT: A common weed of arable and other cultivated land, waysides, generally on rather heavy or saline soils.
FREQUENCY: Continental Europe, but widely naturalised in C and S Britain, Ireland and Scandinavia.
SEASON: July–September.
HABIT: An erect hairless annual, or perennial to 2.5 m, though often less.
LEAVES: Trefoil, with oval, rather sharply toothed leaflets, those of the upper leaves narrower than the lower.
FLOWERS: Yellow, 4–7 mm long, borne in slender, rather lax, racemes from the upper leaves: wing petals longer than the keel petal.
FRUIT: A small oval pod, 3–5 mm long, rough but hairless, brown when ripe.

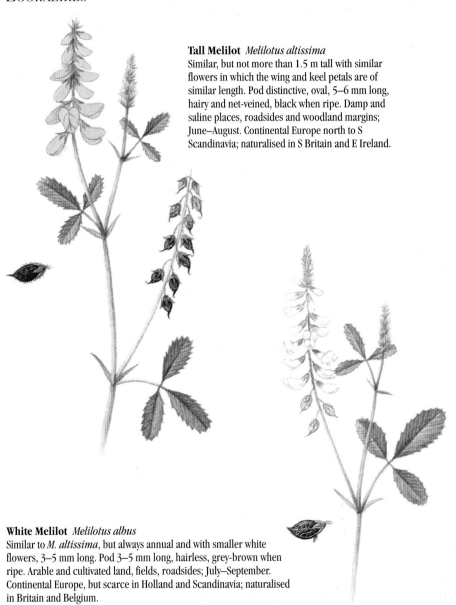

Tall Melilot *Melilotus altissima*
Similar, but not more than 1.5 m tall with similar
flowers in which the wing and keel petals are of
similar length. Pod distinctive, oval, 5–6 mm long,
hairy and net-veined, black when ripe. Damp and
saline places, roadsides and woodland margins;
June–August. Continental Europe north to S
Scandinavia; naturalised in S Britain and E Ireland.

White Melilot *Melilotus albus*
Similar to *M. altissima*, but always annual and with smaller white
flowers, 3–5 mm long. Pod 3–5 mm long, hairless, grey-brown when
ripe. Arable and cultivated land, fields, roadsides; July–September.
Continental Europe, but scarce in Holland and Scandinavia; naturalised
in Britain and Belgium.

Common Bird's-foot Trefoil
Lotus corniculatus

Leguminosae/Fabaceae

The trefoils are bright cheerful little plants widely distributed in the region and most typical of grassy habitats. Several were at one time widely grown as fodder crops. *L. corniculatus* has acquired literally dozens of local names including Eggs and Bacon, Ham and Eggs and Hen and Chickens, as well as the decidedly odd Granny's Toenails and Dutchman's Clogs.

NOTE:
The flowers are much visited by species of bumblebee.

J	
F	
M	
A	
M	
J	❀
J	❀
A	❀ 🌰
S	❀ 🌰
O	🌰
N	🌰
D	

KEY FEATURES: A prostrate plant with trefoil leaves. Flowers pea-shaped, yellow, in a small umbel. Fruit a slender, straight pod.

HABITAT: Short grassy places, verges, heathland, sometimes along the coast.

FREQUENCY: Common throughout and often abundant; naturalised in Iceland.

SEASON: June–September.

HABIT: A prostrate to sprawling perennial, becoming rather woody at the base, hairy or hairless.

LEAVES: Alternate, trefoil, with rounded to lanceolate untoothed leaflets, sometimes slightly notched at the tip.

FLOWERS: Bright yellow to orange-yellow, 10–16 mm long, borne in long-stalked umbels of 2–7.

FRUIT: A slender, straight, smooth pod, 15–30 mm long.

Narrow-leaved Bird's-foot Trefoil *Lotus tenuis* ▶
Similar to *L. coniculatus*, but leaflets linear to linear-lanceolate. Flowers bright yellow, 6–12 mm long, solitary or in groups of 2–4. Lowland grassy places, sand dunes, often coastal; June–August. Throughout, except for N Scandinavia; naturalised in Finland and Norway.

Greater Bird's-foot Trefoil *Lotus uliginosus*
Similar to *L. corniculatus*, but a more upright plant with hollow rather than solid stems, and bluish-green leaves. Flowers 10–18 mm long, in larger heads of 5–12. Damp pastures, ditches, damp woodland pathways and water margins, often on slightly acid soils and usually lowland; June–August. Throughout north as far as S Sweden; naturalised in Norway, Finland and the Faeroes.

Black Medick
Medicago lupulina

Leguminosae/Fabaceae

T he medicks are a large and complicated group in Europe, especially in the Mediterranean region. Many have small yellow flowers and rather similar trefoil leaves, but it is in the details of the fruit pods that most can be distinguished. Black Medick receives its common name from the pods that turn black when ripe.

NOTE:
*The leaves of most medicks
smell of new mown hay.*

J
F
M
A ❖
M ❖
J ❖ ✦
J ❖ ✦
A ❖ ✦
S ❖ ✦
O ✦
N ✦
D

KEY FEATURES: Low annual with trefoil leaves. Flowers small, not more than 3 mm long. Fruit pod equally small, kidney-shaped.

HABITAT: Short permanent grassland, generally over limestone.

FREQUENCY: Throughout, but tending to be coastal in the north of its range; scarce in Ireland and Scotland.

SEASON: April–September.

HABIT: A low, often prostrate, generally hairy annual.

LEAVES: Trefoil leaves with rounded to rhombic leaflets that are usually toothed.

FLOWERS: Yellow, 2–3 mm long, numerous in short, long-stalked, racemes.

FRUIT: Kidney-shaped, 1.5–3 mm long, smooth, black when ripe.

Bur Medick *Medicago minima*
Is an ascending to erect autumn-germinating annual with oval to
heart-shaped leaflets, that are toothed towards the apex. Flowers
bright yellow, 4–5 mm long in clusters of 1–6. Fruit pod
laxly spiralled, 3–5 mm, spiny and somewhat hairy.
Disturbed ground, tracks and sand dunes; May–July.
Continental Europe north to S Sweden; in Britain
confined to the E and SE.

Lucerne *Medicago sativa*
A far more vigorous and distinctive plant to 90 cm
tall, with oval to linear leaflets. Flowers blue to violet,
7–11 mm long, borne in rather short racemes. Fruit
pod spiralled with a hole in the centre, 4–6 mm
across, hairy or not. Widely cultivated for Alfalfa and
commonly naturalised; June–July. Throughout, except
for the far north.

Hop Trefoil
Trifolium campestre

Leguminosae/Fabaceae

The clovers or trefoils are a large group of annual and perennial species with widely varying flower characteristics. The Hop Trefoil gets its common name from the resemblance of the flower clusters to small hops; this is especially so as the flowers fade.

NOTE:
In Trifolium *the fruit pods are small and enclosed within the base of the calyx and they are therefore rather difficult to observe.*

KEY FEATURES: Leaves trefoil. Flowers in rounded clusters. Flowers expanding as the fruits develop, persisting and becoming down-turned and brown eventually.
HABITAT: Dry grassy places, verges, tracks and sand dunes.
frequency: Common throughout, except for the far north and Iceland; naturalised in the Faeroes.
SEASON: June–September.
HABIT: A hairy erect annual to 30 cm, often less.
LEAVES: Leaflets oval with a narrowed base, with a slightly toothed margin.
FLOWERS: Yellow, 4–5 mm long, borne in small rounded heads, eventually becoming pale brown, the flowers persisting and down-turned around the developing fruit.
FRUIT: Pod very small, oval, usually 1-seeded, hidden at the base of the calyx.

J
F
M
A
M
J
J
A
S
O
N
D

◄ Large Hop Trefoil *Trifolium aureum*
Similar to *T. campestre,* but a more robust plant with oblong to rhombic leaflets and golden-yellow flowers 6–7 mm long, browning on ageing. Rough grassy places, woodland margins, scrub and waste places; July–August. Continental Europe except for the far north; naturalised locally in Britain.

▼ Red Clover *Trifolium pratense*
A very distinctive and familiar tufted perennial with large elliptical leaflets that often sport a white crescent in the middle. Flowers reddish-purple or pink, occasionally cream or white, 12–15 mm long, borne in rounded heads with a pair of leaves immediately beneath. Grassy places and cultivated land; May–September. Throughout, except for the far north, the Faeroes and Iceland. Widely grown as a forage crop.

◄ Zig-zag Clover *Trifolium medium*
Similar to *T. pratense,* but with more flexuous stems and plain green leaflets. Flowers reddish-purple, 25–35 mm long, in dense rounded heads. Grassy places, open woods and scrub; May–July. Throughout, except the far north.

White Clover
Trifolium repens

Leguminosae/Fabaceae

Also known as Dutch Clover, this familiar plant is a characteristic of grassy places where it can often dominate. Many children learned from an early age to pull the flowers from the heads and to suck the ends that are sweet with nectar, hence another of its common names, Bee-bread.

KEY FEATURES: Plant with creeping stems that root at the nodes. Leaflets with a pale or dark crescent in the middle. Flowers in dense rounded heads, usually white.

HABITAT: Grassy places, especially meadows and verges, but also lawns, banks and tracksides.

FREQUENCY: Very common throughout apart from the far north, often gregarious and abundant.

SEASON: June–September.

HABIT: A spreading perennial to 50 cm tall, though often lower, with rooting runners.

LEAVES: Leaflets elliptical with translucent veins, bright green with a pale or dark crescent in the centre.

FLOWERS: White or occasionally pale pink, 7–10 mm long, borne in dense rounded heads on leafless stalks, sweetly scented.

FRUIT: Pod linear, constricted between the seeds, protruding from the calyx.

J
F
M
A
M
J
J
A
S
O
N
D

LOOKALIKES

Sulphur Clover *Trifolium ochroleucon*
A rather hairy perennial to 50 cm, with heads of
whitish-yellow flowers, each flower 15–20 mm long,
the heads with leaves immediately beneath. Grassy,
generally shaded or damp places on heavy clay soils;
June–July. Belgium and Germany southwards; local
in E England.

Alsike Clover *Trifolium hybridum*
Similar to White Clover, but more erect and not rooting at the nodes.
Flowers white or purplish, but becoming pink and eventually brown,
7–10 mm long. Meadows and pastures, verges; June–September.
Naturalised throughout except for the far north; native distribution
uncertain as this plant has long been grown for forage.

Strawberry Clover *Trifolium fragiferum*
A low prostrate and creeping perennial with oval to elliptical
leaflets. Flowers pale pink, 6–7 mm long, but swelling and
doubling in size in fruit, then pink and strawberry-like. Grassy
habitats, especially short grazed pastures and commons,
occasionally coastal; July–September. S Sweden southwards;
local in Britain and in Ireland confined mostly to the coast.

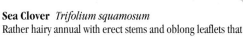

Sea Clover *Trifolium squamosum*
Rather hairy annual with erect stems and oblong leaflets that
are often notched at the tip. Flowers pale pink, 5–7 mm
long, borne in egg-shaped heads with a pair of leaves
immediately beneath. Short coastal turf and salt marshes;
June–July. Britain (Lancashire southwards) and France.

Labiatae/Lamiaceae

Bugle
Ajuga reptans

A very common wayside flower that has been long cherished as a cottage garden plant; today numerous forms have been selected in gardens. Unlike most members of the Labiatae the flowers do not have a prominently developed upper lip to the corolla and this makes the genus easy to identify.

NOTE:
The flowers are much visited by bees.

KEY FEATURES: Plant with square stems and paired leaves. Flowers borne in whorls at the upper leaves; corolla without an upper lip and with protruding stamens.

HABITAT: Woodland, damp grassland and waste places, on calcareous to slightly acid soils.

FREQUENCY: Common throughout, except for the far north, sometimes making extensive stands.

SEASON: April–June.

HABIT: A low spreading hairy perennial with long rooting runners. Stems square, hairy only on two opposing sides.

LEAVES: Oval, usually slightly toothed, deep green but often with a bronze flush, the lower stalked.

FLOWERS: Pale violet-blue, occasionally pink or white, 14–17 mm long, borne in dense whorls which make up long oblong heads. Corolla without a well-developed upper lip and with a 3-lobed lower lip and protruding stamens.

FRUIT: 4 small nutlets at the base of the persistent calyx.

J
F
M
A
M
J
J
A
S
O
N
D

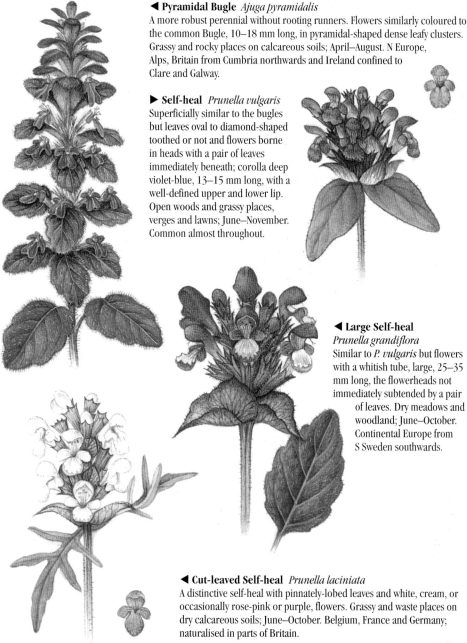

◀ **Pyramidal Bugle** *Ajuga pyramidalis*
A more robust perennial without rooting runners. Flowers similarly coloured to the common Bugle, 10–18 mm long, in pyramidal-shaped dense leafy clusters. Grassy and rocky places on calcareous soils; April–August. N Europe, Alps, Britain from Cumbria northwards and Ireland confined to Clare and Galway.

▶ **Self-heal** *Prunella vulgaris*
Superficially similar to the bugles but leaves oval to diamond-shaped toothed or not and flowers borne in heads with a pair of leaves immediately beneath; corolla deep violet-blue, 13–15 mm long, with a well-defined upper and lower lip. Open woods and grassy places, verges and lawns; June–November. Common almost throughout.

◀ **Large Self-heal**
Prunella grandiflora
Similar to *P. vulgaris* but flowers with a whitish tube, large, 25–35 mm long, the flowerheads not immediately subtended by a pair of leaves. Dry meadows and woodland; June–October. Continental Europe from S Sweden southwards.

◀ **Cut-leaved Self-heal** *Prunella laciniata*
A distinctive self-heal with pinnately-lobed leaves and white, cream, or occasionally rose-pink or purple, flowers. Grassy and waste places on dry calcareous soils; June–October. Belgium, France and Germany; naturalised in parts of Britain.

Skullcap

Scutellaria galericulata

Both the Latin name as well as the common name is derived from the calyx shape that reminded early botanists of the cap or galerum worn by Roman soldiers. The genus contains in excess of a hundred species, although only a handful are in Europe.

J
F
M
A
M
J
J
A
S
O
N
D

KEY FEATURES: Stems square bearing pairs of leaves. Flowers 2 per node. Corolla curved and 2-lipped. Calyx also 2-lipped, the upper lip with a distinctive rounded cap.

HABITAT: Wet marshy places, water margins, on calcareous to neutral soils.

FREQUENCY: Throughout, except for the far north; locally common, sometimes abundant.

SEASON: June–September.

HABIT: A Creeping hairy perennial, with erect branched or unbranched stems to 50 cm.

LEAVES: Opposite, oval to lanceolate, with a shallowly toothed margin, short-stalked or unstalked, hairy or not.

FLOWERS: Bright violet-blue, occasionally pink, 10–18 mm long, borne in pairs amongst the uppermost leaves; corolla tube abruptly upcurved.

FRUIT: 4 small nutlets located at the base of the persistent calyx.

148

Spear-leaved Skullcap *Scutellaria hastifolia*
A slighter plant than *S. galericulata* with arrow-shaped leaves and violet-blue
flowers 15–20 mm long; calyx glandular-hairy. Damp grassland and open woodland;
July–September. Scandinavia, Germany and France; naturalised in East Anglia.

Wood Sage *Teucrium scorodonia*
Looks superficially like a skullcap but the corollas are without
an upper lip and the calyx is bell-shaped with 5 teeth, rather than
2-lipped. A perennial to 60 cm with oval to heart-shaped leaves. Flowers
pale greenish-yellow, only 8–9 mm long. Open woods and sand dunes on
dry non-calcareous soils; July–September. From S Scandinavia
southwards; throughout Britain apart form the extreme north.

Water Germander *Teucrium scordium*
Looks superficially like a mint (*Mentha*) but with a strong garlic smell
when crushed. Flowers purplish, 7–10 mm long, the corolla without an
upper lip with the stamens protruding. Damp places, on calcareous soils;
June–October. Throughout, except the far north; rather rare in Britain.

Ground Ivy
Glechoma hederacea

Labiatae/Lamiaceae

A very widespread and often prolific plant which is often one of the very first to come into flower in the spring, flowering at the same time as the Primrose (*see* p.106) and Daffodil (*see* p.246) but, unlike them, continuing on to flower through the summer months. In former times, before the advent of the hop, Ground Ivy was the chief source of bitter for flavouring beer. Today the dried leaves are sometimes used for herbal teas.

NOTE:
*The flowers are much
visited by various species
of bee.*

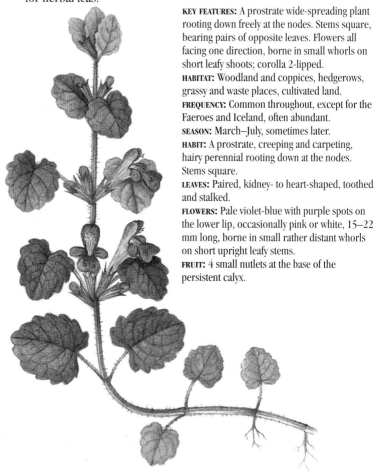

KEY FEATURES: A prostrate wide-spreading plant rooting down freely at the nodes. Stems square, bearing pairs of opposite leaves. Flowers all facing one direction, borne in small whorls on short leafy shoots; corolla 2-lipped.

HABITAT: Woodland and coppices, hedgerows, grassy and waste places, cultivated land.

FREQUENCY: Common throughout, except for the Faeroes and Iceland, often abundant.

SEASON: March–July, sometimes later.

HABIT: A prostrate, creeping and carpeting, hairy perennial rooting down at the nodes. Stems square.

LEAVES: Paired, kidney- to heart-shaped, toothed and stalked.

FLOWERS: Pale violet-blue with purple spots on the lower lip, occasionally pink or white, 15–22 mm long, borne in small rather distant whorls on short upright leafy stems.

FRUIT: 4 small nutlets at the base of the persistent calyx.

J
F
M
A
M
J
J
A
S
O
N
D

Cat-mint
Nepeta cataria

This is one of a number of herbs whose smell cats find wholly intoxicating. The common Catmint of gardens is *Nepeta × faasenii*.

KEY FEATURES: Grey-woolly plant with a smell reminiscent of mint. Leaves paired on square stems. Flowers pale, spotted, in whorls or denser heads; corolla 2-lipped.

HABITAT: Hedgerows and waysides, banks and rocky places, usually on calcareous soils.

FREQUENCY: Widely distributed, though often local in Britain, Belgium, Holland and France; naturalised in Ireland, Germany and in parts of Scandinavia.

SEASON: June–September.

HABIT: An erect, tufted, soft, grey-woolly perennial to 1 m, with square stems.

LEAVES: Paired, oval, generally with a heart-shaped base, toothed and stalked, mint-scented when bruised.

FLOWERS: White with purple spots, 7–10 mm long, in oblong heads, often with one or 2 distinct whorls beneath.

FRUIT: 4 nutlets located at the base of the persistent calyx.

LOOKALIKES

Hairless Catmint *Nepeta nuda*
Similar but a smoother, almost hairless, plant with oblong or oval leaves. Flowers in whorls, pale violet, 6–8 mm long, borne in branched spikes. Open woodland and grassy places; June–September. C and E France; naturalised in Germany.

J
F
M
A
M
J
J
A
S
O
N
D

151

Black Horehound
Ballota nigra

Labiatae/Lamiaceae

A distinctive plant commonly seen along hedgerows throughout the region that is represented by two subspecies in the area. In the ordinary form (subsp. *nigra*), which is more prevalent on the Continent, the foliage is aromatic when crushed, whereas in the second (subsp. *foetida*) the leaves have a strong and unpleasant smell when bruised.

NOTE:
Subsp. nigra *is located on the Continent from E France and Germany eastwards and is naturalised further west, including Britain. Subsp.* foetida *is primarily distributed in Britain and W Europe, northwards to S Sweden.*

KEY FEATURES: Stems square, bearing paired leaves. Calyx funnel-shaped rather truncated at the top and with 5 even, short-triangular lobes or teeth. Fruit 4 nutlets.

HABITAT: Woodland margins, hedgerows, verges and waste ground.

FREQUENCY: Common throughout, but absent from the Faeroes, Iceland and much of Scandinavia; sometimes growing in large colonies.

SEASON: June–September.

HABIT: A robust, scarcely hairy perennial with erect square stems to 1 m, sometimes rather straggly.

LEAVES: Paired, heart-shaped to oval or oblong, short-stalked and with a toothed margin.

FLOWERS: In dense whorls at the upper leaves, lilac or whitish, 12–14 mm long; corolla 2-lipped, the upper lip rather furry.

FRUIT: 4 nutlets, dark brown when ripe, located at the base of the persistent calyx.

J
F
M
A
M
J
J
A
S
O
N
D

Motherwort *Leonurus cardiaca*
A robust hairy or hairless perennial to 2 m, though generally
far less. Leaves hand-like with 3–7 toothed segments. Flowers
white or pale pink, sometimes with purple spots, borne in
dense whorls; upper lip of corolla very furry. Similar habitats
and flowering time to Black Horehound. Throughout, except
the far north, but only naturalised in S Britain.

False Motherwort *Leonurus marrubiastrum*
Similar to Motherwort, but a grey-hairy biennial to 1.2 m, with oval
to rounded, irregularly toothed leaves. Flowers pale pink,
the corolla scarcely longer than the 10-veined calyx. Grassy and
waste places; June–September. Germany; naturalised in France.

White Deadnettle
Lamium album

Labiatae/Lamiaceae

A familiar wild flower of the countryside that flowers over a very long season, even doing so during mild winter weather in some areas. The deadnettles bear leaves reminiscent of those of the true nettle (*Urtica dioica*) but fortunately they lack the stinging hairs. As with many members of the Labiatae the flowers are 2-lipped and bear 4 stamens.

NOTE:
The flowers bear nectar at the base of the tube and are much-visited by various species of bee, especially bumble-bees.

KEY FEATURES: Square stems bearing pairs of leaves. Flowers in tight whorls (verticillasters) at the upper leaf pairs. Corolla 2-lipped. Calyx narrow-campanulate, with 5 more or less equal teeth.

HABITAT: Grassy places, hedgerows, waysides and verges, woodland margins, generally on deep fertile soils.

FREQUENCY: Common almost throughout, except for the far north; naturalised in Ireland and Iceland.

SEASON: March–October; occasionally almost throughout the year.

HABIT: A patch-forming hairy perennial, with rooting stolons and erect flowering stems to 50 cm.

LEAVES: Paired, oval to heart-shaped, stalked and with a toothed margin, faintly aromatic when crushed.

FLOWERS: White, 20–25 mm long, 2-lipped with the tube curved near the base and the upper lip very furry.

FRUIT: 4 small nutlets located at the base of the persistent calyx.

J
F
M
A
M
J
J
A
S
O
N
D

LOOKALIKES

Red Deadnettle *Lamium purpureum*
An aromatic annual to 25 cm, with the upper leaves often flushed with purple. Flowers pinkish-purple, 10–18 mm long, with a straight corolla tube. Cultivated and wasteland; March–December. Throughout; naturalised in Iceland.

Cut-leaved Deadnettle *Lamium hybridum*
Like *L. purpureum*, but the leaves deeply and irregularly toothed and flowers 10–15 mm long. Similar habitats, but especially on arable land; March–October. Throughout, except Iceland.

Henbit Deadnettle *Lamium amplexicaule*
Another small annual species but with distinctive unstalked and clasping upper stem leaves. Flowers pinkish-purple, 14–20 mm long almost erect and with a straight corolla-tube; calyx softly hairy. Cultivated and wasteland; March–December. Throughout, except for the far north and the Faeroes; naturalised in Iceland.

Yellow Archangel
Lamiastrum galeobdolon (syn. *Lamium galeobdolon*)
A distinctive strong-smelling, rampant stoloniferous perennial, often making dense carpets. Leaves dark green, oval and coarsely toothed. Flowers yellow with greenish-brown markings, 17–21 mm long; lower lip with 3 almost equal lobes, the upper lip hooded and furry. Shaded habitats, particularly woods and coppices, usually on heavy calcareous soils; April–July. S Sweden southwards; in Britain mainly in England and Wales.

155

Large-flowered Hemp-nettle
Galeopsis speciosa

Labiatae/Lamiaceae

T he hemp-nettles are a group of annual plants that closely resemble the deadnettles the prime difference being found in the spine-tipped calyx teeth of the former. They are generally associated with cultivated land, particularly arable fields.

J
F
M
A
M
J
J
A
S
0
N
D

KEY FEATURES: Stems square, with yellow hairs. Leaves paired. Flowers 2-lipped, bicolored. Calyx teeth spine-tipped.

HABITAT: Arable land, often in potato fields or on dark peaty soils.

FREQUENCY: Rather local throughout except for the far north; naturalised in Ireland and rare in S England.

SEASON: July–September.

HABIT: A rough-hairy annual with erect stems to 1 m; stems square, usually branched, hairy on opposite sides.

LEAVES: Oval to lanceolate, short-stalked, with a coarsely toothed margin.

FLOWERS: 2-lipped, pale yellow with purple on the lower lip, 27–34 mm long, borne in crowded whorls at the uppermost leaves; upper lip of the corolla furry; calyx with long stiff tips.

FRUIT: 4 small nutlets located at the base of the persistent calyx.

Common Hemp-nettle *Galeopsis tetrahit*
A rough-hairy annual of similar size to
G. speciosa, but with narrower lanceolate
to oval leaves and pinkish-purple flowers,
rarely yellowish or whitish; corolla 15–20
mm long. Arable land, heaths and open
woodland; July–October. Throughout.

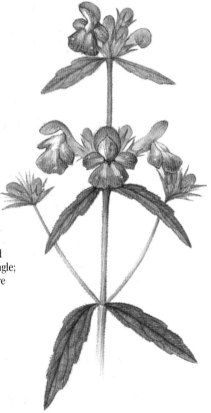

Red Hemp-nettle *Galeopsis angustifolia*
A slighter annual not more than 50 cm tall,
with linear-lanceolate to linear leaves that are
often untoothed. Flowers deep reddish-pink, with a
yellow botch in the throat and flecked with white,
14–24 mm long; calyx with white hairs. Arable land
and bare places, occasionally found on coastal shingle;
July–October. Local in Britain and Ireland, but more
common on the Continent north to S Scandinavia.

Meadow Clary
Salvia pratensis

Labiatae/Lamiaceae

The salvias or clarys are amongst the most attractive members of the deadnettle family. Many have relatively large and colourful flowers that are very attractive to various species of bee. The flowers, like those of most labiates, are 2-lipped, but unlike the majority they contain only 2 instead of the usual 4 stamens; a very useful diagnostic character.

NOTE:
This and a number of European salvias are widely cultivated in gardens, sometimes escaping to become casual or naturalised outside their native range.

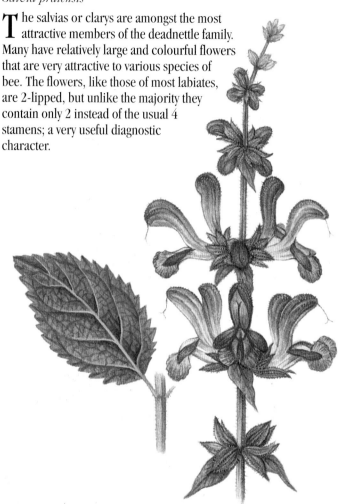

J
F
M
A
M
J
J
A
S
O
N
D

KEY FEATURES: Stems square. Calyx and corolla markedly 2-lipped. Stamens 2 only, hinged in the middle of the filament. Style protruding from the corolla.

HABITAT: Meadows and grassy places, generally on calcareous soils.

FREQUENCY: S Sweden, Germany and Holland southwards; in Britain confined to the south.

SEASON: June–July, occasionally later.

HABIT: A tufted, hairy and slightly aromatic perennial; stems erect to ascending, branched and rather glandular above, to 80 cm.

LEAVES: Oval to oblong, with a heart-shaped base, dark green and somewhat wrinkled above, the lowermost long stalked, but the upper smaller and unstalked.

FLOWERS: Violet-blue, relatively large, 20–30 mm long, borne in congested whorls with 4–6 flowers in each whorl; upper lip of corolla markedly curved.

FRUIT: 4 small nutlets located at the base of the persistent calyx.

Whorled Clary
Salvia verticillata
A rather foetid perennial of similar height to *S. pratensis*, but leaves oval to lyre-shaped with a rather square base, the lower generally with one or 2 pairs of small basal lobes. Flowers purple to lilac-blue, 8–15 mm long, in dense whorls of 15–30. Dry grassy, stony and waste places; C and S France, but widely naturalised on the Continent north as far as S Sweden, as well as in Britain.

Wild Sage
Salvia nemorosa
(syn. *S. sylvestris*)
Similar to *S. verticillata*, but leaves narrow-heart-shaped, without lobes, and flowers violet blue, or sometimes pink or white, 8–12 mm long, in lax whorls of 2–6. Grassy, bare and waste places; June–August. C France and S Germany southwards, but naturalised or casual in Britain, N France, Norway and Sweden.

Wild Clary *Salvia verbenaca*
(syn. *S. horminoides*)
Leaves pinnately-lobed and toothed, the upper leaves and stem often purplish. Flowers blue, violet or lilac, with white marking in the throat, small, 6–10 mm long, borne in whorls of 6–10. Calyx enlarging in fruit. Flowers sometimes cleistogamous and failing to open. Dry grassy places on sandy or calcareous soils; May–August. Britain, Ireland and France; occasionally naturalised elsewhere.

Hedge Woundwort

Stachys sylvatica

Labiatae/Lamiaceae

While many members of the mint family are admired for their aromatic properties, Hedge Woundwort cannot be classed among them, for the whole plant emits a rather nasty powerful astringent smell, especially when it is bruised. There are a number of different species of *Stachys* in the region; they all bear flowers in rather congested whorls, which, make up spike-like inflorescences.

NOTE:
The flowers are visited by various species of bee.

KEY FEATURES: Plant with a foetid smell. Leaves all long-stalked. Stems square and glandular-hairy. Calyx bell-shaped, not 2-lipped. Corolla 2-lipped.
HABITAT: Woodland, hedgerows, margins of cultivated land.
FREQUENCY: Throughout, except for the Faeroes and Iceland, sometimes prolific.
SEASON: June–September.
HABIT: An erect hairy perennial to 1 m, with vigorous spreading rhizomes.
LEAVES: Heart-shaped, slightly hairy, with a toothed margin, all stalked.
FLOWERS: Dull dark reddish-purple, with white markings on the lip, 13–18 mm long, borne in whorled spikes; calyx downy, with equal teeth.
FRUIT: 4 small nutlets located at the base of the persistent calyx.

J
F
M
A
M
J
J
A
S
O
N
D

LOOKALIKES

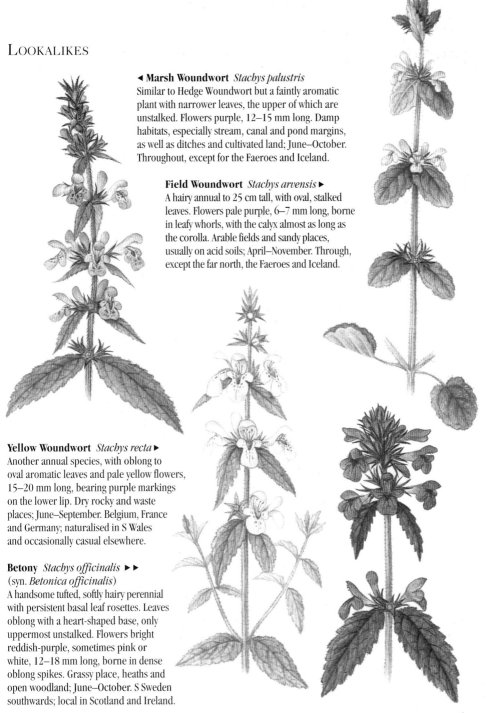

◄ **Marsh Woundwort** *Stachys palustris*
Similar to Hedge Woundwort but a faintly aromatic
plant with narrower leaves, the upper of which are
unstalked. Flowers purple, 12–15 mm long. Damp
habitats, especially stream, canal and pond margins,
as well as ditches and cultivated land; June–October.
Throughout, except for the Faeroes and Iceland.

Field Woundwort *Stachys arvensis* ►
A hairy annual to 25 cm tall, with oval, stalked
leaves. Flowers pale purple, 6–7 mm long, borne
in leafy whorls, with the calyx almost as long as
the corolla. Arable fields and sandy places,
usually on acid soils; April–November. Through,
except the far north, the Faeroes and Iceland.

Yellow Woundwort *Stachys recta* ►
Another annual species, with oblong to
oval aromatic leaves and pale yellow flowers,
15–20 mm long, bearing purple markings
on the lower lip. Dry rocky and waste
places; June–September. Belgium, France
and Germany; naturalised in S Wales
and occasionally casual elsewhere.

Betony *Stachys officinalis* ► ►
(syn. *Betonica officinalis*)
A handsome tufted, softly hairy perennial
with persistent basal leaf rosettes. Leaves
oblong with a heart-shaped base, only
uppermost unstalked. Flowers bright
reddish-purple, sometimes pink or
white, 12–18 mm long, borne in dense
oblong spikes. Grassy place, heaths and
open woodland; June–October. S Sweden
southwards; local in Scotland and Ireland.

Corn Mint

Mentha arvensis

Labiatae/Lamiaceae

A number of mints are to be found in the area. All have aromatic leaves, especially when crushed, although not all are equally pleasing to the nose. The identification of mints is complicated by the fact that numerous hybrids can be found with intermediate characters.

NOTE:
The flowers are visited by both bees and butterflies.

KEY FEATURES: Plant with a stickily-sweet smell, especially when bruised. Stems square. Flowers in dense whorls at the base of the upper leaf pairs. Corolla weakly 2-lipped, with 4 almost equal lobes and protruding stamens.
HABITAT: Damp habitats, woodland and grassy places, arable fields.
FREQUENCY: Throughout, except for the far north; scarcer in N Britain.
SEASON: July–September.
HABIT: A variable hairy perennial with erect to ascending stems, to 60 cm, often less.
LEAVES: Elliptical to oval, shallowly toothed and with a short stalk.
FLOWERS: Lilac to white, sometimes pink, 3–4 mm long, borne in distant dense whorls at the base of the upper pairs of leaves; calyx hairy.
FRUIT: 4 nutlets at the base of the persistent calyx.

J
F
M
A
M
J
J
A
S
O
N
D

Water Mint *Mentha aquatica*
A strongly aromatic plant, often purplish, with oval to oblong pointed leaves. Flowers lilac-pink, 4–6 mm long, borne in dense oblong heads, often with one or two extra whorls of flowers beneath. Swampy habitats, especially water margins and marshes; July–September. Through, except the far north; naturalised in Iceland.

Spear Mint *Mentha spicata*
A sweetly aromatic perennial to 90 cm, with lanceolate to oval, green or greyish, often hairless leaves. Flowers pink or white, 2–3.5 mm long, borne in long, usually branched, spikes. Damp habitats; July–October. Naturalised throughout much of the region; of uncertain origin.

Marjoram

Origanum vulgare

Labiatae/Lamiaceae

O ne of the most popular culinary herbs, the 'oregano' of the Mediterranean which is widely used in cooking. Its delight attracted early herbalists and it has been a feature of cottage gardens from early times. Today it exists in gardens in a number of distinct forms.

NOTE:
The flowers are extremely attractive to many species of butterfly, as well as bees.

J
F
M
A
M
J
J
A
S
O
N
D

KEY FEATURES: Pleasantly and strongly aromatic plant. Stems often purplish. Flowers small, borne in branched, flat-topped clusters. Corolla and calyx weakly 2-lipped, with protruding stamens. Bracts dark purple.

HABITAT: Dry grassy places, scrub, hedgebanks, verges, generally on calcareous soils.

FREQUENCY: Through except for the far north, often local but then sometimes abundant.

SEASON: July–September.

HABIT: A tufted, hairy perennial to 50 cm tall, sometimes more, with purplish, squarish stems.

LEAVES: Paired, oval, untoothed or very slightly toothed, short-stalked or unstalked.

FLOWERS: Purplish-red to pink or white, 4–7 mm, borne in broad, flat-topped clusters with numerous small purplish bracts.

FRUIT: 4 tiny nutlets located at the base of the persistent calyx.

Breckland Thyme *Thymus serpyllum*
A bit like a dwarf Marjoram, this mat-forming perennial has faintly aromatic leaves, when crushed. Stems hairy all round. Leaves linear to elliptic, untoothed. Flowers purple or pinkish, 6–7 mm long, borne in rounded heads. Dry grassy places, often grazed by rabbits, heaths and sand dunes; May–September. Throughout, except Ireland; rare in Britain and confined mainly to the Brecklands.

Large Thyme *Thymus pulegioides*
This species is rather similar to *T. serpyllum*, but it is a larger and coarser and shrubbier plant with the stems hairy only in the angles. Leaves hairy on the margin towards the base. Flowers rose-purple, 6 mm long, in an oblong head. Dry grassy places, banks and hill-slopes, usually on calcareous soils; June–September. S Scandinavia southwards, including Britain and Ireland; Britain most common in the centre and south, scarcer elsewhere.

Common Figwort

Scrophularia nodosa

Scrophulariaceae

T he figworts are a group of often large and rather leafy plants with small and rather insignificant flowers. The little pouched flowers are fascinating to observe closely. The 'fig' has nothing to do with the fruit but is an old name for piles, which the buds were said to resemble, and the plant was at one time used in their treatment. The specific name of the plant refers to the numerous nodules found on the roots.

NOTE:
The rather sombre flowers are visited by wasps.

J
F
M
A
M
J
J
A
S
O
N
D

KEY FEATURES: Tall plant with square stems. Leaves opposite. Flowers small and pouched, weakly 2-lipped with the upper lip 2-lobed and the lower 3. Stamens 4. Fruit a 2-parted capsule.

HABITAT: Hedgerows and woodland margins, water margins and other damp places.

FREQUENCY: Throughout, except for the far north; in Britain, absent from N Scotland.

SEASON: June–September.

HABIT: A tough hairless perennial with erect, often pale green stems to 1 m.

LEAVES: Paired, oval to lanceolate with a heart-shaped base, double-toothed and stalked.

FLOWERS: Small, greenish with a purple-brown upper lip, 7–9 mm long, borne in lax panicles; corolla pouched, with rounded lobes; calyx with 5 equal, rounded lobes shorter than, and pressed closely to, the corolla.

FRUIT: A small 2-parted capsule containing numerous tiny seeds.

LOOKALIKES

◄ **Yellow Figwort** *Scrophularia vernalis*
A softly, glandular-hairy plant, with deeply toothed leaves. Flowers yellow, 6–8 mm long, borne in leafy clusters. Mountain woods, waste places and other shaded or part-shaded habitats; April–June. France and Germany, naturalised further north to S Sweden, and in Britain.

▼ **Water Figwort** *Scrophularia auriculata*
Like *S. nodosa*, but often taller, to 1.2 m, the stems narrowly winged on the angles. Leaves often with a small pair of lobes towards the base. Flowers slightly larger, greenish to purplish-brown. Wet habitats, particularly marshes, fens, pond, river and canal margins; June–September. Britain to Holland and Germany southwards; absent from most of Scotland.

◄ **Green Figwort** *Scrophularia umbrosa*
Like *S. nodosa*, but stems broadly winged on the angles and leaves narrowed at the base. Flowers olive-brown; calyx lobes with membranous margins. Damp and shaded habitats, water margins, fens and marshes; July–September. Britain to Denmark and Germany southwards; Very local in England and Scotland and very rare in Ireland.

Common Toadflax
Linaria vulgaris

Scrophulariaceae

The toadflaxes are closely related to the Snapdragon, *Antirrhinum*, commonly grown in our gardens. The prime difference is in the spurred flowers of the latter. The Common Toadflax is a familiar wayside wild flower, seen through the summer and autumn months, a plant that can resist regular cutting of verges.

NOTE
The flowers are visited by various species of bee.

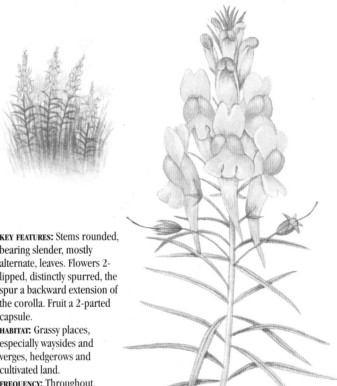

KEY FEATURES: Stems rounded, bearing slender, mostly alternate, leaves. Flowers 2-lipped, distinctly spurred, the spur a backward extension of the corolla. Fruit a 2-parted capsule.

HABITAT: Grassy places, especially waysides and verges, hedgerows and cultivated land.

FREQUENCY: Throughout, except the Faeroes and Iceland.

SEASON: July–October.

HABIT: A patch-forming hairless or partly glandular perennial with spreading rhizomes; flowering stems erect to ascending, to 80 cm, though generally less.

LEAVES: Grey-green, somewhat fleshy, linear to narrow-elliptical, 1-veined, rather crowded and with an untoothed margin.

FLOWERS: Pale to bright yellow, 25–33 mm long, borne in dense racemes; corolla 2-lipped with a closed mouth and a pointed spur 10–13 mm long.

FRUIT: A small 2-parted capsule containing numerous tiny seeds.

J
F
M
A
M
J
J
A
S
O
N
D

LOOKALIKES

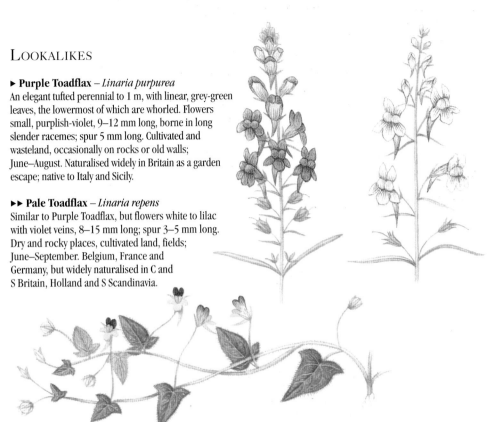

► **Purple Toadflax** – *Linaria purpurea*
An elegant tufted perennial to 1 m, with linear, grey-green leaves, the lowermost of which are whorled. Flowers small, purplish-violet, 9–12 mm long, borne in long slender racemes; spur 5 mm long. Cultivated and wasteland, occasionally on rocks or old walls; June–August. Naturalised widely in Britain as a garden escape; native to Italy and Sicily.

►► **Pale Toadflax** – *Linaria repens*
Similar to Purple Toadflax, but flowers white to lilac with violet veins, 8–15 mm long; spur 3–5 mm long. Dry and rocky places, cultivated land, fields; June–September. Belgium, France and Germany, but widely naturalised in C and S Britain, Holland and S Scandinavia.

Sharp-leaved Fluellen – *Kickxia elatine*
Similar to *Linaria* but with broad leaves. A low often prostrate hairy annual with oval to arrow-shaped leaves. Flowers small, 7–10 mm long, like small toadflaxes, yellowish to bluish with a dark violet upper lip, solitary on long slender stalks. Arable land and other cultivated places; July–October. Throughout, except the Faeroes, Norway and Iceland; local in Britain and Ireland, north to Cumbria.

Round-leaved Fluellen – *Kickxia spuria*
Similar to *K. elatine*, but a more robust plant with oval leaves and hairy flower-stalks. Flowers 10–15 mm with a markedly curved, not straight, spur. Similar habitats and flowering time. S Britain to Holland and Germany southwards; casual further north.

Monkey-flower
Mimulus guttatus

Scrophulariaceae

A lthough not native to Europe this North American plant has become thoroughly at home in the countryside. It is a bright and cheerful plant, long cherished in gardens, from where it presumably escaped during the last century. The common name apparently comes from the broad little flowers with their gaping mouths and spotted cheeks.

NOTE:
The flowers are much visited by bumblebees.

J
F
M
A
M
J
J ❖
A ❖
S ❖ 🐾
O 🐾
N 🐾
D

KEY FEATURES: Rather succulent plant with squarish stems and paired leaves. Flowers with 2-lipped corollas that are closed by 2 ridges, 5-lobed and containing 4 stamens. Fruit a 2-parted capsule.

HABITAT: Wet and damp places, particularly by water margins, marshes or wet rocks.

FREQUENCY: Naturalised almost throughout, except for the far north and the drier and hotter areas.

SEASON: July–September.

HABIT: A tufted annual with hollow erect to ascending stems to 50 cm; stems simple or branched towards the base.

LEAVES: Paired, oval, coarsely toothed, only the lower stalked.

FLOWERS: Bright yellow, usually with reddish-brown spots in the centre, 25–45 mm long, paired at the upper leaves; corolla with a 2-lobed upper lip and a 3-lobed lower lip, the mouth closed by 2 hairy ridges; flower stalks glandular-hairy.

FRUIT: A small 2-parted capsule containing numerous seeds.

Blood-drop-emlets *Mimulus luteus*
Similar to *M. guttatus*, but the flowers are slightly
smaller and covered in red blotches and spots, while
the corolla throat is open. Wet habitats, especially
stream margins and lake margins; June–September.
Naturalised in Scotland, N Wales and parts of
N England; native to Chile.

Musk *Mimulus moschatus*
A smaller stickily-hairy perennial with erect stems
and oval toothed or untoothed, grey-green leaves.
Flowers plain pale yellow, but striped red in the
throat, rather small, 10–20 mm long; mouth of
corolla open. Damp and shaded habitats;
June–September. Naturalised in Britain, Holland,
Belgium, France and Germany; from western
North America.

Marsh Lousewort

Pedicularis palustris

Scrophulariaceae

The louseworts are an interesting and colourful group of plants that are semi-parasitic, being partially dependent on the plants, particularly grasses, which they associate with in the wild. For this reason they are seldom seen in cultivation. Unlike true parasites they do have green leaves and are capable synthesising their own energy.

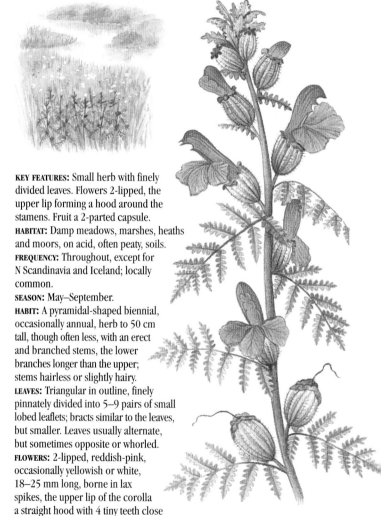

NOTE:
Often grows in association with Yellow Rattle, Rhinanthus minor *(see p.175).*

KEY FEATURES: Small herb with finely divided leaves. Flowers 2-lipped, the upper lip forming a hood around the stamens. Fruit a 2-parted capsule.

HABITAT: Damp meadows, marshes, heaths and moors, on acid, often peaty, soils.

FREQUENCY: Throughout, except for N Scandinavia and Iceland; locally common.

SEASON: May–September.

HABIT: A pyramidal-shaped biennial, occasionally annual, herb to 50 cm tall, though often less, with an erect and branched stems, the lower branches longer than the upper; stems hairless or slightly hairy.

LEAVES: Triangular in outline, finely pinnately divided into 5–9 pairs of small lobed leaflets; bracts similar to the leaves, but smaller. Leaves usually alternate, but sometimes opposite or whorled.

FLOWERS: 2-lipped, reddish-pink, occasionally yellowish or white, 18–25 mm long, borne in lax spikes, the upper lip of the corolla a straight hood with 4 tiny teeth close to the apex, the lower lip broad and 3-lobed. Calyx green, tubular and markedly 2-lipped, with tiny leaf-like tips.

FRUIT: A 2-parted capsule containing numerous tiny seeds, held within the persistent and inflated calyx.

J
F
M
A
M
J
J
A
S
O
N
D

Lookalikes

Lousewort *Pedicularis sylvatica*
A smaller plant, often with the flowers on or close to the ground; stems several, sometimes numerous, unbranched, hairless of with 2 lines of hairs. Flowers pink or red, 15–25 mm long, with the upper lip somewhat curved, with 2 teeth close to the apex; calyx not 2-lipped. Bogs, marshes, moors and open woodland, on usually peaty, acid soils; April–July. Throughout, except the Faeroes, Iceland and N Scandinavia.

Common Cow-wheat

Melampyrum pratense

Scrophulariaceae

An attractive little plant of shaded, particularly wooded habitats, which can be found in bloom from summer until autumn. Like the rattles and louseworts, the cow-wheats are semi- or hemi-parasitic plants, partly reliant on the other plants with which they associate in the wild.

KEY FEATURES: A small, slender plant. Leaves paired and untoothed. Flowers 2-lipped, unstalked, borne in 1-sided spikes. Fruit a 2-parted capsule.

HABITAT: Open woods, scrub and heathland.

FREQUENCY: Throughout apart from the Faeroes, Iceland and the far north.

SEASON: May–October.

HABIT: A small hairless or slightly bristly annual to 25 cm tall, often less, with slender, branched stems, the branches spreading to almost erect.

LEAVES: Paired, linear to oval, untoothed and usually unstalked; bracts similar to the leaves usually narrow-lanceolate and pointed, but with several coarse pointed teeth close to the base.

FLOWERS: Paired, bright yellow to whitish, 10–18 mm long, the upper lip often flushed with red or purple; throat of corolla usually closed.

FRUIT: A 2-parted capsule containing numerous small seeds.

J
F
M
A
M
J
J
A
S
O
N
D

LOOKALIKES

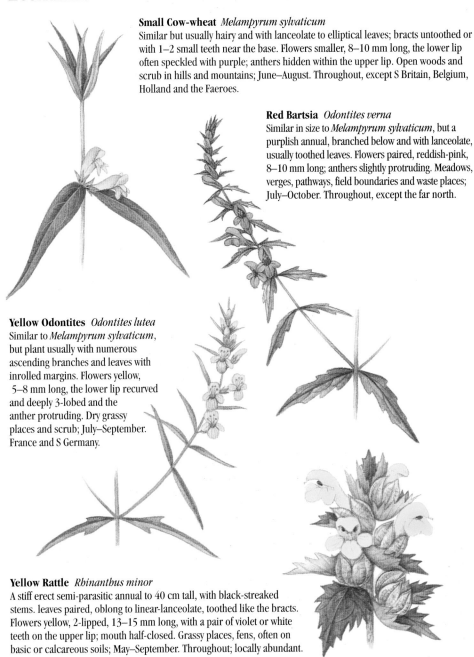

Small Cow-wheat *Melampyrum sylvaticum*
Similar but usually hairy and with lanceolate to elliptical leaves; bracts untoothed or with 1–2 small teeth near the base. Flowers smaller, 8–10 mm long, the lower lip often speckled with purple; anthers hidden within the upper lip. Open woods and scrub in hills and mountains; June–August. Throughout, except S Britain, Belgium, Holland and the Faeroes.

Red Bartsia *Odontites verna*
Similar in size to *Melampyrum sylvaticum*, but a purplish annual, branched below and with lanceolate, usually toothed leaves. Flowers paired, reddish-pink, 8–10 mm long; anthers slightly protruding. Meadows, verges, pathways, field boundaries and waste places; July–October. Throughout, except the far north.

Yellow Odontites *Odontites lutea*
Similar to *Melampyrum sylvaticum*, but plant usually with numerous ascending branches and leaves with inrolled margins. Flowers yellow, 5–8 mm long, the lower lip recurved and deeply 3-lobed and the anther protruding. Dry grassy places and scrub; July–September. France and S Germany.

Yellow Rattle *Rhinanthus minor*
A stiff erect semi-parasitic annual to 40 cm tall, with black-streaked stems. leaves paired, oblong to linear-lanceolate, toothed like the bracts. Flowers yellow, 2-lipped, 13–15 mm long, with a pair of violet or white teeth on the upper lip; mouth half-closed. Grassy places, fens, often on basic or calcareous soils; May–September. Throughout; locally abundant.

Foxglove
Digitalis purpurea

Scrophulariaceae

The Foxglove is one of the best known and cherished wild flowers in the region. Yet it is peculiarly a plant of the lands close to the Atlantic seaboard. It has been long used in medicine, being especially important, even today, in the treatment of various heart conditions. Yet it is an extremely poisonous plant and doses have to be calculated with pinpoint accuracy. The Foxglove is also widely cultivated in gardens, where a number of different forms and colours are known.

NOTE:
The flowers are visited by bees, especially bumblebees. Poisonous.

KEY FEATURES: Leaves soft, in a large rosette in the first year. Flowers drooping, tubular with a pronounced spotted lip. Fruit a 2-parted capsule.

HABITAT: Woodland, hedgerows, scrub, and heaths, often, but not exclusively, on acid soils.

FREQUENCY: Throughout north to S Sweden, but only naturalised in Denmark and Holland; often local but sometimes abundant.

SEASON: June–September.

HABIT: A softly hairy greyish biennial or short-lived perennial, forming a leaf-rosette in the first season, with an erect leafy stem to 1.5 m in the second.

LEAVES: Oval to lanceolate, tapered to a winged stalk, blunt toothed; upper leaves similar but smaller.

FLOWERS: Nodding, borne in a long tapered spike, purple patterned within with darker spots or wings, occasionally pure white; corolla tubular with 5 rather indistinct lobes and a well-defined lower hairy lip, 40–55 mm long. Calyx 5-lobed. Stamens 4.

FRUIT: A small greenish to brownish 2-parted capsule, with pores near the apex, containing numerous small seeds.

J
F
M
A
M
J
J
A
S
O
N
D

Columbine
Aquilegia vulgaris

Ranunculaceae

A popular old cottage garden favourite that is often called Granny's Bonnet or Granny's Night-cap, the wild form of the Columbine is native in many parts of the region. The flowers are unmistakable with their 5 upward-pointing spurs. In gardens they exist in many colours, including those with double flowers or with short or non-existent spurs; these sometimes escape 'into the wild'.

NOTE:
The flowers are visited by bees in search of nectar at the tip of the spurs. Poisonous.

KEY FEATURES: Leaves with many similar leaflets. Flowers with 5 spurs. Fruit a collection of small, pod-like follicles.

HABITAT: Woodland, grassy places, scrub and banks, hedgerows, occasionally in the drier parts of marshes and fens.

FREQUENCY: Throughout, except for the far north, but often rather local, occasionally in large colonies; absent from N Scotland and Ireland.

SEASON: May–July.

HABIT: A stout clump-forming, hairy short-lived perennial, to 80 cm tall, with most of the leaves crowded towards the base of the plant; upper stem and flower-stalks usually sticky with glands.

LEAVES: 2-ternate, with dull green leaflets that are paler beneath, rounded to oblong, toothed to shallowly lobed.

FLOWERS: Purple-blue or violet, rarely white, 30–50 mm across, with 5 spreading petal-like sepals and 5 petals with hooked spurs which are directed upwards; stamens numerous, just protruding.

FRUIT: A cluster of small pod-like follicles that split along the inside to release the seeds.

J
F
M
A
M
J
J
A
S
O
N
D

Cow Parsley
Anthriscus sylvestris

Umbelliferae/Apiaceae

F ew plants are more evocative of early summer than Cow Parsley, its frothy clouds of bloom lining pathways and verges in profusion. It is a great delight and a herald of the summer months to follow. It is scarcely surprising that this almost ubiquitous plant should have acquired a plethora of common names; of these perhaps the most charming is Queen Ann's Lace, but others include Hedge Parsley, Fairy Lace and Lady's Lace.

NOTE:
One of the earliest umbels to come into flower; this and its prolific nature make it easy to identify.

J
F
M
A
M
J
J
A
S
O
N
D

KEY FEATURES: A stout branched, only slightly hairy plant. Leaves finely cut into numerous small divisions. Flowers in umbels. Fruit elliptical, 2-parted, brown or black when ripe.

HABITAT: Hedgerows, verges, and other rough grassy places, woodland margins.

FREQUENCY: Common throughout, except the far north; often abundant.

SEASON: May–June, occasionally later.

HABIT: A robust branched, bushy biennial or perennial to 1.5 m tall; stems hollow, lined, and speckled.

LEAVES: The lower leaves 3-pinnate, with numerous small acute segments, generally rather dull green; upper leaves smaller with few prime segments.

FLOWERS: White, 3–4 mm across, borne in umbels with 415 spokes (rays), without bracts at the base of the main umbels; outer florets with 1–2 enlarged petals, otherwise with 5 petals like the inner florets.

FRUIT: Elliptical, 7–10 mm long, 2-parted, with a short beak and a bristly base, dark brown or black when ripe.

LOOKALIKES

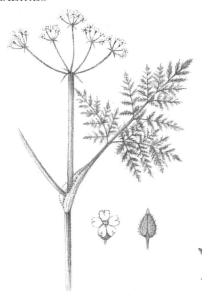

Bur Parsley *Anthriscus caucalis*
An annual to 70 cm with the stem usually purplish towards the base. Umbels with only 2–6 rays and flowers smaller, 2 mm across. Fruit distinctive, even in the young state, egg-shaped, 3 mm long, covered with hooked bristles which readily attach themselves to clothing etc. Dry places, particularly rough grassland, waste ground and hedgerows, on light well-drained soils; May–June. Throughout, north to S Sweden, but not in N Scotland or Ireland.

Rough Chervil
Chaerophyllum temulem (syn. *C. temulentum*)
Very like Cow Parsley but a rough-hairy plant with solid stems, to 1 m. Leaves dark green, eventually turning purple. Flowers white, 2 mm across, in compound umbels that nod in bud. Fruit 4–7 mm long, narrow-oblong, tapered to the beak apex and ridged throughout its length (in *Anthriscus* ridged only near the base). Rough grassy places and semi-shaded habitats, on well-drained soils; May–July. Throughout except the Faeroes, Iceland, Norway and Finland.

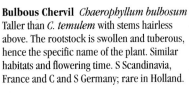

Bulbous Chervil *Chaerophyllum bulbosum*
Taller than *C. temulem* with stems hairless above. The rootstock is swollen and tuberous, hence the specific name of the plant. Similar habitats and flowering time. S Scandinavia, France and C and S Germany; rare in Holland.

Wild Carrot

Daucus carota

Umbelliferae/Apiaceae

A handsome plant which is rather distinctive in seed when the rays of the umbel curve upwards and, together with the bracts, become decidedly concave, hence another common name for the plant, Bird's-nest. The wild carrot has a thin whitish root that is very different from that of the cultivated carrot, subsp. *sativus*, which is believed to have been developed from the wild plant by early man.

NOTE:
Coastal forms, often found on sand dunes or cliffs, are far shorter and more densely hairy, with the rays less contracted in the fruiting umbels; these are assigned to subsp. gummifer.

KEY FEATURES: Flowers in rather rounded, compound umbels, surrounded at the base by a ruff of dissected bracts. Fruiting umbels concave. Fruit small, covered in regular short spines.

HABITAT: Rough grassy places, meadows, verges and waysides, cliff tops and sand dunes, on well-drained soils and usually at low altitudes.

FREQUENCY: Throughout, except the far north; sometimes in large numbers.

SEASON: June–August.

HABIT: An erect, hairy or hairless annual or biennial; stems solid, usually ridged, branched above, to 1 m.

LEAVES: 2–3-pinnate, feathery-looking, divided into numerous linear to lanceolate segments; uppermost leaves often bract-like, or at least much reduced. Bracts conspicuous, often 3-lobed, forming a ruff round the base of the main (primary) umbels.

FLOWERS: White, 2 mm, numerous borne in secondary umbels; primary umbels rather rounded, with at least 10 rays, the central (uppermost) floret sometimes purple. Bracts and rays incurving strongly as the fruits develop.

FRUIT: 2-parted, elliptical, 2–4 mm long, with regular rows of short spines.

J
F
M
A
M
J
J
A
S
O
N
D

Burnet-saxifrage *Pimpinella saxifraga*
Stems hollow, to 70 cm. The lower leaves pinnate with 3–9 broad, toothed, leaflets, while the upper leaves are have more finely cut divisions and inflate bases to the leaf-stalks. Flowers white or pinkish borne in umbels without bracts and in which the rays do not curve upwards in fruit. Fruit rounded and with slender ridges, 2 mm long, hairless. Rough and grazed meadows, rocky places, on calcareous and base-rich soils; June–September. Throughout, except the far north; rare in N Ireland and N Scotland.

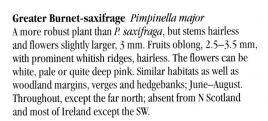

Greater Burnet-saxifrage *Pimpinella major*
A more robust plant than *P. saxifraga*, but stems hairless and flowers slightly larger, 3 mm. Fruits oblong, 2.5–3.5 mm, with prominent whitish ridges, hairless. The flowers can be white, pale or quite deep pink. Similar habitats as well as woodland margins, verges and hedgebanks; June–August. Throughout, except the far north; absent from N Scotland and most of Ireland except the SW.

Hogweed

Heracleum sphondylium

Umbelliferae/Apiaceae

One of the best known and most characteristic hedgerow and verge umbellifers, coming into flower as Cow Parsley (*see* p.178) fades and sometimes almost as prolific. The large white umbels are unmistakable and, long after the flowers and fruits have gone, the ashen stems stand gaunt through the first weeks of winter. Like the Giant Hogweed (*see* Note below) the juice of stem and leaves can cause a skin reaction in sunlight, leading to blistering, which can be severe.

KEY FEATURES: A large stout plant with umbels to 20 cm across, occasionally larger. Stems rough with bristles, hollow. Outer florets of secondary umbels with 1 or 2 enlarged petals. Fruit flattened and broadly winged.

HABITAT: Rough grassy places, verges and banks, waysides, open woodland, on a variety of soils, but especially calcareous and base-rich ones.

FREQUENCY: Throughout except the far north, often gregarious and sometimes abundant.

SEASON: June–September, sometimes almost throughout the year, especially mown verges.

HABIT: A stout bristly biennial or short-lived perennial, to 2 m, though often less; stems ridged and hollow.

LEAVES: Large, pinnate, with often 5 broad, lobed and toothed leaflets; upper leaves with reduced blades but with the stalk much enlarged, inflated and sheath-like.

FLOWERS: In large compound umbels with 12–25 rays, white or occasionally washy pink, each flower 5–10 mm across, the outer florets usually with uneven, enlarged petals; petals deeply notched.

FRUIT: 2-parted, flattened, elliptical to rounded, 7–10 mm long, with 4 dark resin canals towards the top.

J
F
M
A
M
J
J
A
S
O
N
D

NOTE: *The Giant Hogweed,* H. mantegazzianum, *from the Caucasus, is widely naturalised in Europe, especially in Britain. It is a very substantial plant with thick stems as high as 5 m tall in favoured localities. The large umbels can be 50 cm across and have more than 50 rays. The juice is photosensitive in sunlight and can cause very serious skin blistering.*

LOOKALIKES

Ground Elder *Aegopodium podagraria*
Another white-flowered umbel, but distinctive on account of its vigorous patch-forming habit. Plant to 1 m tall in flower, though often less, with bright green ternate or 2-ternate leaves; leaflets lanceolate to oval, pointed, with a sharply toothed margin; upper leaves reduced and with a short inflated stalk. Umbels rounded, with 10–12 rays but no bracts; flowers white 2–3 mm across. Fruit egg-shaped, with slender ridges, 3–4 mm long. Shaded places, cultivated and waste ground, banks, close to old buildings and abandoned gardens; May–August. Throughout, except the far north, the Faeroes and Iceland. An often invasive and tenacious weed of cultivation.

Wild Angelica
Angelica sylvestris

A very handsome umbel of damp habitats, which is sometimes grown in gardens as an ornamental subject. The distinctive purple coloration of much of the plant is a useful diagnostic character. In the umbellifer flower the ovary is located below the other flower parts, the calyx is minute or absent altogether and the petals are 5; there are characteristically 2 styles per flower.

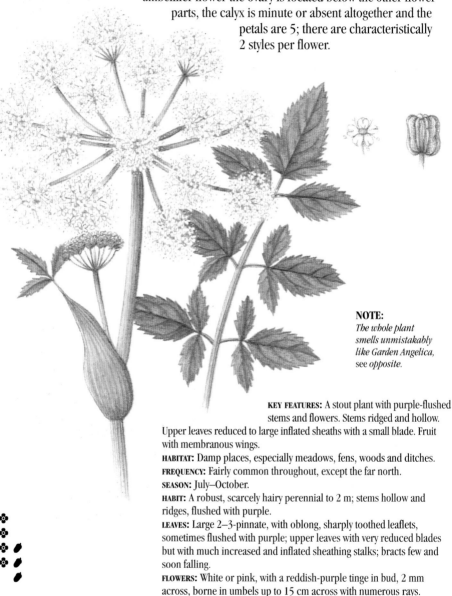

NOTE:
The whole plant smells unmistakably like Garden Angelica, see opposite.

KEY FEATURES: A stout plant with purple-flushed stems and flowers. Stems ridged and hollow. Upper leaves reduced to large inflated sheaths with a small blade. Fruit with membranous wings.

HABITAT: Damp places, especially meadows, fens, woods and ditches.

FREQUENCY: Fairly common throughout, except the far north.

SEASON: July–October.

HABIT: A robust, scarcely hairy perennial to 2 m; stems hollow and ridges, flushed with purple.

LEAVES: Large 2–3-pinnate, with oblong, sharply toothed leaflets, sometimes flushed with purple; upper leaves with very reduced blades but with much increased and inflated sheathing stalks; bracts few and soon falling.

FLOWERS: White or pink, with a reddish-purple tinge in bud, 2 mm across, borne in umbels up to 15 cm across with numerous rays.

FRUIT: 2-parted, oval, 4–5 mm long, with broad membranous wings.

J
F
M
A
M
J
J
A
S
O
N
D

184

LOOKALIKES

Garden Angelica *Angelica archangelica*
A pleasantly aromatic perennial of similar proportions to Wild Angelica, but even more robust. Stems green, occasionally flushed with purple towards the base. Flowers greenish or cream, 3–4 mm across, borne in large umbels up to 25 cm across, with numerous rays. Fruit oblong, 6–8 mm long, with corky wings. Damp places, especially meadows, water margins, ditches, thickets and waste places; June–September. The Faeroes, Iceland, Holland, Germany and much of Scandinavia, but naturalised widely from gardens in much of Britain, Belgium and France; sometimes abundant. It is the candied stems of this plant that are used to decorate cakes, but the stems and roots have long been used for medicine and for adding to liqueurs.

Alexanders
Smyrnium olusatrum

Umbelliferae/Apiaceae

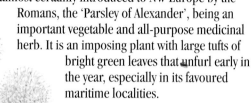

T his is another alien that is thoroughly naturalised in parts of the region. It was almost certainly introduced to NW Europe by the Romans, the 'Parsley of Alexander', being an important vegetable and all-purpose medicinal herb. It is an imposing plant with large tufts of bright green leaves that unfurl early in the year, especially in its favoured maritime localities.

KEY FEATURES: A large hairless plant. Upper branches opposite. Uppermost leaves yellow-green. Fruit black when ripe.
HABITAT: Hedgebanks, woodland margins, waste ground, verges and cliffs, often near the sea.
FREQUENCY: NW and C France southwards and south-eastwards; widely naturalised in Britain and Holland; local inland.
SEASON: April–June.
HABIT: A stout hairless biennial to 1.5 m; stems eventually hollow, with the upper branches opposite.
LEAVES: Large, triangular in outline, 3-ternate, with bright deep green and shiny oval, toothed, leaflets. Upper leaves much smaller, with inflated stalks, yellow-green.
FLOWERS: Yellow, in compound umbels, each flower 5-parted, 3 mm across, without sepals; umbels with 7–15 rays.
FRUIT: 2-parted, egg-shaped, 7–8 mm long, with slender ridges, black when ripe.

J
F
M
A
M
J
J
A
S
O
N
D

LOOKALIKES

Perfoliate Alexanders *Smyrnium perfoliatum*
A less robust and less coarse plant to 80 cm, occasionally taller, with angled stems that are hairy at the nodes. Upper branches alternate. Upper leaves heart-shaped, clasping the stem, chrome-yellow. Fruits smaller, only 3–3.5 mm long and brownish-black when ripe. Woodland and rocky habitats; May–July. Naturalised in Britain, France, Denmark and Germany. Widely cultivated in gardens as a decorative plant.

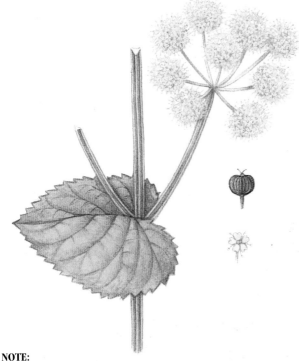

NOTE:
*The flowers of both species
are visited by a variety of
insects including bees, flies
and beetles.*

Cypress Spurge
Euphorbia cyparissias

Euphorbiaceae

T he spurges are a very large and interesting group of plants which all produce milky latex when cut. The flowers are small but are surrounded by large and conspicuous bracts that are very decorative and often long-lasting; for this reason many are cultivated in gardens. The plant in question gets its name from its feathery shoots that are reminiscent of a young cypress.

KEY FEATURES: Plant hairless, producing white latex when cut. Shoots feathery, with linear leaves. Flower clusters surrounded by bright greenish-yellow bracts. Fruit a 3-parted capsule.
HABITAT: Grassy and rocky places, scrub, waste places, cultivated ground (especially gardens).
FREQUENCY: Holland and Germany southwards; widely naturalised in Britain and Scandinavia, especially in the south.
SEASON: April–June.
HABIT: A tufted, rhizomatous, patch-forming, hairless perennial with feathery shoots to 50 cm tall; stems densely leafy, usually branched near the base.
LEAVES: Alternate, crowded, linear, dull green at first but later in the year turning yellow and reddish.
FLOWERS: Borne in 9–18-rayed umbels, rather insignificant, yellowish-green, but surrounded by similarly coloured rounded to kidney-shaped bracts that form small cups around the flowers.
FRUIT: A small 3-parted granular capsule, containing 3 seeds, exploding when ripe.

NOTE:
The flowers of spurges are generally petalless, male and female being separate but on the same plant; in many the one to few-stamened male flowers are borne on a common hypanthium together with a solitary female flower that consists of just the ovary and a feathery style.

J
F
M
A
M
J
J
A
S
O
N
D

Sun Spurge *Euphorbia helioscopia*
An annual of similar size, although small depauperate plants are to
be found on impoverished ground or thin soils. Stem usually solitary
and erect bearing oval leaves which are slightly toothed in the upper
half. Bracts similar in shape to the leaves, yellowish. Umbels with up
to 5 main rays, with flowers in the ray forks. Fruit capsule smooth,
unwinged. Cultivated, waste and disturbed ground, sometimes along
roadsides; May–August. Throughout, except the far north.

Petty Spurge *Euphorbia peplus*
A hairless green annual like the Sun Spurge, but stems
branched from the base. Leaves oval to rounded, short-stalked
and untoothed; bracts similar in size to the leaves and the same
colour, but more triangular capsule smooth but shallowly
keeled on the back of each valve. Similar habitats;
April–October. Throughout north as far as C Scandinavia;
absent from the Faeroes and Iceland.

Scented Mayweed

Matricaria recutita (syn. *Tripleurospermum recutita*)

Compositae/Asteraceae

T he mayweeds present a challenge to the botanist and, for the beginner, are often very tricky to tell apart. This is not helped by the fact that they belong to several different, albeit closely related genera. The nature of the flowerheads, the position of the rays and the shape of the disk are useful diagnostic features.

NOTE:
The flowers are visited by bees and butterflies, as well as flies. In the daisy family the flowerheads consist of numerous small flowers or florets crammed into a dense head and surrounded at the base by closely overlapping floral bracts.

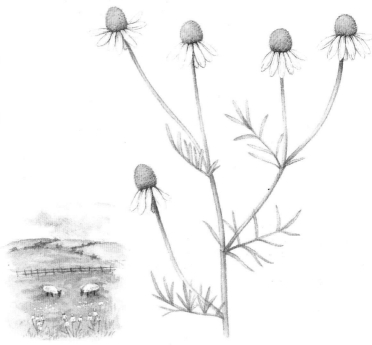

J
F
M
A
M
J
J
A
S
O
N
D

KEY FEATURES: Plant with finely dissected leaves, aromatic when bruised. Flowerheads daisy like, with a conical, hollow central disk; rays downturned.

HABITAT: Cultivated land, especially arable, waste and disturbed land, saline areas, on sandy or loamy soils.

FREQUENCY: Throughout, except for Ireland, the Faeroes and Iceland; probably naturalised in much of northern Europe; often abundant.

SEASON: May–November.

HABIT: A hairless annual with branched, ascending to erect stems to 60 cm, often less.

LEAVES: Alternate, feathery, bright green, divided into numerous linear segments; aromatic with a strong sweet smell when fresh.

FLOWERS: Daisy-like, solitary, flowerheads, 10–25 mm across, with white rays that soon become down-turned; central disk yellow, conical and hollow.

FRUIT: A small single-seeded achene, difficult to observe; each flowerhead consists of many such achenes.

LOOKALIKES

Scentless Mayweed
*Tripleurospermum inodorum (*syn. *Matricaria perforata)*
Similar to Scented Mayweed, but plant unscented and the flower disks flatter and solid. Flowerheads 20–40 mm across. Similar habitats, but on a wide range of soils; July–September. Throughout, except for the far north.

Corn Camomile *Anthemis arvensis*
Similar to Scented Mayweed, but with slightly aromatic leaves and pleasantly scented flowers. Flowerheads 20–30 mm across, with spreading white rays and a solid, conical yellow disk. Similar habitats, on calcareous or sandy soils; June–August. Throughout, except the Faeroes and N Scandinavia.

Daisy *Bellis perennis*
A very familiar weed of grassy places, especially lawns. Plant a small perennial to 10 cm tall, with all the leaves in basal rosettes. Flowerheads white with a yellow disk, 15–30 mm across; rays numerous, narrow, often tipped or flushed with purplish-red underneath. Flowering almost year-round. Throughout.

Common Fleabane
Pulicaria dysenterica

Compositae/Asteraceae

A common plant of damp places which has a curious smell (often said to be a mixture of chrysanthemum with a hint of carbolic). For this reason it was said to be a good flea repellent in medieval times, and bunches of it were hung in houses.

NOTE:
Pulicaria *and* Inula *are very similar, differing in details of the pappus, the hair or scale-like attachments of the achenes; in both the pappus consists of a tuft of hairs, but in* Pulicaria *the outer row is replaced by a row of closely-fused scales.*

KEY FEATURES: A softly downy plant. Stem leaves clasping with unstalked bases. Flowerheads all yellow, daisy-like, backed by numerous narrow downy bracts.
HABITAT: Damp places, particularly river and canal banks, ditches, marshes and wet meadows.
FREQUENCY: Throughout, except the far north.
SEASON: August–September.
HABIT: A downy, stoloniferous perennial to 60 cm, with erect stems that are branched in the upper part.
LEAVES: Basal oblong with a narrowed base, usually withered by flowering time; stem leaves heart- or arrow-shaped, clasping the stem with unstalked bases.
FLOWERS: Golden-yellow daisy heads, 15–30 mm across, borne in lax, flat-topped clusters; rays numerous, narrow and rather short, the disk flat.
FRUIT: A single-seeded achene, scaly above.

J
F
M
A
M
J
J
A
S
O
N
D

Elecampane *Inula helenium*
A robust perennial, sometimes reaching 2
m or more, with oval to elliptical leaves, the
upper unstalked. Flowerheads large and
bright yellow, 60–80 mm across; rays long
and narrow; outer floral bracts recurved.
Old meadows, waste ground, orchards and
copses, roadsides; July–August. Widely
naturalised throughout except for the
Faeroes, Iceland and the far north. Native
to W Asia.

Irish Fleabane *Inula salicina*
Rather like a small version of *I. helenium*, but not more than 75 cm tall
and with linear-lanceolate to narrow-oval, grey-green, net-veined
leaves. Flowerheads 25–40 mm across, wit long slender rays. Woods,
fens, marshes and rocky places, at low altitudes, local; July–August.
Ireland and Continental Europe, except the far north.

Butterbur

Petasites hybridus

Compositae/Asteraceae

A n interesting plant whose flowers appear early in the year before the huge leaves develop. In the days before refrigeration, the pliable leaves were used to wrap butter in, being both moist and cool. The cone-like flowerheads are quite impressive, especially as they appear as winter fades into spring.

KEY FEATURES: Leaves very large and all basal. Flowerheads aggregated into large cone-like inflorescences, either male or female. Florets with short rays. Fruithead a typical 'clock'.

HABITAT: Damp often part-shaded places, woodland, wet meadows, river and streamsides, roadsides.

FREQUENCY: Britain (except N Scotland) to Holland and Germany southwards, but naturalised in S Scandinavia; often forming extensive colonies, but local.

SEASON: March–May.

HABIT: A vigorous patch-forming, hairy perennial with only basal leaves and inflorescences arising before the leaves appear.

LEAVES: Large, to 1 m across, broad heart-shaped, with a long stalk and an irregularly toothed margin, grey-downy beneath.

FLOWERS: Pale reddish-violet, not scented, borne in large conical inflorescences to 50 cm tall, the male flowerheads fewer 7–10 mm across, the female more numerous and smaller, 3–6 mm across.

FRUIT: A 'clock', consisting of a collection of achenes with an attached 'parachute'.

J
F
M
A
M
J
J
A
S
O
N
D

White Butterbur *Petasites albus*
Similar to *P. hybridus*, but leaves white-downy beneath, and
flowerheads fragrant, yellowish-white to white. Similar habitats and
flowering time. S Scandinavia, Germany and France; naturalised in
England and E Scotland.

▲ **Winter Heliotrope**
Petasites fragrans
Leaves and flowers appearing at the same time.
Leaves not more than 20 cm across, kidney to
heart-shaped, rather shiny above and slightly
hairy beneath. Flowerheads vanilla-fragrant,
pinkish-white, few borne in a broad raceme.
Similar habitats as well as waste and cultivated
land. Widely naturalised from the Mediterranean
region, in Britain, Belgium, France and Denmark.

Coltsfoot *Tussilago farfara*
Rather similar leaf to Winter Heliotrope but leaves mealy-white beneath,
and above when young. Flowerheads solitary, yellow, 15–35 mm across,
borne on scaly stalks from ground level, appearing in advance of the
leaves. Arable fields, banks, roadsides, hedgerows, sand dunes and
shingle; February–April. Throughout, except the far north.

Yarrow

Achillea millefolium

Compositae/Asteraceae

A strong-smelling and familiar wayside flower, long cultivated in gardens, where various colour forms exist. It is also a familiar weed of lawn and verges, being extremely resistant to mowing. The plant has attracted a variety of common names including Milfoil, Staunchweed and Poor Man's Pepper. The finely divided foliage, reflect the Latin name; *millefolium* literally means 'thousand leaf'.

NOTE:
The flowers are visited by a variety of insects including bees, flies and butterflies.

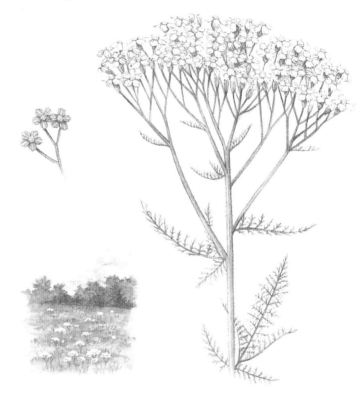

J
F
M
A
M
J
J
A
S
O
N
D

KEY FEATURES: Very finely divided, strongly aromatic, foliage. Flowerheads small but clustered into flat-topped inflorescences, each head with both rays and a disk.

HABITAT: Grassy places, meadows and pastures, as well as lawns, verges and hedgerows, waste places, often on calcareous soils.

FREQUENCY: Throughout, sometimes abundant.

SEASON: July–October.

HABIT: A tufted, stoloniferous, hairy perennial, with stiff erect leafy stems to 60 cm.

LEAVES: Feathery, narrow-oblong, finely divided into numerous tiny segments; strongly aromatic when bruised.

FLOWERS: White to pink, occasionally reddish, the individual heads small 4–6 mm across, but massed together into bold flat topped inflorescences; flowerheads with a small disk and several short, broad rays; disk white or cream.

FRUIT: A collection of small achenes, buried in the persistent disk.

LOOKALIKES

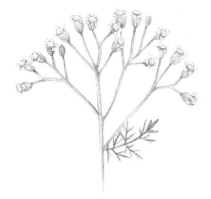

Noble Yarrow *Achillea nobilis*
Similar to common Yarrow, but a non-stoloniferous plant. Leaves with larger divisions, rather flat and flowerheads 3 mm across, yellowish-white with a yellow disk; rays very short, only 1 mm long. Dry grassy and rocky places; July–August. France and Germany; naturalised or casual in Britain and N Europe.

Sneezewort *Achillea ptarmica*
Readily distinguished by its lanceolate, saw-edged leaves and larger flowerheads, 12–18 mm across, borne in lax, branched clusters; rays white, while the disk is greenish-white. Damp grassy habitats, marshes and water margins, on acid to neutral soils; July–September. Throughout, except the far north; naturalised in Iceland.

Oxeye Daisy
Leucanthemum vulgare

Compositae/Asteraceae

O ne of the most familiar wild flowers of the summer landscape, the Oxeye or Moon Daisy is as thoroughly at home in meadows as along motorways. It is an early coloniser in such places, provided it is not overcome by weedkillers, and can make impressive stands within very few years.

NOTE:
The flowers are visited by a variety of insects, including bees, butterflies and flies.

J
F
M
A
M
J
J
A
S
O
N
D

KEY FEATURES: Leaves toothed but not lobed; stem leaves, alternate, clasping. Flowerheads large and daisy-like, with long rather broad strap-shaped rays.

HABITAT: A wide range of grassy places, particularly meadows, downs and verges, but also banks, open woodland and cliffs, on calcareous to slightly acid soils.

FREQUENCY: Common almost throughout; naturalised in the Faeroes and Iceland.

SEASON: May–September.

HABIT: A patch-forming stoloniferous, often hairless, perennial with erect flowering stems to 80 cm, though often less; stems ridged, often branched in the upper part.

LEAVES: Dark green, the basal oval, stalked, while the stem leaves are oblong and clasp the stem with unstalked bases; all leaves coarsely toothed.

FLOWERS: Solitary daisies, 25–50 mm across, with long white rays and a prominent yellow disk; rays numerous, strap-shaped, overlapping to some extent, often pinking as they age.

FRUIT: Small single-seeded achenes, imbedded in the persistent disk.

Corn Marigold *Chrysanthemum segetum*
Similar in stature to the Oxeye Daisy, but a greyish, somewhat fleshy, annual with all-yellow flowerheads, 35–55 mm across. Arable fields and other cultivated land, waste and disturbed ground; June–August. Throughout, except for N Scandinavia and Iceland, but local and declining in most places.

Feverfew *Tanacetum parthenium*
An aromatic biennial or short-lived perennial, with stiff, erect, branched stems. Leaves often rather yellowish-green, pinnately-lobed. Flowerheads like small Oxeye Daisies, 10–25 mm across, numerous borne in large wide-branched clusters. Scrub and rocky places, cultivated land, waysides, often on calcareous soils; July–September. Widely naturalised in Britain, Ireland and much of Continental Europe north to S Scandinavia; native to SE Europe.

Tansy *Tanacetum vulgare*
Like Feverfew, but leaves with narrower, more saw-toothed, segments and flowerheads yellow and button-like, without ray florets, borne in flat-topped clusters. Similar habitats and flowering time. Throughout, except the far north; naturalised in Ireland.

Common Ragwort

Senecio jacobaea

Compositae/Asteraceae

A familiar plant of meadows, often seen in large numbers, the Common Ragwort is an injurious weed that can poison livestock. Despite this, it is a handsome plant much frequented by a variety of insects, including bees and butterflies. Although loathed by farmers it is, nonetheless, the national flower of the Isle of Man.

NOTE:
Forms without rays to the flowerheads are usually referred to var. flosculosus.

KEY FEATURES: A tall plant with pinnately-lobed leaves, which have a malodorous characteristic, especially when bruised. Flowerheads daisy-like, all of one colour; floral bracts equal, in a single row.

HABITAT: Overgrazed meadows, poor pastures and waste places, open woodland, banks and sand dunes, on a variety of soils.

FREQUENCY: Throughout, except for the far north, sometimes abundant; naturalised in Finland.

SEASON: June–November.

HABIT: A variable hairy or almost hairless perennial, occasionally a biennial, with erect stems to 1.5 m, although generally less; stems stiff, branched above.

LEAVES: Deep green, pinnately-lobed, the lowermost stalked and generally withered by flowering time, the upper unstalked and half-clasping the stem.

FLOWERS: Yellow, the heads 15–25 mm across, borne in large flat-topped clusters; rays 12–15; floral-bracts with a dark tip.

FRUIT: An achene with a whitish pappus.

J
F
M
A
M
J
J
A
S
O
N
D

LOOKALIKES

Oxford Ragwort *Senecio squalidus*
Rather like a scaled down version of Common Ragwort, but plant more diffuse and not more than 50 cm tall, with the upper leaves more deeply dissected; flowerheads bright yellow, of similar size, with 12–13 rays normally; floral-bracts unequal and black-tipped. Waste and disturbed ground, embankments, old walls; April–December. Widely naturalised from S Europe, in Britain, France and Denmark; local or casual elsewhere.

Groundsel *Senecio vulgaris*
An annual to 25 cm tall with shiny-green, pinnately-lobed leaves, only the lower stalked. Flowerheads yellow, small, 4–5 mm, without rays; outer floral-bracts very short. Cultivated, waste and disturbed ground; Flowering all the year round. Throughout.

Sticky Groundsel *Senecio viscosus*
A sticky, foetid annual a bit like Groundsel, but generally taller, the flowerheads pale yellow, 6–10 mm, with short recurved rays; floral-bracts plain green. Waste and disturbed ground, roadsides, embankments and sand dunes, shingle; July–October. Britain to Holland and Germany southwards; naturalised widely further north and in Ireland.

Heath Groundsel *Senecio sylvaticus*
Similar to Sticky Groundsel, but a non-sticky rather yellowish-green hairy annual. Flowerheads smaller, 4–6 mm. Similar habitats, as well as open woodland and heaths; July–September. Throughout except for much of the north.

Wild Teasel

Dipsacus fullonum

Dipsacaceae

A familiar thistle-like plant that is both bold and handsome. In former times the prickly heads were used for the carding of wool, literally teasing the fibres apart before they can be spun. The plant has curious leaves that surround the stem in pairs with a cup-like base that fills with water. Despite popular belief, these pools are benign and the plant does not devour insects that fall into the small leaf pools.

NOTE:
The flowers are greatly attractive to bees and butterflies. In the autumn birds, especially goldfinches, are keen on the seeds.

KEY FEATURES: Stiff prickly plant. Leaves paired and forming distinctive cups around the stem. Flowereheads oblong, very bristly, surrounded by long spiny bracts at the base.

HABITAT: A variety of habitats on dry clay soils, especially field and woodland margins, hedgebanks and embankments or river margins.

FREQUENCY: C and S Britain, rare in Ireland, Holland to Germany southwards; naturalised in Denmark; sometimes making extensive colonies.

SEASON: July–August.

HABIT: A stiff, erect biennial, to 2 m, branched in the upper half, forming a low leaf-rosette in the first year; stems prickly.

LEAVES: Paired, cupped around the stem, elliptical to linear-lanceolate, shallowly toothed, the lowermost withered by the time the plant comes into flower, prickly along the main veins beneath.

FLOWERS: Thistle-like bristly heads 3–8 cm long, with concentric rings of small pinkish-purple flowers opening from the base upwards; heads surrounded at the base by very long, curved, spine-like stiff bracts.

FRUIT: Small dry achene with a papery calyx, hidden amongst the bristles of the persistent flowerhead.

J
F
M
A
M
J
J
A
S
O
N
D

LOOKALIKES

Small Teasel *Dipsacus pilosus*
Similar, but a slighter plant without 'cupped' leaves and with small rounded flowerheads, only 1.5–2 cm across, bearing whitish flowers. Damp or shaded places, usually on calcareous soils; August–September. Britain (Yorkshire southwards) and Denmark and Germany southwards.

Lesser Burdock *Arctium minus* ▲
Superficially teasel-like but *Arctium* belongs to the Compositae. A large leafy biennial with heart-shaped leaves which have hollow stalks. Flowerheads egg-shaped, purple, 15–25 mm across, surrounded by numerous hooked floral-bracts that persist in fruit and catch onto clothing readily. Various habitats, particularly woodland margins and verges; July–September. Throughout, except the far north.

◄ **Greater Burdock** *Arctium lappa*
Similar to Lesser Burdock, but leaf-stalks solid and flowerheads larger 20–42 mm across, the floral bracts shiny golden-green. Similar habitats and flowering time. Throughout, except the far north, the Faeroes and Iceland.

Arctium tomentosum
Similar to the other burdocks but flowerheads small, 12–20 mm, with the floral-bracts enveloped in white cottony hairs. Similar habitats and flowering time. Throughout, except the far north, but rare and casual in Britain and Ireland and much of the north.

203

Carline Thistle

Carlina vulgaris

Compositae/Asteraceae

A handsome and attractive thistle-like plant widely grown in gardens. The flowers are rather insignificant but the flowerheads are surrounded by a circle of long slender floral bracts that persist everlasting-like as the seeds develop. During dull damp weather the heads remain tightly closed but during warm dry spells they open, and this feature persists even when the heads are dead.

NOTE:
The flowerheads are visited by various species of bee and butterfly.

KEY FEATURES: A low plant with thistle-like leaves. Flowerheads surrounded by long slender, stiff, shiny bracts. Florets 5-lobed, small and crammed into large flat disks.
HABITAT: Dry, generally grazed grassland, sand dunes, often on calcareous soils.
FREQUENCY: Throughout, except the far north, but often rather local; only coastal in N Ireland and Scotland.
SEASON: July–September.
HABIT: A very prickly biennial forming a large leaf-rosette at ground level in the first year; in the second year smooth stems arise to 60 cm and by the time the plants are in flower the basal leaves have withered.

J
F
M
A
M
J
J
A
S
O
N
D

LEAVES: Thistle-like, alternate, narrow-oblong, with a deep-spiny wavy margin, cottony with hairs, especially beneath.
FLOWERS: Flowerheads 15–40 mm across, surrounded by numerous slender, stiffly pointed, shiny, yellow floral-bracts; florets in a dense disk, yellowish-brown.
FRUIT: Dry achenes embedded in the persistent disk of the flowerhead.

LOOKALIKES

Stemless Carline Thistle *Carlina acaulis*
A lower short-lived perennial, or a biennial, which is quite stemless. Leaves in a flat basal rosette, elliptic oblong, pinnately-lobed, with a spiny margin, sometimes downy beneath. Flowerheads resting on the ground in the middle of the leaf-rosettes, 35–60 mm across, surrounded by numerous silvery or pinkish, stiffly pointed floral-bracts; disk florets whitish to purplish-brown. Grassy and rocky mountain habitats; June–September. C and E France and S Germany southwards and eastwards.

Creeping Thistle
Cirsium arvense

Compositae/Asteraceae

One of the commonest thistles seen in the countryside and regarded by many farmers and gardeners as a pernicious weed. However, it is a handsome plant and attracts a wide variety of insects when in flower. In the autumn the characteristic fluffy seeds, 'thistle-down' wafts across the countryside in the slightest breeze.

NOTE:
Cirsium *and* Carduus *are much confused. The prime distinction is seen in the fruit pappus; in* Cirsium *the pappus hairs are feathery, while in* Carduus *they are simple.*

J
F
M
A
M
J
J
A
S
O
N
D

KEY FEATURES: Leaves extremely spiny. Stems not spiny or winged. Flowerheads numerous and relatively small. Floral-bracts closely overlapping, with a short spine tip.
HABITAT: Meadows, verges and other grassy places, arable and cultivated land, open woodland, on a variety of soils, but favouring fertile ones.
FREQUENCY: Common throughout, often forming extensive colonies; naturalised in the Faeroes and Iceland.
SEASON: June–September.
HABIT: A vigorous stoloniferous perennial, forming large patches, with erect stems to 1.2 m; stems somewhat cottony, usually branched but unwinged and non-spiny.
LEAVES: Alternate, pinnately-lobed, with a very spiny margin, the upper leaves unstalked, cottony beneath.
FLOWERS: Heads pale purple to lilac, small, 15–25 mm across, borne in branched clusters; floral-bracts usually purplish, closely overlapping, with a short spine tip.
FRUIT: A collection of achenes, each with a white feathery pappus.

LOOKALIKES

▶ **Spear Thistle** *Cirsium vulgare*
A non-stoloniferous biennial forming a large spiny
rosette in the first year. The stems have wide spiny
wings right to the top. Flowerheads purple, 20–40 mm
across; floral-bracts straight, with a yellowish spine.
Similar habitats to the Creeping Thistle; July–October.
A common weed throughout, except the far north.

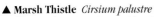

▲ **Marsh Thistle** *Cirsium palustre*
A tall biennial to 1.2 m. Stems with spiny wings right to the top. Flowerheads
purple, occasionally white, 10–20 mm across; floral-bracts purplish,
weakly spiny. Damp places, woodland clearings and margins, rough grassy
places, marshes and hedgerows; July–September. Throughout, except the
far north and Iceland.

▶ **Welted Thistle** *Carduus acanthoides*
A tall hairy biennial to 2 m. Stems winged and spiny to just below the
flowerheads. Flowerheads reddish-purple, 10–25 mm, solitary or
several together; floral bracts slightly spreading, weakly spined. Damp
meadows and woods, water margins, hedgerows; June–August.
S Sweden southwards; rare in N Scotland and much of Ireland.

Woolly Thistle

Cirsium eriophorum

Compositae/Asteraceae

A conspicuous thistle in the landscape, this handsome species has large woolly flowerheads and is very distinctive and unlikely to be confused with other thistles in the region. Like all thistles, the flowerheads are greatly attractive to a whole host of different insects, but particularly bees and butterflies.

NOTE:
The British plant is generally referable to subsp. britannicum.

J
F
M
A
M
J
J
A
S
O
N
D

KEY FEATURES: A bold, stout plant, forming a large leaf-rosette in the first year and flowering in the second. Stems unwinged and not spiny. Leaves deeply cut and very spiny. Flowerheads large, with the recurved, spine-tipped floral-bracts enveloped in cottony hairs.

HABITAT: Dry habitats, especially rough grassland, scrub, roadsides and embankments, on calcareous soils usually.

FREQUENCY: C and S Britain, Holland to Germany southwards; often rather local.

SEASON: July–September.

HABIT: A bold hairy biennial, to 1.5 m tall in flower, with a large leaf-rosette in the first season; stem stout, not winged or spiny, bristly.

LEAVES: Large and pinnately-lobed, with long rigid spines, white-cottony beneath.

FLOWERS: Large reddish-purple, solitary flowerheads, 25–50 mm across, with the floral-bracts recurved and spine-tipped, enveloped in cottony hairs.

FRUIT: A collection of achenes, each with a feathery pappus, shuttlecock-shaped.

LOOKALIKES

Melancholy Thistle
Cirsium heterophyllum (syn. *C. helenoides*)
A stout leafy perennial, patch-forming. Stems smooth, unwinged. Leaves large and flat, often unlobed, with a soft-prickly margin, white-cottony beneath. Flowerheads purple, rarely white, 35–50 mm across, solitary or in small clusters. Damp places, woodland, meadows and verges, usually on calcareous or base-rich soils; June–September. Through, except Belgium and Holland; naturalised in Iceland; absent from S Britain.

Meadow Thistle *Cirsium dissectum*
Rather like *C. eriophorum*, but a rhizomatous perennial. Leaves not deeply dissected, with a softly spiny margin. Flowerheads purple, 25–30 mm, usually solitary; floral-bracts not spreading, only the outer spine-tipped. Wet meadows and roadsides; June–August. C and S Britain, Ireland, Holland to Germany southwards; naturalised in Norway.

Tuberous Thistle *Cirsium tuberosum*
Perennial with smooth non-spiny stems. Leaves green on both surfaces, pinnately-lobed, with a softly spiny margin. Flowerheads long-stalked, purple, 20–30 mm across, solitary on long stalks; floral bracts erect, cottony below. Grassy places, especially in the hills, scrub, on calcareous soils; June–August. S Britain, France and Germany; naturalised in Belgium.

Musk Thistle

Carduus nutans

Also known as Nodding Thistle, this is a familiar plant of the summer landscape making a large and bold plant that is highly attractive to insects of various sorts. The plant gets its Latin name from the unusual nodding flowerheads which make it an easy thistle to identify.

J
F
M
A
M
J
J
A
S
O
N
D

KEY FEATURES: A stout, very prickly plant. Stems white-cottony, winged and spiny except beneath the flowerheads. Flowerheads nodding to half-nodding; floral-bracts long, spine-tipped and recurved.

HABITAT: Grassy places and arable land, roadsides and waste land.

FREQUENCY: S Sweden southwards; in Britain absent from N Scotland and rare in Ireland; naturalised in Norway.

SEASON: May–September.

HABIT: A tall biennial to 1.5 m, branched from the base, forming a large spiny rosette in the first year. Stems with spiny wings, except below the flowerheads.

LEAVES: Large deeply pinnately-lobed and very spiny, coolly on the raised veins.

FLOWERS: Bright reddish-purple, the heads 30–50 mm across, nodding to half-nodding, solitary or several together; floral-bracts narrow, spine-tipped and recurved.

FRUIT: A collection of achenes, each with a pappus of simple hairs.

LOOKALIKES

Welted Thistle *Carduus acanthoides*
Another large biennial, reaching as much as 2 m tall in flower. Stems erect and
branched, spiny-winged except immediately below the flowerheads. Leaves shallowly
pinnately-lobed, weakly spiny. Flowerheads reddish-purple, 10–25 mm across, solitary
or in small clusters; floral-bracts with a weak spine tip, slightly spreading. Rough
grassy places, especially meadows, roadsides, embankments and water margins;
June–August. S Sweden southwards; absent from N Scotland, and in Ireland,
naturalised in Norway.

Common Knapweed
Centaurea nigra

Compositae/Asteraceae

A delightful summer flower greatly sought out by both bees and butterflies. Another common name for the plant is Hardheads, which aptly describes the flowerheads, especially in bud.

NOTE:
The commonest species of Centaurea *in most of the region. Hybridises freely with* C. jacea.

J
F
M
A
M
J
J
A
S
O
N
D

KEY FEATURES: A rough-hairy plant with stems characteristically thickened below the flowerheads. Leaves simple, somewhat toothed or untoothed. Flowerheads relatively small but numerous, the floral-bracts very closely overlapping, with a black, deeply fringed, top.

HABITAT: Rough grassy places, embankments, verges and hedgerows, cliffs, on a wide variety of soils.

FREQUENCY: Common throughout most of the British Isles, and on the Continent from C Scandinavia southwards.

SEASON: June–September.

HABIT: A rough-hairy perennial, with erect often branched stems, to 1 m.

LEAVES: Alternate, the lower elliptical to oval, somewhat toothed and stalked, but the upper unstalked and generally untoothed, rather grey-green.

FLOWERS: Heads purple, 20–40 mm across, solitary or in branched clusters, the florets all more or less equal in size; floral-bracts very tightly overlapping, with a black, fringed, upper half which conceals the lower half.

FRUIT: An achene, without a pappus.

LOOKALIKES

Brown Knapweed *Centaurea jacea*
Similar to Common Knapweed, but flowerheads smaller, 10–20 mm across, purple, occasionally white, with the outer florets longer than the inner; floral-bracts with a pale brown, irregularly fringed, margin. Rough grassy, places and open woods, waste ground; August–September. Throughout, except the far north.

Greater Knapweed *Centaurea scabiosa*
A robust perennial to 1.5 m, with all the leaves grey-green and pinnately-lobed. Flowerheads large, 30–50 mm across, purple, with the outer florets considerably longer than the inner; floral-bracts with a brown or black 'eyelash' fringed margin. Similar habitats; July–September. Through, except the far north and Iceland.

Perennial Cornflower *Centaurea montana*
A patch-forming rhizomatous, cottony-grey perennial with oval or oblong, untoothed and unlobed leaves, to 80 cm tall, generally less. Flowerheads violet or blue, occasionally white, 60–80 mm across, with the outer florets much larger than the inner; floral bracts with a blackish-brown fringed margin. Dry open places, on calcareous soils; June–August. Belgium and Germany southwards; casual or naturalised from gardens elsewhere, particularly in Britain and Finland.

Cornflower *Centaurea cyanus*
A slender erect annual to 80 cm, with grey-cottony, generally unlobed, leaves. Flowerheads blue or violet-blue, occasionally white or purple, 15–30 mm across, with the outer florets much larger than the inner. Arable land, disturbed and waste places; June–August. Throughout, except the far north, often casual and generally declining; rare in Britain, but widely cultivated.

213

Devil's-bit Scabious

Succisa pratensis

Dipsacaceae

A pretty scabious-like plant found almost throughout the region. It differs principally from *Scabiosa* in the 4- not 5-lobed florets and in the non-membranous extension of the epicalyx. Like the scabious, the flowers are eagerly sought by both bees and butterflies.

NOTE:
Readily mistaken for Sheep's-bit, Jasione montana *(see* opposite*), a member of the Campanulaceae, which prefers drier habitats and has more rounded paler blue flowerheads with the style and not the stamens protruding.*

J
F
M
A
M
J
J
A
S
O
N
D

KEY FEATURES: Leaves generally untoothed. Flowers in rounded heads, with the outer florets slightly larger than the inner, with the stamens protruding; epicalyx present.
HABITAT: Damp places on calcareous soils, particularly meadows, rocky grassland and stream-margins.
FREQUENCY: Throughout, often common and gregarious.
SEASON: July–October.
HABIT: A tufted, hairy perennial to 1 m tall, with slender, moderately branched stems.
LEAVES: Leaves opposite, the basal oval and untoothed, often blotched with purple, the upper smaller and often lanceolate, sometimes slightly toothed.
FLOWERS: Heads dark violet-blue to lilac, occasionally pink or whitish, solitary, rounded, 15–25 mm across; florets almost equal in size, sometimes all female.
FRUIT: A small achene with a persistent papery calyx.

214

Sheep's-bit *Jasione montana*
In the Campanulaceae but with a similar look to Devil's-bit Scabious. A smaller annual or biennial plant with alternate, lanceolate to narrow-oblong leaves that usually have a wavy margin. Flowerheads pale blue to pink or white, rounded 10–18 mm across, with the florets of equal size; styles protruding, not the stamens. Dry rough grassy places, heaths, rocky places and cliffs; May–August. Throughout, except parts of the far north, the Faeroes and Iceland; local in much of Britain, except more widespread in the east and south.

Jasione perennis (syn. *J. laevis*)
A perennial with numerous non-flowering shoots and narrow-oblong leaves; bracts toothed. Flowerheads always blue. Mountain habitats, dry meadows in particular. Belgium, France and Germany; naturalised in Finland.

Field Scabious
Knautia arvensis

Dipsacaceae

A popular wild flower of high summer and early autumn, whose flowerheads are highly attractive to butterflies as well as bees. The plant has acquired a host of local names including Blue Bonnets, Lady's Pincushion and Pincushion Flower and these all describe the flowerheads rather well.

NOTE:
The florets may be hermaphrodite or female, the female flowerheads tending to be somewhat smaller.

J
F
M
A
M
J
J
A
S
O
N
D

KEY FEATURES: An elegant plant with slender erect stems. Leaves pinnately-lobed. Flowerheads rather flat and pincushion-like, with the outer florets rather larger than the inner; florets 4-lobed.

HABITAT: Meadows, open woodland and, verges and embankments, generally on dry calcareous soils.

FREQUENCY: Throughout, except the far north; naturalised in the Faeroes and Iceland. season: July–September.

HABIT: A tufted, hairy perennial to 1 m tall; stems slender, branched above, often with purple spots or blotches.

LEAVES: The basal in rosettes, the other paired; most leaves pinnately-lobed, although the uppermost pairs may be unlobed.

FLOWERS: Variable in colour from pale lilac to bluish-violet, occasionally purple, 20–40 mm across, rather flat heads with the outer florets rather larger than the inner; florets 4-lobed with the stamens protruding.

FRUIT: An achene with a persistent papery calyx.

LOOKALIKES

Wood Scabious *Knautia dipsacifolia* (syn. *K. sylvatica*)
Similar to *K. arvensis*, but a more robust plant to 1.5 m with
bright green leaves that are toothed not lobed. Flowerheads
bluish-violet to lilac, 25–40 mm across. Shady places, woodland
and woodland margins; June–September. Mountains of France
and Germany.

Small Scabious *Scabiosa columbaria* ▲
Very similar to *Knautia*, but the florets 5-lobed. A perennial to 80 cm tall
with the upper leaves finely 2-pinnately-lobed, the lower lobed or unlobed.
Flowerheads bluish-lilac, 20–40 mm across, the outer florets slightly
larger than the inner. Achene with a membranous funnel on top. Dry
grassy places on calcareous soils; June–August. S Sweden southwards;
in Britain absent from N Scotland, and not in Ireland.

Scabiosa canescens ▶
Similar to *S. columbaria*, but lower leaves all lanceolate, toothed but unlobed.
Flowerheads blue or lilac, 15–25 mm across, the outer florets twice the size of
the inner. Similar habitats; July–September. Continental Europe from S Sweden
southwards.

Goat's-beard
Tragopogon pratensis

Compositae/Asteraceae

The large 'clock' fruits of the Goat's-beard are a characteristic feature of the verges and fields during the summer. It is a fascinating plant, more beautiful in fruit than in flower. The flowerheads open in the early morning and are shut by midday, hence another local name for the plant is Johnny-go-to-bed-at-noon.

J
F
M
A
M
J
J
A
S
O
N
D

KEY FEATURES: Plant with milky juices or latex, when cut. Leaves alternate, long and tapering, untoothed. Flowerheads dandelion-like but surrounded by a halo of soft, pointed floral-bracts. Fruit a large silvery 'clock'.

HABITAT: Grassy places, cultivated land, verges, occasionally on sand dunes.

FREQUENCY: Throughout, except the far north; sometimes abundant.

SEASON: June–July.

HABIT: A slender, generally hairless annual or short-lived perennial, often with unbranched stems, to 75 cm tall.

LEAVES: Alternate, rather fleshy, grey-green, narrow-lanceolate, tapered to a fine tip, channelled, the margin not toothed; base half-clasping the stem.

FLOWERS: Heads pale yellow, 18–40 mm across, closed by midday, surrounded by long leaf-like floral-bracts which are longer than the florets; inner florets shorter than outer.

FRUIT: A large 'clock' to 12 cm across, composed of numerous elliptical achenes each with an attached 'parachute'.

LOOKALIKES

Tragopogon dubium

Like *T. pratensis*, but a shorter plant with the flower-stalks much expanded immediately below the flowerhead; floral bracts 8–12. Dry woodland and woodland margins. E France and Germany; naturalised in Belgium.

Chicory *Cichorium intybus*

A large tall perennial to 1.2 m, often less, producing white latex when cut. Basal leaves pinnately-lobed to deeply toothed, short-stalked, but the upper leaves small, lanceolate, toothed or untoothed and with stem-clasping bases. Flowerheads clear bright blue, occasionally pink or white, 24–40 mm across, borne in branched spikes, opening in bright weather only; floral bracts shorter than the florets. Rough grassy places, field boundaries, verges and waysides, waste ground; July–October. Throughout, except the far north, probably naturalised in much of the north of its range.

Compositae/Asteraceae

Smooth Sow Thistle
Sonchus oleraceus

A common weed of cultivation and waste places which is also known locally as Milk Thistle, and Silver and Gold due to the seeds that change colour as they ripen from greeny-yellow to brown. The 'silver' being the silky pappus attached to each seed. In some places this plant becomes an abundant weed, although being an annual it is relatively easy to eradicate.

NOTE:
Plants found on impoverished or very dry soils can be very depauperate.

J	
F	
M	
A	
M	
J	❖
J	❖ 🌰
A	❖ 🌰
S	🌰
O	🌰
N	
D	

KEY FEATURES: A rather succulent plant producing white latex when cut. Plant more or less hairless with pinnately-lobed leaves. Leaf-margin softly prickly. Flowerheads dandelion-like, but clustered. Fruit a small 'clock'.

HABITAT: Cultivated, waste and disturbed ground on fertile, slightly acid to calcareous soils.

FREQUENCY: Common almost throughout, except the far north, sometimes abundant.

SEASON: June–August.

HABIT: A tall, more or less hairless, annual with an erect stem to 1.5 m, though often less; stems pale green, angled, sometimes branched.

LEAVES: Alternate, deeply pinnately-lobed, clasping the stem with triangular basal lobes; margin softly prickly.

FLOWERS: Flowerheads golden-yellow, 20–25 mm across, dandelion-like, borne in lax clusters; inner floral-bracts narrower and much longer than the outer.

FRUIT: A small white 'clock', each achene with an attached parachute-like pappus.

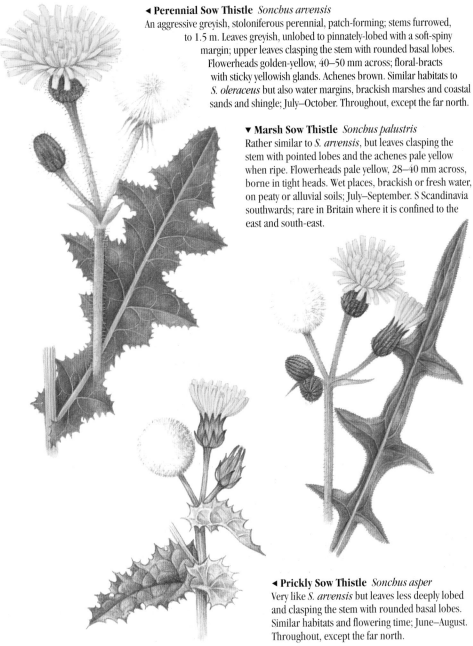

◄ **Perennial Sow Thistle** *Sonchus arvensis*
An aggressive greyish, stoloniferous perennial, patch-forming; stems furrowed, to 1.5 m. Leaves greyish, unlobed to pinnately-lobed with a soft-spiny margin; upper leaves clasping the stem with rounded basal lobes. Flowerheads golden-yellow, 40–50 mm across; floral-bracts with sticky yellowish glands. Achenes brown. Similar habitats to *S. oleraceus* but also water margins, brackish marshes and coastal sands and shingle; July–October. Throughout, except the far north.

▼ **Marsh Sow Thistle** *Sonchus palustris*
Rather similar to *S. arvensis*, but leaves clasping the stem with pointed lobes and the achenes pale yellow when ripe. Flowerheads pale yellow, 28–40 mm across, borne in tight heads. Wet places, brackish or fresh water, on peaty or alluvial soils; July–September. S Scandinavia southwards; rare in Britain where it is confined to the east and south-east.

◄ **Prickly Sow Thistle** *Sonchus asper*
Very like *S. arvensis* but leaves less deeply lobed and clasping the stem with rounded basal lobes. Similar habitats and flowering time; June–August. Throughout, except the far north.

Prickly Lettuce
Lactuca serriola

Compositae/Asteraceae

An interesting plant that is slightly thistle-like but bears panicles of small dandelion-type flowers. The upper leaves are held in a vertical plane that is generally orientated north to south, a curious feature that makes this an easy plant to identify. It is probably a native to NW Europe but has spread considerably in recent years.

J
F
M
A
M
J
J
A
S
O
N
D

KEY FEATURES: Leaves prickly along the margins and midrib. Upper leaves vertical and clasping the stem, Flowers small and dandelion-like. Fruit a small 'clock'.

HABITAT: Disturbed and waste land, sand dunes, on open sites.

FREQUENCY: Throughout except the far north and Ireland; in Britain confined mainly to England and S Wales.

SEASON: July–September.

HABIT: A tall greyish annual or biennial, to 2 m, though often less; stems stiff, hairless or somewhat bristly, branched only in the inflorescence.

LEAVES: Oblong shallowly pinnately-lobed, with a bristly margin and along the midrib beneath; upper leaves held vertically, clasping the stem with unstalked bases.

FLOWERS: Pale yellow, 11–13 mm across, dandelion-like, borne in large pyramidal panicles.

FRUIT: A small 'clock'; each achene with a white pappus like a tiny parachute.

LOOKALIKES

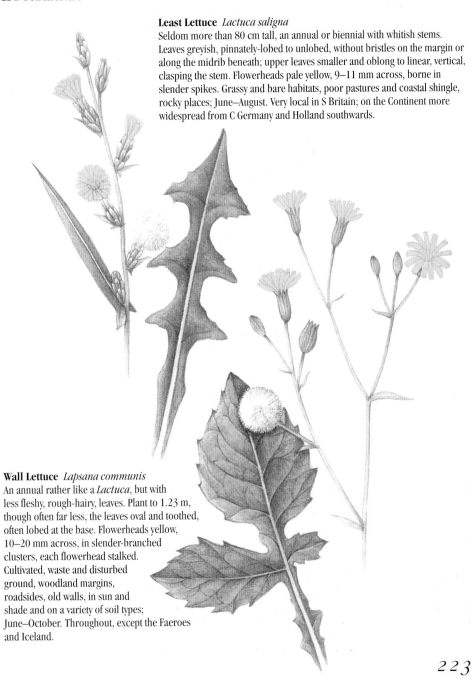

Least Lettuce *Lactuca saligna*
Seldom more than 80 cm tall, an annual or biennial with whitish stems.
Leaves greyish, pinnately-lobed to unlobed, without bristles on the margin or
along the midrib beneath; upper leaves smaller and oblong to linear, vertical,
clasping the stem. Flowerheads pale yellow, 9–11 mm across, borne in
slender spikes. Grassy and bare habitats, poor pastures and coastal shingle,
rocky places; June–August. Very local in S Britain; on the Continent more
widespread from C Germany and Holland southwards.

Wall Lettuce *Lapsana communis*
An annual rather like a *Lactuca*, but with
less fleshy, rough-hairy, leaves. Plant to 1.23 m,
though often far less, the leaves oval and toothed,
often lobed at the base. Flowerheads yellow,
10–20 mm across, in slender-branched
clusters, each flowerhead stalked.
Cultivated, waste and disturbed
ground, woodland margins,
roadsides, old walls, in sun and
shade and on a variety of soil types;
June–October. Throughout, except the Faeroes
and Iceland.

223

Dandelion

Taraxacum officinale

Compositae/Asteraceae

F ew plants are as familiar as the common Dandelion. Thoroughly at home in a wide variety of habitats it must be one of the commonest flowers in the region. The common name comes from the French *dent de lion* or lion's tooth, a reference to the typical jagged leaves. The charming fruitheads, or 'clocks', are known to nearly every child who delights in blowing the seeds away.

NOTE:
The genus Taraxacum *is a formidable one, with in excess of 200 microspecies recognised in Britain alone.*

KEY FEATURES: A rosette-leaved, rather fleshy plant; stemless and producing white latex when cut. Leaves with jagged margins. Flowerheads solitary, borne on leafless, hollow scapes. Fruit a 'clock'.

HABITAT: Grassy places, both mown and unmown, cultivated land, verges and waysides, often abundant.

FREQUENCY: Throughout, usually gregarious, sometimes dominant in a meadow.

SEASON: March–October.

HABIT: A perennial with one or several leaf-rosettes at ground level, to 40 cm tall in flower, often less.

LEAVES: Bright green, horizontal to erect, winged, coarsely lobed usually and with a lobed stalk; lobes backward-facing, often somewhat toothed.

FLOWERS: Mid-yellow, 25–50 mm across, solitary on long fleshy, yet hollow, scapes; all florets rayed, the outer longer than the inner, usually purple-striped beneath. Floral-bracts dark bluish-green, the outer recurved but the inner erect.

FRUIT: A white 'clock', each achene with a typical stalked parachute on the top, which carries the fruit through the air on the slightest breeze.

J
F
M
A
M
J
J
A
S
O
N
D

LOOKALIKES

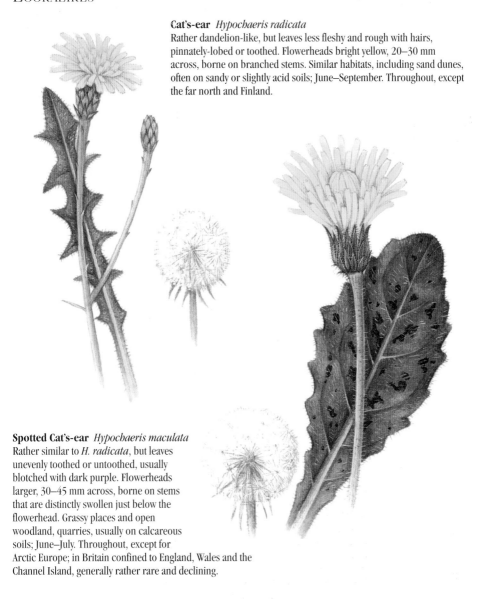

Cat's-ear *Hypochaeris radicata*
Rather dandelion-like, but leaves less fleshy and rough with hairs, pinnately-lobed or toothed. Flowerheads bright yellow, 20–30 mm across, borne on branched stems. Similar habitats, including sand dunes, often on sandy or slightly acid soils; June–September. Throughout, except the far north and Finland.

Spotted Cat's-ear *Hypochaeris maculata*
Rather similar to *H. radicata*, but leaves unevenly toothed or untoothed, usually blotched with dark purple. Flowerheads larger, 30–45 mm across, borne on stems that are distinctly swollen just below the flowerhead. Grassy places and open woodland, quarries, usually on calcareous soils; June–July. Throughout, except for Arctic Europe; in Britain confined to England, Wales and the Channel Island, generally rather rare and declining.

Compositae/Asteraceae

Smooth Hawk's-beard
Crepis capillaris

The genus *Crepis* is a large one with more than 20 species in the region, most of which look rather similar. They are a bit like *Taraxacum* in their basal leaf-rosettes, but they tend to have smaller flowers borne on branched leafy stems.

KEY FEATURES: Leaves shiny, the basal in a rosette. Stem branched. Flowers dandelion-like; florets all rayed. Floral-bracts in 2 series, the outer much shorter.

HABITAT: Grassy places, verges, heaths, waste places, sometimes on old walls.

FREQUENCY: Throughout Britain; on the Continent from Holland and Germany southwards, but naturalised in S Scandinavia.

SEASON: June–November.

HABIT: An annual or biennial with a branched, erect stem to 75 cm tall, hairless or slightly hairy.

LEAVES: Mostly in a basal rosette, shiny green, lanceolate, toothed to pinnately-lobed, rather dandelion-like, stalked; stem leave similar but smaller and sparser and clasping the stem with pointed basal lobes.

FLOWERS: Heads yellow, often reddish beneath, 10–15 mm across, borne in lax, branched clusters; floral-bracts lanceolate, downy.

FRUIT: A 'clock', the achenes with a white shuttlecock-shaped pappus.

J
F
M
A
M
J
J
A
S
O
N
D

LOOKALIKES

Marsh Hawk's-beard *Crepis paludosa*
A rather taller, more leafy rhizomatous perennial. Leaves dark green, elliptical, sharply toothed and clasping the stem. Flowerheads deep yellow to dull orange, 15–25 mm across; floral-bracts with sticky black glands. Damp and shady habitats; July–September. Throughout, except the far north.

Crepis tectorum
A slightly hairy annual with leafy stems. Basal leaves few, toothed to pinnately-lobed; stem leaves linear to narrow-lanceolate. Flowerheads plain yellow, 15–25 mm across; floral-bracts linear-lanceolate, hairy. Dry grassy and sandy habitats; June–September. Continental Europe, except the far north.

Mouse-ear Hawkweed
Hieracium pilosella (syn. *Pilosella officinarum*)
Like a hawk's-beard, but with a brown brittle pappus to the achenes. A white-haired stoloniferous perennial with elliptical, untoothed leaves, white-felted beneath. Flowerheads lemon-yellow, 20–30 mm across, solitary on leafless scapes. Grassy and waste places, hillslopes, sand dunes, old walls. June–September. Throughout, except the far north.

Orange Hawkweed *Hieracium aurantiacum*
A distinctive patch-forming stoloniferous perennial with blackish hairs. Flowerheads orange-brown to orange-red, 13–15 mm across, in tight clusters. Grassy and waste places, cultivated land; June–August. Scandinavia, Germany and France, but naturalised widely in Britain and Ireland, Belgium, Holland, Denmark and Iceland.

Ramsons

Allium ursinum

Alliaceae

The alternative vernacular names of Wild Garlic, Stink Bombs or Stinking Nanny perhaps gives a better impression of this strong-smelling woodland plant that can carpet the ground in some places, inhabiting similar places to the Bluebell (*see* p.230), but rarely growing intermixed with them. Despite the very strong stench of garlic, Ramsons are quite mild flavoured and have been used widely in the past; the leaves especially were used to flavour stews and soups, sandwiches and salads.

NOTE:
In all alliums the flower umbels are enclosed in bud in a membranous spathe which eventually splits to reveal the flowers within.

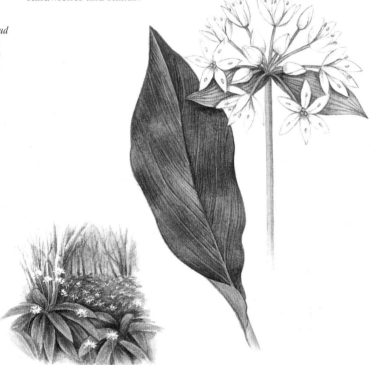

J
F
M
A
M
J
J
A
S
O
N
D

KEY FEATURES: Plants with 2–3 large flat elliptical leaves. Flowers borne in distinctive heads or umbels; each flower star-shaped with 6 petal-like segments (tepals) and 6 stamens. Fruit a 3-parted capsule.
HABITAT: Woods, scrub and hedgerows.
FREQUENCY: Locally abundant, from S Scandinavia and Scotland southwards.
SEASON: April–June.
HABIT: Bulbous plant with 2–3 basal leaves when mature; to 45 cm tall in flower.
LEAVES: Narrow to broad-elliptic, flat, dark green, with parallel veins, smelling powerfully of garlic when crushed.
FLOWERS: Borne in dense rounded umbels at the end of leafless 2–3-angled scapes; flowers white, starry, 12–20 mm across; tepals all similar and elliptical, pointed.
FRUIT: A small 3-lobed capsule containing numerous seeds.

Triquetrous Leek *Allium triquetrum*
Leaves 2–3, linear, triangular in cross-section. Flowers nodding in a 1-sided umbel, narrow bell-shaped, 10–18 mm long, white with green mid-veins. Naturalised in W and SW Britain and S Ireland from the Mediterranean region.

Few-flowered Leek *Allium paradoxum*
Similar to *A. triquetrum*, but leaf solitary and strap-shaped and flowers broader bells, few to an umbel and often partly replaced by bulbils. April–May. Naturalised in Britain, Denmark and Germany southwards; from the Caucasus and Iran.

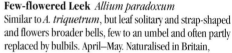

Crow Garlic *Allium vineale*
Like *A. paradoxum*, but leaves 2–4, linear and almost cylindrical and flowers pink, red or greenish-white, 2–4.5 mm long, mixed with bulbils; stamens protruding. Dry grassy and rocky habitats through, apart from the far north; June–August.

Chives *Allium schoenoprasum*
Forms dense tufts of slender cylindrical leaves, Flowers narrow bell-shaped, 7–15 mm long, lilac or pale purple with a deeper midvein to the tepals, borne in dense rounded heads. Cultivated and wild grassy and rocky places; June–August. Throughout, except the Faeroes and Iceland.

Sand Leek *Allium scorodoprasum*
Plant generally solitary with 3–5 linear, flat leaves and dense rounded heads of pale lilac to deep purple flowers; flowers bell-shaped, 5–8 mm long, with protruding stamens. Sandy and grassy places, hedgebanks; June–August. Throughout except the far north; absent from S England.

229

Liliaceae/Hyacinthaceae

Bluebell

Hyacinthoides non-scripta

(syn. *Endymion non-scriptus*, *Scilla non-scripta*)

O ne of the most popular and endearing of wild flowers, the Bluebell has a surprisingly limited range in the wild being primarily associated with areas close to the Atlantic and away from the inner Continent. A woodland coloured misty blue by Bluebells in the late spring is an unforgettable sight and one to rival the sheets of colour seen in the Mediterranean and other parts of the world. In Scotland the Bluebell is *Campanula rotundifolia* (*see* p.94), while the plant in question is the 'Wild Hyacinth'. It is scarcely surprising that this charming plant has been much written about over the centuries.

NOTE:
Widely cultivated in gardens where it hybridises with the Spanish Bluebell, Hyacinthoides hispanica *(see opposite); these hybrids occasionally become naturalised in the wild, especially along hedgerows.*

KEY FEATURES: Leaves linear, all basal. Flowers nodding, borne on long leafless scapes. Corolla (or perianth) 6-parted, part-tubular, nodding. Bracts 2 per flower.
HABITAT: Primarily deciduous woodland and heaths, but venturing into open grassy places and along hedgerows and even on cliff tops (especially close to the sea).
FREQUENCY: Widespread in Britain and Ireland, France, Holland and Belgium; naturalised in Germany and parts of Scandinavia.
SEASON: April–June.
HABIT: A hairless bulbous perennial with basal leaves, to 50 cm tall in flower.
LEAVES: Linear, deep bright green and rather succulent, 3–6 per bulb, keeled beneath, generally arching over the ground at maturity.
FLOWERS: Violet-blue pendent, tubular-bells, 14–20 mm long, rarely white or pinkish, borne in a 1-sided raceme, fragrant; each flower with a pair of bluish bracts; perianth of 6 tepals with 6 stamens inside and the ovary.
FRUIT: An erect, 3-parted capsule, containing many black seeds.

J
F
M
A
M
J
J
A
S
O
N
D

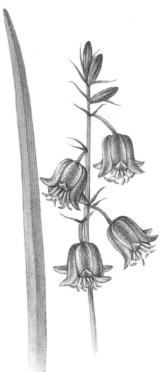

Spanish Bluebell
Hyacinthoides hispanica (syn. *Endymion hispanicus*)
Similar to the Bluebell, but often forming large clumps, with broader leaves, generally up to 8 per bulb. Flowers blue, occasionally pink or white, broad bells, 12–20 mm long, borne in a stout raceme, not 1-sided not drooping at the apex. Shaded habitats and cultivated ground; May–June. Naturalised from gardens in Britain and France, perhaps elsewhere.

Spring Squill *Scilla verna*
A small plant not more than 15 cm tall, with 2–7 thread-like leaves. Flowers violet-blue, rarely white, star-like, 10–16 mm across, borne in short, often few-flowered, racemes, sometimes several racemes per bulb; each flower with a single bract. Rocky and grassy places, particularly sea cliffs and in the mountains; April–June. W Britain, E Ireland, the Faeroes, W France and Norway.

Common Solomon's-seal

Polygonatum multiflorum

Liliaceae/Convallariaceae

A popular garden plant, but a native in many parts of the region. It is not a particularly showy plant but a fascinating one with its arched stems that gradually unfurl to reveal the leaves which slant upwards whilst, at the same time, the clusters of flowers droop demurely below.

NOTE:
The usual Solomon's seal of gardens is a hybrid between P. multiflorum *and* P. odoratum.

J
F
M
A
M
J
J
A
S
O
N
D

KEY FEATURES: Plant with stiff leafy stems bearing alternate leaves; leaves with parallel veins. Flowers in small clusters held below the arched stems, tubular-bell-shaped, with 6 short lobes; stamens 6 hidden within the flower. Fruit a small berry.
HABITAT: Woodland and scrub, usually on calcareous soils; lowland or mountains.
FREQUENCY: Throughout except for the far north and Ireland.
SEASON: May–June.
HABIT: A rhizomatous, hairless perennial, with stiff leafy stems to 80 cm that are usually arched or oblique, round and smooth.
LEAVES: Alternate, all on the stem, elliptical to lanceolate, plain green, with rib-like parallel veins; unstalked; margin untoothed.
FLOWERS: In drooping clusters of 2–6, held close to the stem beneath the foliage, tubular bells 9–20 mm long, greenish-white, tipped by 6 short lobes, unscented.
FRUIT: A small berry, green at first but bluish-black when ripe.

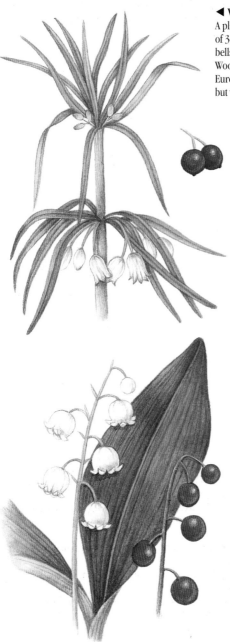

◀ **Whorled Solomon's-seal** *Polygonatum verticillatum*
A plant with distinctive linear or lanceolate leaves borne in whorls
of 3–8 up the erect stem. Flowers solitary or 2–3, greenish-white
bells, 5–10 mm long. Berry red at first but becoming dark purple.
Woods, scrub and rocky places; June–July. Throughout Continental
Europe, except the far north; in Britain rare and confined to Perth,
but widely cultivated.

▲ **Angular Solomon's-seal**
Polygonatum odoratum
Like *P. multiflorum*, but a shorter plant with angled
stems. Flowers solitary or paired, scented, not constricted
in the middle. Similar habitats and flowering time.
Continental Europe north to S Sweden; in W Britain and
the Inner Hebrides.

◀ **Lily-of-the-valley** *Convallaria majalis*
A popular and widely cultivated plant forming patches,
each short stem bearing a pair of dull green, elliptical
leaves. The scapes of highly scented flowers arise from
ground level to the same height as the leaves and are
partially hidden by them; flowers white, rounded bells,
5–9 mm across, drooping 1-sided racemes. Woods,
scrub, mountain meadows, occasionally in rocky places;
May–June. Throughout, except the far north and Iceland.

Snowdrop
Galanthus nivalis

Amaryllidaceae

The Snowdrop is one of the most endearing of wild flowers with a long association in cultivation. It is so much at home in our woodlands and churchyards that is often assumed to be a native plant; however, its origins are almost certainly further east in Europe. It is a harbinger of spring and, like the Winter Aconite, among the first flowers to brave the New Year. In some areas the Snowdrops can be found in countless numbers and are a truly breathtaking sight.

NOTE:
Two other species, G. elwesii *and* G. plicatus, *are found naturalised in the area, especially in churchyards. They sometimes hybridise.*

KEY FEATURES: Plants with 2 basal leaves. Flowers solitary and pendent, with 3 longer outer sepals and 3 short inner, notched petals. Ovary located outside at the base of the flower.

HABITAT: Damp deciduous woodland, copses, meadows, streamsides, verges, churchyards, and abandoned cultivation.

FREQUENCY: France and Germany; widely naturalised in Britain, Holland and Scandinavia.

SEASON: January–March, occasionally later.

HABIT: Clump-forming hairless bulbous perennial; each bulb bearing 2 leaves and a solitary flower borne on a long slender scape, to 20 cm tall at the most, often less.

LEAVES: Paired, grey-green and rather fleshy, linear, only partly developed at flowering time.

FLOWERS: Solitary and pendent white, 12–25 mm long, the outer tepals (sepals) oval and unmarked, the inner (petals) half the length, with a notched end with a green crescent towards the tip; scape with a spathe just below, and arching over, the flower.

FRUIT: A 3-parted capsule, containing a number of seeds.

J
F
M
A
M
J
J
A
S
O
N
D

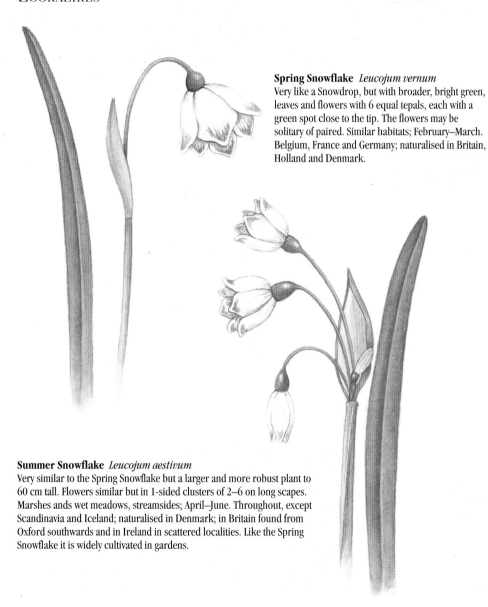

Spring Snowflake *Leucojum vernum*
Very like a Snowdrop, but with broader, bright green, leaves and flowers with 6 equal tepals, each with a green spot close to the tip. The flowers may be solitary of paired. Similar habitats; February–March. Belgium, France and Germany; naturalised in Britain, Holland and Denmark.

Summer Snowflake *Leucojum aestivum*
Very similar to the Spring Snowflake but a larger and more robust plant to 60 cm tall. Flowers similar but in 1-sided clusters of 2–6 on long scapes. Marshes ands wet meadows, streamsides; April–June. Throughout, except Scandinavia and Iceland; naturalised in Denmark; in Britain found from Oxford southwards and in Ireland in scattered localities. Like the Spring Snowflake it is widely cultivated in gardens.

Bee Orchid

Ophrys apifera

Orchidaceae

*O**phrys** is an extraordinary genus of plants in which the lip of the flower is elaborated and often intricately patterned, often mimicking the bodies of insects or spiders. These bizarre flowers are fascinating to observe close to. Relatively few species are to be found in western and northern Europe, whereas in the Mediterranean region they have proliferated in profusion.

NOTE: *Plants are often unpredictable from year to year, appearing in large numbers in one locality some years and few the next. Most orchids are protected and must not be picked.*

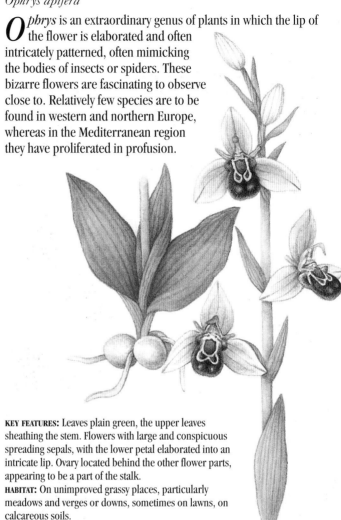

KEY FEATURES: Leaves plain green, the upper leaves sheathing the stem. Flowers with large and conspicuous spreading sepals, with the lower petal elaborated into an intricate lip. Ovary located behind the other flower parts, appearing to be a part of the stalk.

HABITAT: On unimproved grassy places, particularly meadows and verges or downs, sometimes on lawns, on calcareous soils.

FREQUENCY: C and S Britain, Belgium, France and Germany; generally local but sometimes in large colonies.

SEASON: June–July.

HABIT: A tuberous perennial with a basal rosette of leaves that first emerges in the autumn and a solitary erect stem to 45 cm tall.

LEAVES: All plain green and somewhat shiny, hairless, the basal and lower lanceolate, the stem leaves sheathing.

FLOWERS: Bee-like, generally 2–7 in a lax spike; sepals spreading, elliptical, pink or purplish, as long as the lip; lateral petals short and pinkish-green; lip (the lower petal) 10–13 mm long, reddish-brown, with a yellowish pattern enclosing a shield-shaped zone, with 2 basal furry lobes.

FRUIT: A narrow-oblong, 3-parted capsule containing very many tiny dust-like seeds.

J
F
M
A
M
J
J
A
S
O
N
D

Fly Orchid *Ophrys insectifera*
A slender more elegant plant than the Bee Orchid with narrow-lanceolate shiny leaves. Flowers in a long narrow spike, with spreading green petals and a fly-like lip 9–10 mm long; lip deep violet brown, 3-lobed, the large central lobe notched at the tip and with a small mirror-like pale violet-blue zone in the centre. Woods, coppices, fens and rough grassy places; May–June. Throughout, except the far north and Iceland; rare in Ireland and confined primarily to the Burren, and absent from N England and Scotland.

Early Spider Orchid *Ophrys sphegodes*
Similar to the Bee Orchid, but basal leaves broad-lanceolate. Flowers with yellowish-green sepals and lateral petals; lip spider-like, a similar size but pale to dark brown or blackish-brown, with an X- or H-shaped bluish-violet pattern in the centre. Short turf, roadsides and rocky places, embankments, in exposed sites, on calcareous soils; April–June. SE Britain, Belgium, France and Germany; always local. Rare and protected in Britain.

Early Purple Orchid

Orchis mascula

Orchidaceae

The true orchids, *Orchis*, have far less bizarre, and often more brightly coloured, flowers than *Ophrys*. The flowers still have a lip that can be intricately shaped and patterned. The Early Purple Orchid is a handsome plant and one of the commonest orchids seen in the region, often flowering in woods at the same time as the Bluebell (*see* p.30). *Orchis* means testicles and refers to the pair of swollen underground tubers that support and nourish the plant from season to season.

NOTE:
In the flowers of all members of the orchid family the pollen is usually concentrated into two regular masses or pollinia.

KEY FEATURES: Leaves shiny deep green, usually with prominent purple-black blotches. Flowers with a large lip and erect lateral sepals, the upper sepal and lateral petals forming a hood; spur present. Ovary located below the other flower parts and appearing to be a part of the flower-stalk.
HABITAT: Deciduous woodland, scrub, grassy places, verges and banks.
FREQUENCY: Throughout, except Iceland and the far north; often local but sometimes forming large colonies.
SEASON: April–June.
HABIT: An erect, hairless perennial, to 50 cm tall, though often less, with most of the leaves in a basal rosette; stem solitary and erect.
LEAVES: Purple-spotted, the basal 3–5, narrow-oblong, shiny deep green, the upper leaves 2–3, closely sheathing the stem.
FLOWERS: Borne in oblong spikes, purple, occasionally pinkish or white, with an unpleasant tom-cat smell; lateral sepals erect and wing-like, while the upper sepal and petals form a hood over the fertile parts of the flower; lip 6–8 mm long, diamond-shaped, shallowly 3-lobed, with a few spots in the paler or whitish central part, spurred behind.
FRUIT: A narrow-oblong 3-parted capsule, containing countless tiny, dust-like seeds.

J
F
M
A
M
J
J
A
S
O
N
D

LOOKALIKES

Green-winged Orchid *Orchis morio*
Similar to the Early Purple Orchid and sometimes mistaken for it, but the leaves are always unspotted, and the all the sepals as well as the lateral petals form a close, generally green-veined, hood. Flowers generally more variable in colour from purple to purplish-violet, to reddish, pinkish or white, but with the lateral sepals generally green-veined. Grassy places, open scrub, abandoned quarries or sand pits. May–June. Throughout, except the far north; absent from N Scotland.

Lady Orchid *Orchis purpurea*
A more robust orchid with plain, shiny green leaves, to 70 cm tall, often less. Flowers in large oblong spikes, the sepals and lateral petals forming a close brownish-purple hood and with a white or pale pink, purple-dotted, lip; lip 10–15 mm long, lobed, with 2 narrow 'arms' and 2 broader 'legs'. Woodland and scrub, occasionally on grassy slopes or road verges; May–June. S Britain (rare and protected), Denmark and Germany southwards.

Burnt-tip Orchid *Orchis ustulata*
Like a scaled down version of the Lady Orchid, rarely more than 15 cm tall. Flowers deep brownish-purple or maroon in bud, the hood paling somewhat; lip 4–8 mm long, white or pale pink with purple spots. Grassy habitats and open scrub, on calcareous soils, often in hilly or mountain regions; May–June. S Sweden southwards; in Britain from Cumbria southwards but very local and declining.

Pyramidal Orchid

Anacamptis pyramidalis

Orchidaceae

T he Pyramidal Orchid is very closely related to *Orchis*, differing in the non-sheathing stem leaves and the long slender spur to the flowers. The plant gets its name from the dense pyramidal (or cone-shaped) cluster of flowers, although as the later flowers open the inflorescence generally becomes decidedly more oblong. Although widespread and locally common, this is a species that has been taking advantage of new situations in recent years, such as roundabouts and motorway verges.

NOTE:
Hybridises with the Fragrant Orchid where the two grow in close proximity to one another.

KEY FEATURES: Leaves all narrow-oblong and pointed, not spotted nor sheathing the stem. Flowers with a long slender, down-turned, spur and an evenly 3-lobed lip.
HABITAT: Unimproved meadows and other grassy places, particularly verges and embankments, but also along woodland rides and sand dunes, most often on calcareous soils.
FREQUENCY: Locally common throughout, except the far north, the Faeroes and Iceland.
SEASON: June–August.
HABIT: A tuberous hairless perennial with a solitary, erect stem to 60 cm.
LEAVES: Plain green, narrow-oblong, usually pointed, the stem leaves not clasping, smaller than the lower leaves.
FLOWERS: In a broad pyramidal spike, pale to bright pink, purplish-red or white, unscented; lateral sepals spreading and wing-like, but the upper sepal and the petals forming a close hood; lip small, 6–8 mm long, evenly 3-lobed, with 2 ridges in the centre but otherwise unmarked, with a long slender, down-curved spur behind.
FRUIT: A narrow-oblong 3-parted capsule containing countless tiny dust-like seeds.

J
F
M
A
M
J
J
A
S
O
N
D

LOOKALIKES

◄ **Fragrant Orchid** *Gymnadenia conopsea*
Rather similar to the Pyramidal Orchid, but flowers pink, reddish-lilac or white, borne in a long cylindrical spike, vanilla-scented. Leaves all linear-lanceolate. Lip 3-lobed, 3.5–5 mm long, plain and unridged. Similar habitats as well as fens and marshes, especially on calcareous soils; June–July. Throughout, except the far north.

▲ **Lesser Butterfly Orchid** *Platanthera bifolia*
A distinctive plant with a basal pair of oval leaves. Flowers white tinged with green, borne in an oblong spike, sweetly fragrant; lateral sepals spreading, the upper sepal and petals forming a close hood; lip narrow-oblong, 8–12 mm long. Extended behind into a long spur, 25–30 mm long that is not expanded at the tip. Open woodland, scrub, meadows, damp heaths and marshy ground; June–July. Throughout, except Iceland.

◄ **Greater Butterfly Orchid** *Platanthera chlorantha*
Similar to *P. bifolia*, but a stouter plant with greener flowers which bear a faint vanilla fragrance. Spur shorter, 18–27 mm long, somewhat expanded at the tip. Pollinia diverging, whereas they are parallel in *P. bifolia*. Similar habitats and distribution but scarcer in the north.

Common Spotted-Orchid
Dactylorhiza fuchsii

Orchidaceae

The spotted or marsh orchids are a distinctive group characterised by dense spikes of brightly coloured flowers and leaves that do not sheath the stem. As the common name indicates most of the species have attractively spotted foliage. The Common Spotted Orchid is perhaps the one most often seen in the area, especially in drier habitats. Large colonies can make a very arresting sight.

NOTE:
On damper ground, especially old industrial sites, this species may grow in association with D. praetermissa *and in such instances hybrid swarms are frequent.*

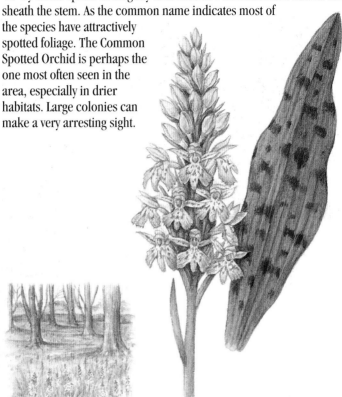

KEY FEATURES: Leaves spotted, all similar, not sheathing the stem. Flowers in dense spikes; lip 3-lobed, with looped-line markings or dots.
HABITAT: Dry grassy habitats, meadows, verges, fens, woodland and woodland margins, generally on calcareous soils.
FREQUENCY: Throughout, except the far north, usually gregarious and sometimes in very large colonies.
SEASON: June–early August.
HABIT: An erect tuberous, hairless perennial with a solitary stem, sometimes grouped, to 50 cm tall, although often less.
LEAVES: 7–12, lanceolate to narrow-lanceolate, pointed, mid to deep green, with dark transverse-oval spots; bracts usually shorter than the flowers.
FLOWERS: Variable, white to reddish-purple and pink, borne in dense cylindrical spikes; lateral sepals spreading and wing-like, while the upper sepal and the petals from a close hood; lip 3-lobed, 7–11 mm long, lobed to halfway or more, with the middle lobe smaller and tooth-like, symmetrically patterned with loops of dote or dashes; spur the same length as the ovary.
FRUIT: A narrow-oblong 3-parted capsule containing numerous tiny dust-like seeds.

J
F
M
A
M
J
J
A
S
O
N
D

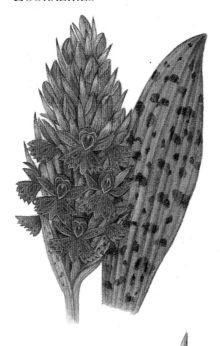

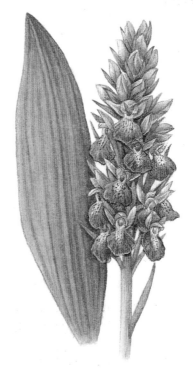

◄ Broad-leaved Marsh-orchid *Dactylorhiza majalis*
Similar to *D. fuchsii*, but leaves 4–8, broader, oblong to broad-lanceolate, and often with large dark spots or blotches, the bracts longer than the flowers. Lip 9–10 mm long, with the central lobe unmarked; spur shorter than the ovary. Damp habitats, especially meadows, marshes and fens, on calcareous soils; May–July. Britain and Ireland, Continental Europe from S Sweden southwards; in Britain confined to W Scotland and the Hebrides.

▲ Southern Marsh-orchid *Dactylorhiza praetermissa*
Plant with unspotted, plain leaves and bright purple-red flowers; lip 3-lobed, 10–12 mm long, with a central cluster of small spots. Plant to 75 cm tall. Similar habitats sand flowering time to *D. majalis*. Throughout, except Ireland, Iceland and much of Scandinavia.

◄ Heath Spotted-orchid *Dactylorhiza maculata*
Rather like *D. fuchsii*, but the lip of the flower shallowly lobed, with the tooth-like central lobe often shorter than the side lobes. In addition the leaves are usually sharply pointed, with rounded spots. Woodland, grassy places and moor, on damp, primarily acid, soils; June–early August. Throughout; locally common.

243

Marsh Helleborine

Epipactis palustris

T he helleborines are an interesting and distinctive group of orchids, generally with rather subtly coloured flowers and characteristically ribbed leaves, with long parallel veins. The flowers, borne in long elegant spikes, are usually half-nodding and have equal spreading sepals and petals, while the lip is folded or joined in the middle with the basal part forming a sort of cup. Most are to be found in scattered colonies, rarely making the spectacular displays of some of their cousins.

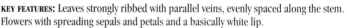

KEY FEATURES: Leaves strongly ribbed with parallel veins, evenly spaced along the stem. Flowers with spreading sepals and petals and a basically white lip.

HABITAT: Marshes, fens and other damp places, occasionally in dune slacks.

FREQUENCY: Throughout, except the far north, then Faeroes and Iceland; locally common and sometimes forming sizeable colonies.

SEASON: July–August.

HABIT: A rhizomatous, patch-forming perennial, with erect, downy stems to 45 cm tall, occasionally taller, which are usually purplish towards the base.

LEAVES: 4–8, oblong to lanceolate, decreasing in size up the stem, pointed, folded lengthways.

FLOWERS: Up to 50 in a long raceme with the lowermost flowers opening first; sepals greenish with faint violet or purplish-brown streaks, while the petals are white with a pinkish base; lip 9–10 mm long, white with a yellow blotch towards the base and purple lines, the tip oval and with a frilly margin.

FRUIT: An oblong 3-parted, hairy capsule containing numerous tiny dust-like seeds.

J
F
M
A
M
J
J
A
S
O
N
D

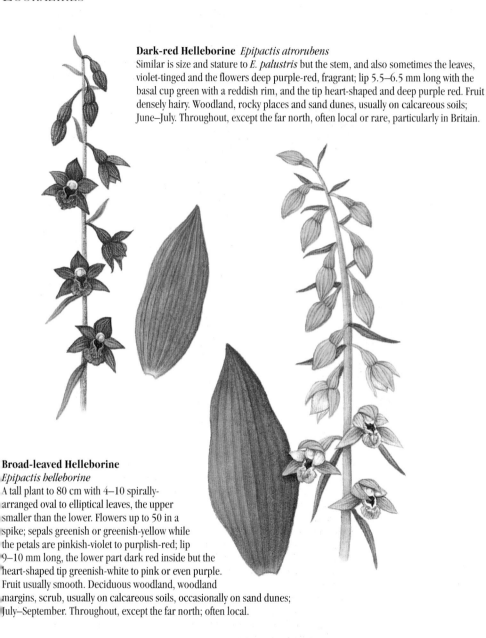

Dark-red Helleborine *Epipactis atrorubens*
Similar is size and stature to *E. palustris* but the stem, and also sometimes the leaves, violet-tinged and the flowers deep purple-red, fragrant; lip 5.5–6.5 mm long with the basal cup green with a reddish rim, and the tip heart-shaped and deep purple red. Fruit densely hairy. Woodland, rocky places and sand dunes, usually on calcareous soils; June–July. Throughout, except the far north, often local or rare, particularly in Britain.

Broad-leaved Helleborine
Epipactis helleborine
A tall plant to 80 cm with 4–10 spirally-arranged oval to elliptical leaves, the upper smaller than the lower. Flowers up to 50 in a spike; sepals greenish or greenish-yellow while the petals are pinkish-violet to purplish-red; lip 9–10 mm long, the lower part dark red inside but the heart-shaped tip greenish-white to pink or even purple. Fruit usually smooth. Deciduous woodland, woodland margins, scrub, usually on calcareous soils, occasionally on sand dunes; July–September. Throughout, except the far north; often local.

245

Daffodil

Narcissus pseudonarcissus

Amaryllidaceae

T he Daffodil is so well known that it scarcely warrants describing yet again. It is one of the true gems of the spring and it is little wonder that it should have acquired a host of local names with Lent Lily, Lenten Lily and Easter Lily being the most explicit. The true wild daffodil is a refined plant which has given rise to a host of garden forms and hybrids, many with a coarser and brasher countenance; these are sometimes naturalised in the wild, especially on large estates where the first would have no doubt been planted.

NOTE:
Hybrids with N. poeticus, *called* N. × incomparabilis, *are sometimes found in the wild. They are essentially like the daffodil but with a small cup-like yellow corona.*

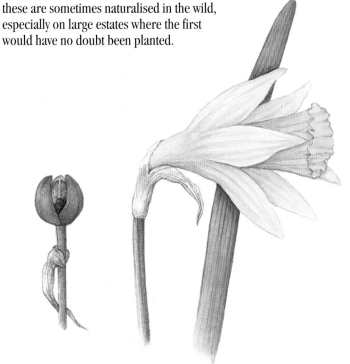

J
F
M
A
M
J
J
A
S
O
N
D

KEY FEATURES: Leaves linear and grass-like but rather fleshy. Flowers solitary on leafless stems or scapes. Sepals and petals (tepals) equal in size and colour. The centre of flower dominated by a large flair-ended trumpet.

HABITAT: Meadows and open deciduous woodland, waste ground and hedgerows; lowlands and mountains.

FREQUENCY: Britain, France, Holland and Germany; widely cultivated and naturalised elsewhere; locally abundant.

SEASON: April–June.

HABIT: A hairless, bulbous perennial, often clump-forming with all the leaves basal.

LEAVES: Linear, rather fleshy, grey-green, to 12 mm wide, usually 2–5 per bulb.

FLOWERS: Solitary, half-nodding, cream to pale yellow with a deep yellow trumpet (corona), 20–35 nn long, the 6 tepals all similar in size and shape and forward pointing, the trumpet with a frilled and slightly flared rim; spathe papery and pale brown or whitish, enclosing the flower in bud.

FRUIT: A 3-parted capsule containing a number of seeds.

▲ **Tenby Daffodil** *Narcissus obvallaris*
A similar but stiffer plant with uniformly yellow flowers
in which the tepals are more or less at right angles. Only
known form SW Wales, but widely cultivated in gardens.

Poet's Narcissus *Narcissus poeticus* ▶
Similar in proportion to the Daffodil although often somewhat taller, with the
leaves slightly grooved, to 10 mm wide. Flowers 40–50 mm across, white with
a very small rim-like corona that is yellow with a crisped red or brownish rim.
Tepals elliptical, often slightly twisted. Flowers very sweetly perfumed.
Primarily moist meadows, particularly in mountain regions; April–June.
C and E France, but naturalised in Britain, Belgium and Germany.

Yellow Iris

Iris pseudacorus

Iridaceae

Also known as the Yellow Flag or Jacob's Sword, this is a familiar plant of moist places and waterways. The characteristic flower shape has been suggested as the source of the *fleur de lys*. It is widely cultivated in gardens where forms with variegated leaves and pale cream flowers are known.

NOTE:
In the Iris Family there are normally 6 tepals (petal-like structures), comprising both sepals and petals, and 3 stamens, while the ovary is situated clearly below the other flower parts.

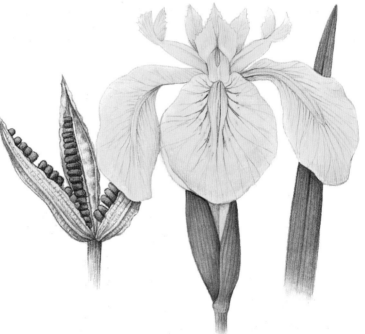

KEY FEATURES: Leaves long and sword-like. Flowers 3-parted, the outer segments being large and distinctive 'falls' the inner upright 'standards'. Ovary located below the other flower parts.

HABITAT: Moist places, especially freshwater margins, ditches, and wet meadows.

FREQUENCY: Throughout, except Iceland; frequent and sometimes abundant.

SEASON: June–August.

HABIT: A stout, rhizomatous, patch-forming, hairless perennial, with erect, somewhat branched flowering stems to 1.5 m, often less.

LEAVES: Deep green and sword-like, tapered to a pointed tip, with a conspicuous raised midrib; spathes (surrounding the flowerbuds) green and leaf-like, but much smaller.

FLOWERS: Yellow, 70–100 mm across, the falls broad and rounded or oval with green dots and veins in the centre. Standards rather short, erect, more or less equalling the 3 yellow style-arms.

FRUIT: An oblong 3-parted capsule, to 9 cm long, containing numerous greenish-brown seeds in neat rows.

J
F
M
A
M
J
J
A
S
O
N
D

LOOKALIKES

Stinking Iris *Iris foetidissima*
Also known as the Roast Beef Plant because of the curious smell of the crushed leaves, this plant forms dense tough clumps of deep green, often rather curved, foliage, to 60 cm tall. The iris flowers are quite demure, being dull violet tinged with yellow, 55–80 mm across, with the falls lightly veined. In fruit, however, this is a spectacular plant, with the green capsules turning brown and splitting during the winter to reveal numerous bright red berry-like seeds. Open woodland and hedgerows, occasionally on sand dunes; May–July. Britain and France, but widely cultivated.

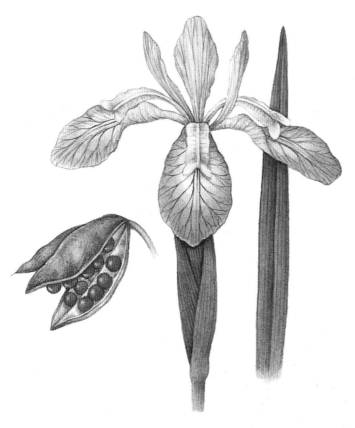

Araceae

Lords and Ladies
Arum maculatum

A familiar and yet rather bizarre plant of woodland and hedgerows well known to all country folk, this plant has acquired a plethora of common names including Cuckoo Pint, Jack-in-the-pulpit, Devils and Angels, Willy Lily and Cows and Bulls. One particularly curious feature of the flowers is that the pollen emits a faint glow of light at night, hence it has also been called Shiners and Fairy Lamps.

NOTE:
The flowers are pollinated by flies which fall into the spathe-tube and are trapped below a ring of hairs located above the flowers. After pollination the spathe relaxes and the insects are free to escape.

KEY FEATURES: Leaves arrowhead-shaped. Inflorescence terminated by a long appendage or spadix that is surrounded by a large and conspicuous spathe. Fruit a head of right berries.
HABITAT: Woodland, hedgerows, banks and ditches, field boundaries, often on neutral to calcareous soils.
FREQUENCY: Britain to Holland and Germany southwards; occasionally naturalised elsewhere.
SEASON: April–May.
HABIT: A tuberous, patch-forming, hairless perennial to 25 cm tall with leaves clasping the base of the erect flower stems.
LEAVES: Appearing in the late winter and early spring, arrow-shaped with a blunt apex, shiny bright green, often with small black blotches.
FLOWERS: Small and inconspicuous, borne on a stem with the female flowers at the base the male higher, but surrounded by the tube of the spathe. Spathe large and conspicuous yellowish-green or pale green, flushed and spotted with purple; spadix truncheon-like, deep purple usually.
FRUIT: A head, 3–4 cm long, of green berry-like seeds that turn bright orange-red when ripe in the autumn.

J
F
M
A
M
J
J
A
S
O
N
D

illustration ½ life size

Large Cuckoo Pint *Arum italicum*
Similar, but a rather larger plant, the
leaves appearing in the late autumn
and with conspicuous white veining
and the spathe plain greenish-yellow;
spadix the same colour as the spathe.
Fruiting spikes large, 10–15 mm long.
Hedgerows and disturbed land;
April–May. S Britain and France;
naturalised in Holland.

Meadow Saffron
Colchicum autumnale

A lso called Autumn Crocus (it is not related to *Crocus*
which has 3 stamens and linear leaves), this bulbous
plant bears it 4–6 cm long, goblet-shaped, pink or
lilac-purple flowers in the autumn, while
the tuft of shiny leathery, elliptical leaves
arise in the late winter. *Colchicum* flowers
have 6 equal tepals and 6 stamens. Damp
meadows and other grassy places, woodland
margins, on neutral or calcareous soils;
August–September. C and S Britain, SE Ireland,
Holland to Germany southwards; naturalised in
Denmark and S Scandinavia.

J
F
M
A
M
J
J
A
S
O
N
D

Index